ISBN 0-87666-455-9

AQUARIUM PLANTS
their identification, cultivation and ecology
by dr. karel rataj
and
thomas j. horeman

Distributed in the U.S.A. by T.F.H. Publications, Inc., 211 West Sylvania Avenue, P.O. Box 27, Neptune City, N.J. 07753; in England by T.F.H. (Gt. Britain) Ltd., 13 Nutley Lane, Reigate, Surrey; in Canada to the book store and library trade by Clarke, Irwin & Company, Clarwin House, 791 St. Clair Avenue West, Toronto 10, Ontario; in Canada to the pet trade by Rolf C. Hagen Ltd., 3225 Sartelon Street, Montreal 382, Quebec; in Southeast Asia by Y.W. Ong, 9 Lorong 36 Geylang, Singapore 14; in Australia and the south Pacific by Pet Imports Pty. Ltd., P.O. Box 149, Brookvale 2100, N.S.W., Australia. Published by T.F.H. Publications, Inc. Ltd., The British Crown Colony of Hong Kong.

Cover: *Lagarosiphon major.* Photo by Dr. Herbert R. Axelrod.

Frontispiece: A planted aquarium photographed by Ruda Zukal.

All photos in this book are by Ruda Zukal unless specifically credited otherwise.

N.B. *The senior author, Prof. Dr. Karel Rataj, has not been able to verify completely the identification of those photographs credited to Mr. T. Horeman.*

Contents

1

Introduction

*This book has been written for
lovers of aquariums and terrariums.*

Until now the literature dealing with aquarium plants could be divided into two groups. The first group is represented by the numerous books written by educated laymen. In spite of great efforts by their authors, these books usually contain a number of fallacies and errors that are in due course passed on repeatedly by later writers of other books. These errors are commonly found in the descriptions of the biological conditions necessary for cultivating aquatic plants, as well as in the taxonomic sections where incorrect names are used for the species. The second group of books is those written by botanists who have a great deal of knowledge, usually highly specialized, about the cultivation of plants, their structure, and their classification. Unfortunately these authors often lack even a basic understanding of aquarium science, the practical aspect which is of interest to most readers. These often technical books may give a great amount of information on species which cannot even be cultivated under aquarium conditions or, even worse, about plants which turn into pesty weeds that the aquarist finds difficult to remove from his tank.

The authors are aware that this book is incomplete. Some plants cultivated in aquariums have not been described scientifically at the time of writing and only their commercial names can be given. Other groups of plants require a thorough revision before we can be sure of the proper name for the species. In recent years the senior author has revised more than 30,000 herbarium specimens from the major botanical institutes of the world and has described about 30 new species of the genera *Echinodorus*, *Sagittaria*, *Aponogeton*, and *Cryptocoryne*, the major groups of aquarium plants. The revised nomenclature of these important genera is presented here for aquarists for the first time.

In addition to general information on raising and identifying aquarium plants, we have also included descriptions of methods used to ensure the reproduction of aquatic plants under cultivation. In many cases these methods are more elaborate than the average aquarist would like. If the major aim of the aquarist is simply raising plants for decorating the aquarium, the best thing to do would be to purchase well developed mature plants from professional cultivators of aquarium plants.

The present book is the joint effort of our chosen specialized fields. Dr. Karel Rataj is a distinguished botanist from Sumperk, Czechoslovakia, who has specialized in the study of the taxonomy and ecology of aquatic plants. Among his many important works might be mentioned his revisions of the important aquarium genera *Echinodorus, Cryptocoryne* and *Sagittaria.* Mr. Thomas J. Horeman, of Surrey, England, has made many journeys throughout South America and the Far East to collect aquatic plants. In the course of this activity he has discovered a number of new species, including *Echinodorus horemanii,* and has propagated and distributed them commercially. Thus the reader should be able to profit from the combined experience of both a technical botanist and a practical botanist for the first time in an aquarium book.

2

The Importance of Plants
in the Aquarium

Biological balance is the basis of a good relationship between living organisms. The aquarium hobby is mostly interested in the keeping of fish in indoor aquariums, but since the lives of fish are closely interwoven with the lives of the plants, aquatic vegetation is an integral part of aquarium science.

Plants are the basis of life on earth. They are producers, the only organisms able to develop organic substances from inorganic mineral elements and their compounds. All animals are consumers, their bodies being unable to utilize inorganic substances directly. The basic food of herbivores is plants, so even the largest carnivorous animals are indirectly dependent on plants. In addition, plants are the greatest single source of oxygen in the atmosphere. Without oxygen animal life on earth would not be possible.

The secret of the remarkable production by plants of both oxygen and organic food substances is of course photosynthesis. During the day the plant consumes nutrients (mineral substances) and obtains carbon dioxide from the atmosphere or from the water, where it has been released as a by-product of animal respiration. In the presence of sunlight and the complex compound chlorophyll, starches and sugars are produced and oxygen eliminated as a waste material. At night the plants reverse their role, breathing in oxygen and eliminating carbon dioxide, but during this time most fish are inactive and their need for oxygen is minimal.

It is not our intention to discuss the details of these fundamental functions of plants and their importance to the aquarium. These are matters well known to everybody, with the details easily available in any basic biology book. We wish to deal first with other principles of aquarium keeping commonly used and readily understood by the aquarist, and then with the cultivation of aquatic plants and their use in the aquarium.

Leafy plants are very useful for the spawning of egg-scattering fish like these tetras (*Hyphessobrycon* species). Those eggs caught among the leaves of the plant usually escape predation by the parent fish. Photo by R. Zukal.

In passing it might be mentioned that many of the aquarium plants described in the following pages are actually amphibious, growing both in and out of the water. If they are carefully watered once a week (even less with some species) they can also be used as potted plants outside the aquarium. The shiny green leaves and often bright infloresences of *Cryptocoryne* are certainly as attractive in the living room as in the aquarium.

Our main goal in writing this book has been to acquaint readers with the practical and, to some extent, theoretical aspects necessary for the choice and cultivation of water plants. If our readers are successful in cultivating even one or two of the more exacting species, we will be satisfied.

3

General Principles for the Cultivation of Aquatic Plants

In order to give aquarium plants a perfectly suitable medium, we must first be aware of the conditions existing in their native habitat. Most aquarium plants come from tropical and subtropical areas, with a few from the warmer parts of the temperate zone. Often the aquarist will see in print or hear in discussions the assumption that tropical soils are fertile and rich in nutrients; this is of course in error. As a rule the soil in the tropics is poor because

Aerial view of Rio Purus, a tributary of the Amazon River, taken during the dry part of the year. Note the great scouring effect of water currents on the banks. Photo by Dr. H.R. Axelrod.

Root system of the water hyacinth (*Eichhornia crassipes*). Photo by Dr. D. Sculthorpe.

great quantities of organic substances, arising from defoliation and by the death of tropical vegetation, are consumed by the soil organisms so quickly that the decomposition of this material is faster than the rate at which it is replaced. High temperatures and high humidity make possible such a quick decomposition or mineralization of organic substances that the tropical soil is poorer in nutrients than ordinary field soil in temperate climates.

Plants in their natural environments are continually damaged by animals and by weather conditions such as floods. They grow in water that for at least part of the growing period is muddy and full of impurities that settle on the leaves and impede the functioning of the plants. The bottom of tropical pools and streams is often peaty, and peat is of course a very poor source of nutrients.

In the aquarium we cannot adhere to all these natural conditions because in a confined habitat they are obviously detrimental to the plants. Instead we prepare a much better medium which has many of the advantages of the natural environment without its disadvantages.

Unlike most land plants, aquatic plants are not dependent solely on nutrition obtained through the root system. They are able to receive nutrients through the whole surface of the plant body, especially the epidermis of the leaves. Such typically submersed plants as *Ceratophyllum* and *Utricularia* do not form roots at all, while *Elodea* and *Najas* form only very short ones. For this reason the composition of not only the soil but of the water is of great importance, as the water must contain many mineral substances ab-

The leaves of the bladderwort (*Utricularia*) are modified into small bladders capable of ingesting minute organisms like *Daphnia* but not fish fry. Bladderworts do not develop roots.

sorbed directly by the plant. This must be taken into consideration when establishing an aquarium and selecting the planting medium.

There has long been a controversy over whether such rooted submersed plants as *Cryptocoryne* and *Echinodorus* receive the majority of their nutrients through the leaves or the roots. Either answer is partially correct, as the method of absorption varies with different concentrations of nutrients in the medium. As a general rule, the more diluted the solution, the more accessible the minerals. If there is a very heavy concentration of nutrients in the soil, only the small percentage dissolved in the water will actually be available to the plant.

Occasionally aquarists have good luck growing plants for several months or longer when using such normally objectionable bottom materials as peat, garden soil, industrial fertilizer, or clay. This is because we are never really quite certain about the proper-

The elongated tubers of the underwater banana plant (*Nymphoides aquatica*) contain reserve food material. Photo by Dr. D. Sculthorpe.

Plants of various species and origin can be combined artistically in a single tank provided their requirements do not conflict.

ties of the substrate just from its name. It is necessary to determine many factors, such as the pH, the proportions of the major nutrients (nitrates, phosphates, etc.), the presence or absence of certain important microelements, the amount of humus, etc. Not many aquarists are able to test for all this necessary information without access to a well equipped laboratory. Commercial soil testing kits are available for some of the substrate components, but not for all.

The safest and most uniform method of setting up the planted aquarium is to start off with plain washed sand or gravel and for the first year or so use only plants with strong and well developed rhizomes. The rhizomes should have enough stored food reserves to last the plant at least several months. Good starting plants include the stronger species of *Echinodorus*, *Cryptocoryne*, *Lagenandra*, *Aponogeton*, and *Crinum*. In a newly established aquarium we cannot grow such plants as *Myriophyllum*, *Ludwigia*, or *Cabomba*, as these lack reserve food supplies.

Start the aquarium by purchasing good quality rather coarse sand from a reputable dealer. Make sure the sand is washed clean of all impurities. On the bottom of the aquarium install a good quality undergravel filter to ensure the circulation of the oxygenated water through the sand and around the roots of the plants. This speeds the decomposition of organic substances such as fish feces and food remains to the mineral state and provides a constant temperature throughout the aquarium. By using a sand substrate together with an undergravel filter we can be confident that the water will not contain a surplus of organic substances and will be supplied with sufficient mineral nutrients necessary for the good development of the plants.

To obtain maximum growth and longevity from your plants, the undergravel filter should preferably be the type consisting of numerous small perforated plastic tubes. With this type of filter there is no gap between the base of the aquarium and the sand bed. Thus there is no place for debris to build up where it cannot be decomposed by the proper bacteria in the presence of oxygen. The tube-type filter also has less chance of getting tangled in the growing roots of the plants.

For the first year the substrate is poor in nutrients, but with the passing of time it becomes richer and richer due to the accumulation and decomposition of fish and plant wastes. The type of fish kept can to some extent determine how fast nutrients accumulate, as some fish are naturally "dirtier" than others. Thus most of the live-bearers, including the swordtails, platies, mollies, and guppies, produce dirtier and richer bottoms than the tetras of similar size. In the normal aquarium there is plenty of detritus, usually more than necessary for the plants. It must on occasion be cleaned out, as only the detritus under the surface of the sand is really necessary for the plants to obtain sufficient nutrients. An aquarium two or three years old is an ideal environment for the growth and development of all species of aquatic plants.

It is important that the detritus in the sand should be decomposed in the presence of oxygen. This decomposition, called aerobic, does not occur when the substrate medium is air-tight. Air-tight media include such things as peat, clay, and garden soil. Anaerobic decomposition (decomposition in the absence of air) results in the formation of poisonous gases such as hydrogen sulphide. These gases appear as bubbles which leak out of the bottom when the plants are pulled out; the roots will be brown or black. Hydrogen sulphide can destroy both plants and fish. Industrial fer-

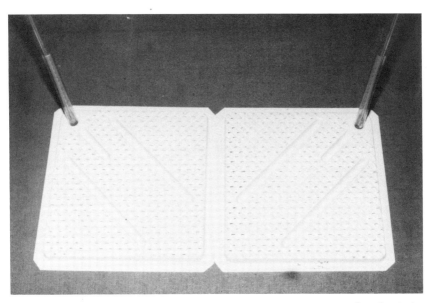

Inexpensive type of undergravel filter with a continuous base of perforated plastic material.

This undergravel filter consists of a series of parallel rows of perforated plastic tubes. Photo courtesy Eureka Products Company.

A small fish population can provide the plants in an aquarium with enough nutrients so that the addition of fertilizers is truly unnecessary.

tilizers are a source of hydrogen sulphide, so they should not be used in the aquarium. Fish produce enough nutrients for the plants.

When we talk of a *poor* substrate or a medium which has to be supplied with nutrients, we do not mean a base without any compounds or with added fertilizers or soil; we are simply referring to an aquarium with a substrate formed of clean, washed sand. A planting medium in a newly established tank or in an aquarium with a small number of fish is poor. It is *moderately rich* to *rich* when composed of washed sand in an established tank containing a reasonable number of fish for a period of six to eight months.

Readers should not be influenced by various publications and pictures illustrating tiny plants grown in clean sand and giant plants growing in fertilized soil or industrial nutrients. How would such pictures look when taken one, two, or three years later? By then the influence of anaerobic decomposition and poisonous gases will have become obvious. If you do not believe this, just check the aquariums of the professionals who acclimatize newly imported plants—you will find only clean, washed sand, never soil or fertilizers.

4

Illumination of the Aquarium

If an aquarium is to fulfill its esthetic function, it must be brightly illuminated. Artificial light is an absolute necessity for the development of plants. It is even more important than the quality of the water.

The length of the day changes in the temperate zone with the change of seasons. In spring the day is as long as the night on March 21. Then the days get longer and are at their longest on the first day of summer (June 21). The shortest day of the year is the first day of winter (December 21). On this day the night lasts 16 hours and the day only 8. During summer the days are essentially longer than the nights. In the tropics the length of a day and a night are equal, each of them lasting about 12 hours. In the temperate zone plants have in consequence much more light than in the tropics when totalled for the year. We therefore say that temperate plants are long-day plants while tropical plants are short-day plants. Only during the time of the spring and autumn equinoxes do our aquariums have a tropical day. For that reason tropical plants usually put out flower buds and flower by slow growth one to three months later. Tropical plants do not mind a longer period of light than they are accustomed to; it even helps speed their growth and the development of roots and leaves.

A long day in the temperate zone does not allow tropical plants to flower, since it acts as a brake on development of the sexual organs. On the other hand, they do not thrive well on a short winter day of 8 to 10 hours. They lose their leaves and some of the more sensitive plants may die. If we want the aquarium to be decorative all year long we must prolong the light period during the winter. The plants require a day of at least 12 hours every day of the year.

The most important principle of aquarium lighting is that the duration of the light is more important than the intensity if everything else is constant. While it is not of drastic importance whether an aquarium is lit with 40, 60, or 100 watt bulbs (presuming the

17

For safety the lighting system should fit the size and construction of the tank. An ill-fitting and improperly installed lighting set-up can be very dangerous. Courtesy of O'Dell Manufacturing Company.

minimal lighting intensity for the plants is reached), it is essential to consider for how long and at what time they are lit. It has already been stated that tropical plants are short-day plants and require light for 12 hours a day. The necessary hours of light cannot be replaced by more intensive light sources operating for a shorter period of time. It is not necessary to measure the intensity of the light in lux (a unit of illumination equal to 1 lumen per square meter; a lumen is the amount of light which falls on an area of 1 square centimeter placed 1 centimeter from a standard candle) as long as the plants can easily become accustomed to weak or strong light, but tropical plants cannot get used to too short of a day.

A lightmeter can be of great help to those who would like to monitor the light requirements of their plants. Photo by Dr. H.R. Axelrod.

By additional artificial light we mean the *prolongation* of daylight in winter, not the increase of the intensity during the natural day. In practice this means that in winter it is necessary to prolong the plants' day by about 4 hours. It does not matter whether this period of additional light is given in the morning before dawn or in the evening after dusk. It also does not matter whether the 4 hours is given as a unit or divided between morning and evening. In order to keep the plants on a regular rhythm or schedule, the light should be given at the same time each day. Thus the day should not be prolonged in the morning one time and in the evening the next.

If an automatic time switch is available, this greatly simplifies the keeping of a regular lighting schedule. The extra lighting can be turned on automatically at, say, 3:30 p.m. and kept operating until at least 8:00 p.m. If the light can be kept on until 10:00 p.m., so much the better. Plants kept under this schedule will have the same growth rate all year long and will develop as well during the winter as during the summer.

Plants react best to light which is predominantly in the red and blue wavelengths. Such lighting is readily available in the form of special fluorescent tubes, such as the Gro-Lux type, sold in most aquarium and plant shops.

The importance of the length of daylight is often underestimated by aquarists, and we are convinced that failures with some sensitive tropical plants are caused largely by short winter days.

A collector pulling out a *Cryptocoryne* from its shady natural habitat in a small stream in Singapore. Photo by Lee Chin Eng.

DO SHADE-LOVING PLANTS EXIST?

Many experts believe that shade-loving plants do not exist. Among aquarium plants the cryptocorynes have the most familiar reputation as shade-loving plants. It is true that in nature most of them grow mainly in shaded situations where no other low-growing vegetation exists. Do they live in deep shade because it meets their requirements best or because they have been forced there through competition? In our opinion there is no doubt that they have been forced into the shade.

The soil in the tropics is very poor, and plants which grow rapidly do so due to their strong root system. Cryptocorynes have a relatively weak root system and are not able to extract the needed nutrients from the soil. In a natural tropical society of plants cryptocorynes are not able to compete with other, more aggressive species which can outgrow and suffocate them. For this reason cryptocorynes have had no other "choice" than to colonize the most shaded situations where competition does not exist. They have a great ability to survive in subdued light. Only in artificial culture can we see how much some cryptocorynes love sunlight and how well some species do under its direct rays.

The same applies to their submersed forms, but only if given the right quality of water. It is not a question here of shade-loving plants but of water in shady areas. In a permanent half-shade or in permanent artificial light water holds its good qualities. If water is alternately sunlit and shaded, sudden changes take place. There are changes in the number and species of protozoans, algae, and bacteria. In consequence both chemical and physical qualities of the water change and these changes effect a negative growth in the development of plants.

Even if the above explanation is nearer to the real situation than most other explanations, nothing changes the fact that the best position for an indoor aquarium is a place away from the window and sunlight. The plants will improve with the assistance of artificial light. The important thing is to prepare the most constant and favorable conditions of development throughout the year. Do not be afraid of plenty of light even with "shade-loving" plants, but protect your aquarium from undesirable fluctuations of light intensity. It has been reliably demonstrated that many shade-loving plants easily become accustomed to a much stronger intensity of light and that plants occurring in nature in constantly lit localities usually become easily accustomed to a constant half-shade in the aquarium. Exceptions will be mentioned with the descriptions of the individual species of plants.

5

Fully Aquatic and Amphibious Plants in Nature and the Aquarium

In nature aquatic and amphibious plants live in various types of still and moving waters. They are found in or on the banks of rivers, streams, backwaters, ponds, lakes, marshes, and swamps, as well as in man-made irrigation ditches or canals. In some areas of the world these plants are to be found on worked land where marsh culture products such as rice are grown and where various kinds of aquatic and marsh plants occur as weeds.

Every type of natural water is characterized by certain peculiarities which influence to a greater or lesser degree the plant communities existing there. The qualities of these waters and the conditions which they provide for water plants are partly variable, partly invariable. To the constant qualities belong the composition of the substrate (the soil on the bottom) and the quality of the water (nutrients, pH, etc.). The other qualities of the medium are subject to greater change as a rule. These variable factors include the depth of the water, its temperature and transparency, and its velocity, among others.

THE TRANSPARENCY OF THE WATER

Transparency of water depends on the presence of suspended insoluble substances which in turn determine the quantity of light that can penetrate the water surface and make life possible for the plants. Light intensity is especially important in relation to photosynthesis, of course. In waters of high clarity the light penetrates for several meters, as in clear lakes, but in most waters penetration is for only a few meters; in very heavily silted dark waters the light penetrates for a meter or less. Transparency of the water determines not only the depth to which plants can successfully grow,

Heteranthera can also be grown successfully outside the water. Photo by G.J.M. Timmerman.

but also some aspects of their coloration. In greater depths or in less translucent waters the plants have a brownish or reddish color mixed with their basic green leaves; in clear waters they are entirely green.

THE DEPTH OF THE WATER

Their depth below the surface often determines the way of life of the plant much as it does their structure and color. In consequence some plants are always found in the lower layers of water, while others live rather nearer the surface. Several groups can be distinguished.

1) Submersed plants that are rooted in the bottom and have leaves and stems that grow permanently under water. They may also flower under water and produce seeds there. The flowers or leaves do not always reach the surface and are not adapted to a life above water. This group includes many aquarium plants such as *Vallisneria*, *Barclaya*, and *Ottelia*.

Vallisneria is a completely submersed form of plant. This plant is not recommended for small tanks.

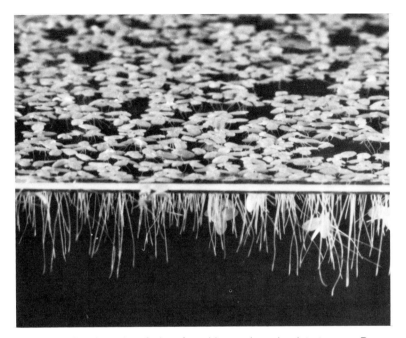

Lemna is a floating type of plant found in ponds and quiet streams. Removal of excess growth in aquariums is recommended for this prolific plant.

2) Plants rooted in the bottom but with leaves reaching the water surface. They usually have well developed roots and fragile stems with which to resist the pressure of the current. They flower as a rule above the water surface and, unlike the preceding group, they develop more conspicuous flowers. Land forms can develop. *Myriophyllum* and *Heteranthera*, among others, are representative of this group.

3) Floating plants that live in the surface layer of the water. Their roots float freely and their leaves may be on the surface, as in *Lemna* and *Limnobium*, under water, as in *Utricularia*, or above water, as in *Eichhornia*. The flowers are always above water and are pollinated in the air.

4) Amphibious plants that can grow under water as well as on dry land. In the water they develop submersed as well as floating leaves and/or emersed aerial leaves. When the water dries, land forms arise. These are mainly bankside plants, of which many are important in the aquarium. Typical genera include *Echinodorus*, *Sagittaria*, and *Cryptocoryne*.

Sagittaria, being an amphibious form, grows under water as well as on land.

THE NUTRIENTS IN THE WATER

The minerals necessary to plants are termed nutrients. Every species has its own special requirements, although a large number of species will need the same materials in about the same proportions. Natural waters contain certain groups or proportions of mineral elements, and plants have evolved in such a way as to be able to occupy waters containing certain concentrations of minerals. It is possible to classify natural water in several groups, each according to its nutritional value.

1) Waters poor in nutrients (oligotrophic) and containing less than 0.01g dissolved material per liter. In waters like these relatively few plants grow, and all are specialized.

2) Waters rich in organic substances and inhabited largely by amphibious plants with emersed leaves. For submersed plants such

Asian fish dealers utilize water hyacinth (*Eichhornia*) to protect their fish from too much light. Photo by Lee Chin Eng.

waters are mostly unsuitable. These organically rich waters arise in the aquarium if a planting medium rich in humus, such as horticultural soil or peat, is used. Submersed leaves usually become unkempt and then decay.

3) Waters rich in mineral substance (eutrophic) and having plenty of basic mineral nutrients and a very small quantity of organic substances. This is the most suitable water for the aquarium containing clean, washed sand. Fish feces fall into the sand and decompose into mineral substances. A biological filter which accelerates the decomposition of organic substances into mineral ones helps greatly.

4) Waters with a superabundance of mineral substances (brackish) are found on soils rich in salts and at the mouth of rivers entering the sea. Few species grow here, and they are generally specialized and unsuitable for the aquarium.

TEMPERATURE AND HEATING OF THE AQUARIUM

Aquariums are generally heated for the benefit of the fish, not the plants. Tropical plants usually need temperatures ranging from 66° to 77° F (19° to 25° C), which fortunately corresponds to the requirements of tropical fish. Aquatic plants from the temperate zone can all stand temperatures of about 68° F (20° C) except those from cold spring waters, which are not recommended for home aquariums anyway.

It is not necessary to go into details of water temperature in relation to their cultivation in aquariums with a temperature of 68° to 77° F (20° to 25° C). If we have an aquarium with fish from the temperate zone, the aquarium being left unheated in the winter and reaching low temperatures of 50° to 59° F (10° to 15° C), we should likewise use temperate plants from Europe and North America. At the other extreme are spawning aquariums where the temperature is often increased to 82° to 86° F (28° to 30° C); here only tropical plants can be used, as temperate or subtropical species die at such high temperatures.

For the greatest efficiency in heating, tubular submersed heaters should be used. These should be installed in the aquarium when the sand bottom is added and should preferably be covered by the sand. In this way uniform heating of all the water occurs as does heating of the substrate. Thus the plants have a constant temperature in both leaves and roots. Short heaters set vertically may heat only the water near the surface, while the bottom water and sand remain cold. By introducing circulation of the water through a filter or by heavy aeration, a uniform temperature is reached in the water but the substrate remains cold. In a cold medium the plant roots reduce their activities and assimilate a smaller amount of nutrients than is needed by the leaves, which are functioning in warm water. Cryptocorynes are very sensitive to these temperature differentials. We are convinced that this is a very frequent cause of "*Cryptocoryne* disease."

An undergravel filter draws the water through the sand substrate, removing temperature differences between the water and the sand bottom. The temperature of the whole plant body is thus about the same, a factor which favors the prosperous development of the plant.

6

The Arrangement of Indoor Aquariums

Although an indoor aquarium can be designed and maintained for any of several purposes, it should always be attractive. The design and planting should not only suit the needs of the plants and fish but should also be as perfect as possible esthetically.

Clean, washed sand, rather coarse in texture, is the most suitable substrate material for the aquarium. The surface of the bottom material should not be flat, but should slope down toward the front, terrace-like, with some irregular indentations. It should be reinforced and decorated with rocks of various sizes. The only suitable rocks are those made of hard and insoluble materials which will not change the quality of the water. Limestone and sandstone are quite unsuitable. The most commonly used rocks are those composed of silica, quartz, granite, slate, and other similarly stable materials. In order to present a natural impression the rocks should be of a uniform type; if they vary in color the aquarium will appear unnatural.

In addition to rocks, such items as old branches, parts of tree trunks, and stumps are all useful decorative material in the aquarium. Any wood placed in the tank should be neither fresh nor rotten. Old pieces of trees which have lain for years in a pond and are impregnated with mineral substances from the water are best. These will usually be very hard and dark. Old jagged roots dug from peat bogs are especially good.

The aquarium is not a copy of nature. We do not usually choose plants according to their geographical distribution, but instead try to build up a collection of plants which will thrive in the aquarium conditions we are able to give them. Thus the temperature, light, available space, available nutrients, pH, and similar factors determine to a great extent which plants can be kept in a specific aquarium.

Marsilea, greatly resembling the ordinary four-leaf clover, can enhance the beauty of the fore part of the tank with a low layer of green growth. Photo by Dr. D. Sculthorpe.

It also goes without saying that the density and kind of growth is chosen according to whether or not the aquarium will be inhabited by fish and the kinds and number of fish kept. In accordance with this, the types of plantings for aquariums can be divided into several groups.

1) The aquarium as a decoration, without fish. This aquarium is a tasteful ornament which, in conjunction with suitably chosen floral decorations, will create a pleasant appearance in the home. Such an aquarium requires less care than ordinary indoor pot-plants and should be a part of the decor of every home that has central heating, as it helps reduce moisture lost to the heating system. An indoor aquarium often enables one to cultivate those plants which cannot stand dry air and which do not thrive in a room with central heating.

The beauty of a planted tank can be maintained by the regular removal of excess growth. Some species grow at a much faster rate than others depending on the light and nutrient conditions in the tank.

This type of aquarium is usually planted with the least exacting plants, mainly those that propagate vegetatively. Often only a single species is used; *Vallisneria* with spirally coiled leaves (*V. americana*) is recommended. This plant grows abundantly over the whole aquarium and produces fine visual effects with an underwater light source.

In addition it is possible to furnish the bottom with low-growing plants to cover the whole floor of the aquarium and create a lower layer of vegetation. Here *Sagittaria subulata, Marsilea browni, Echinodorus quadricostatus,* or *E. tenellus* is suitable. The green carpet on the bottom is complemented by plants with long floating and densely leaved stems (*Myriophyllum, Anacharis, Elodea, Egeria, Lagarosiphon*) or with 2 or 3 tufts of a large-leaved plant whose leaves reach the water surface and do not develop from rhizomes or root runners (*Aponogeton, Echinodorus*).

Some plants can be ruined by freshwater snails such as *Planorbis*. Photo by M. Chvojka.

Aquariums planted in this manner require very little maintenance. In order to prevent them from becoming overgrown by algae, a few snails may be added. Water should be added every 2 to 4 weeks to replace that lost through evaporation. These decorative aquariums can be placed in a flower corner with potted plants or separately; potted plants grow very well in the vicinity of aquariums because of the humid atmosphere.

2) An aquarium with fish and plants, serving exclusively as a decoration. This type of tank should meet the same basic conditions as the first type: it should be decorative, increase the humidity, and require little attention. In order for not only the plants but also the fish to be conspicuous, the aquarium should not be planted with any species that grows over-abundantly, because this would mean frequent disturbing of the aquarium in order to thin excess plantlife. Tall plants are not used except for those which do not reproduce vegetatively. This is so the aquarium remains permanently in the condition in which it was first arranged.

The senior author's planted indoor tank complemented by various species of house plants.

Shown is an aquarium installed as an integral part of the wall and room decor. Determining the right position for an aquarium requires some thought and advance planning. Photo by J. Elias.

Geophagus jurupari, a popular aquarium fish from South America, digs in the substrate often in search of food resulting in the uprooting of plants. Photo by H. Hansen.

From the first everything is done that will contribute to the stability of the aquarium's appearance. The bottom is arranged in an irregular fashion and a big rock or tree root is placed in the aquarium to create the basic decoration. All stones are allowed to become covered with aquatic mosses, and the tree roots are covered with decorative ferns. The taller plants should be mostly *Aponogeton, Echinodorus,* and the larger species of *Anubias* and *Lagenandra.* They may be complemented by the smaller *Cryptocoryne nevillii, Sagittaria,* or *Marsilea.* We can also create within the tank a dark, densely overgrown corner with common species of such genera as *Hygrophila* or *Bacopa.* If we want to have greenery just below the surface of the water, use a tuft of *Elodea, Heteranthera,* or *Myriophyllum.*

In an aquarium of this type there should be only a few species of fish. *Pterophyllum* (angelfish), *Paracheirodon innesi* (neons),

Brachydanio (danios), and a few pairs of red platies or swordtails are good.

3) An aquarium for the fish specialist. Here the plants are of secondary importance because they are there only to fulfill the relatively minor decorative and biological purposes expected of them. Their maintenance should occupy the time of the aquarist as little as possible. Of the species whose vegetative propagation is rapid, the small plants forming a green lawn over the bottom prove most useful. Of the taller plants, only those that do not reproduce vegetatively (or do so very slowly) can be kept; otherwise they would soon overgrow the aquarium and have to be thinned. Plants must also be chosen that will thrive in the water conditions given to the fish. Thus if mainly tetras are kept, the plants must require or at least tolerate an acid medium (*Cryptocoryne*). If livebearers are the aquarist's main interest, *Echinodorus, Sagittaria,*

This male *Macropodus cupanus* has built its bubblenest using some branches of *Riccia*. The plant keeps the nest from breaking up easily.

This beautiful display tank with tiger barbs (*Capoeta tetrazona*) is greatly enhanced by the inclusion of actively growing water plants. A good lighting system ensures the growth of the plants. Photo by Dr. D. Terver, Nancy Aquarium, France.

It is also possible to keep plants in a home tank as long as the plants receive the required amount of light and nutrients. Photo by Dr. Herbert R. Axelrod.

Olean water, a rich bottom, and accessibility to sunlight ensure the survival of aquatic plants in this area of Lake Malawi, Africa. Photo by Dr. Herbert R. Axelrod.

Bacopa moniera is one of many aquarium plants cultivated commercially.

Vallisneria, and *Anacharis* are among the best choices. Mosses do well in tanks with killifishes and are useful in spawning the fish. Cichlids require robust and broad-leaved plants with firm leaves (such as *Echinodorus* and some varieties of *Vallisneria*); the roots of these plants should be protected by stones around the base of the stem so they cannot be dug out by the fish. These and other factors greatly limit the number of really satisfactory plants for each specialized aquarium, and the number is further reduced if the aquarist wishes to keep South American fish with South American plants, African fish with African plants, etc.

4) An aquarium for the plant specialist. Little can be said about this type of aquarium. The preference is usually confined to certain plant groups (such as *Aponogeton, Echinodorus, Cryptocoryne,* etc.), so the aquarist usually has a fairly good knowledge of the requirements of the plants and how they limit his arrangement of the aquarium. These aquariums are planted with a large number of species and, if the subject matter concerns the species of

a single family, it is always necessary to complement these with other plants of a different structure. Otherwise such an aquarium is certainly valuable but has little decorative effect.

5) Biotic aquariums. These are aquariums which represent as accurately as possible a section of aquatic life in a particular area. The plants are therefore chosen not according to their overall appearance in the aquarium, but strictly on how they fit into the geographic area being reproduced in the tank. The aquarium is planted to resemble a tropical Asian jungle, an African lake, or a lagoon in the Amazon basin of Brazil, among many other possibilities. The esthetic appearance of the finished aquarium must of course be given some consideration. It is also natural that the fish should conform to the area from which the plants were obtained. Some plants typical of the main geographic areas are:

Wide-leaved plants are ideal spawning substrates for armored catfish like *Corydoras aeneus.*

Cryptocoryne siamensis var. *kerri.*

Cryptocoryne axelrodii.

Cryptocoryne affinis.

Anubias congensis is a well known plant from the African continent.

South America: *Echinodorus* (except *E. cordifolius* and *E. berteroi*), *Heteranthera*, *Myriophyllum aquaticum*, *M. elatinoides*, *Alternanthera*, *Hydrocleis*, and *Cabomba*, among others.

Central America: *Bacopa amplexicaulis*, *Cabomba*, *Elodea*, *Ludwigia*, *Echinodorus cordifolius*, *E. berteroi*, *E. tenellus*, *Myriophyllum hippuroides*, *M. pinnatum*, *Sagittaria graminea*, and *S. subulata*.

Africa: here is the smallest choice of plants, and one can mention only *Anubias*, *Lagarosiphon*, *Baldellia*, and *Ranalisma*.

Tropical Asia (including Indonesia): *Cryptocoryne* spp., *Aponogeton natans*, *A. undulatus*, *A. crispus*, *Barclaya*, *Blyxa*, *Hygrophila*, *Lagenandra*, *Limnophila*, and *Vallisneria gigantea*.

Tropical Australia: *Aponogeton elongatus* and *Marsilea brownii*.

7

Algae in the Aquarium

Algae are an ever-present but unnecessary and sometimes dangerous part of the flora of every aquarium. The majority of them are harmful to higher plants because they settle on the leaves and reduce the photosynthetic efficiency of these organs. Some species cover the glass sides of the aquarium and shade the interior; they also prevent the aquarist from observing his fish and plants. The harmless filamentous green algae are also not welcome in the aquarium although they add a natural touch when present in small quantities. Unfortunately they are seldom present in small quantities for long, as they soon cover the bottom from their rapid growth. They can also be dangerous to small fish and fry, which might get stuck in the tangle of filaments and suffocate.

As a general rule, algae are considered weeds in the aquarium as their growth cannot be easily regulated. They are a weed which regularly gets into the water with food, fresh water, new plants, and through the surface with air-borne spores. Each species of alga has definite requirements with respect to the quality of the medium, and it develops only under the correct conditions. The most important of these conditions are temperature, duration and intensity of illumination, the mineral and organic substances in the water and substrate, the species and number of fish inhabiting the aquarium, and the kind and number of pieces of apparatus (such as filters, bubblers, etc.) which effect the movement of the water.

Algae can be fought by removing the causes of development of the specific groups. Generally any species of alga can be destroyed or suppressed by changing the conditions: increasing or decreasing illumination, increasing filtration and aeration, or—most drastic —moving the entire aquarium to a new location. Specific ways of checking individual groups of algae are discussed below. A chemical is now available which will subdue or kill all algae even when used in dosages safe for higher plants and fish in the aquarium. In heavily planted aquariums, however, any chemical can theoretically be dangerous to the plants and should be used with caution.

Algae are responsible for the green color of this standing pool in Indonesia.
Photo by Dr. Herbert R. Axelrod.

Newly hatched fry of *Herotilapia multispinosa* find temporary refuge in a clump of vegetation in this spawning tank. Photo by H.J. Richter.

The Chinese algae eater (*Gyrinocheilus aymonieri*) can keep the aquarium walls and plant surfaces free from algae.

GREEN ALGAE (CHLOROPHYTA)

Green algae abound in nature and are distributed all over the earth, although most species are found in freshwater. They reproduce mostly vegetatively but can also develop microscopic sexual organs resulting in minute spores. These spores are easily introduced into the aquarium with water, plants, or through the air.

In appearance greens vary greatly from unicellular forms which float freely in the water to multicellular filaments attached to stones or other plants. The unicellular forms may be so abundant as to color the water green or may be attached to plants, the aquarium glass, decorations, and the substrate. The filaments may produce dense tangles among the higher plants. Because their requirements resemble those of many higher plants, they are often common in the aquarium but do little harm unless present in very large numbers. They produce oxygen as well as the higher plants.

The minute species can be very troublesome when they attach to the leaves of plants and decrease their food-making efficiency. They are usually firmly attached and cannot be easily removed. Since they attach mainly to the older leaves and to stems, seldom to young leaves, the infested leaves can be cut off and removed from the aquarium. Algal films on the glass can be removed by various types of aquarium scrapers and sponges.

Filamentous green algae are seldom a nuisance unless they are allowed to reproduce excessively. Unattached filaments should be removed from the aquarium regularly with a net. Most attached filaments are only a few centimeters long and do not interfere with the higher plants. Some look very attractive and can even serve as spawning media for fish.

Ventral view of the Chinese algae eater showing the mouth adapted for scraping off algae.

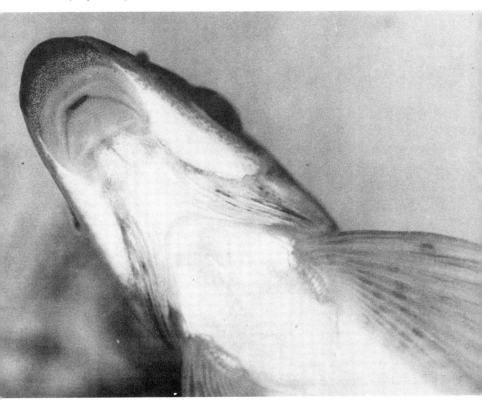

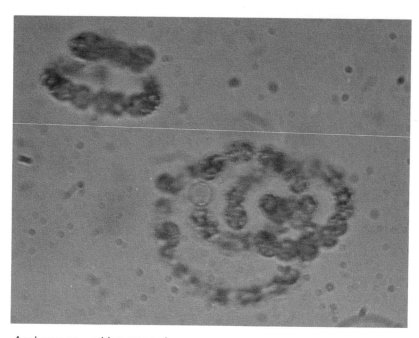

Anabaena sp., a blue-green alga.

Cladophora, a green alga. Photo by Frickhinger.

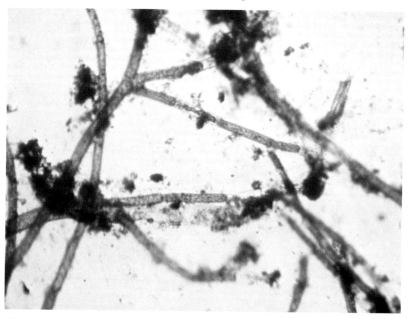

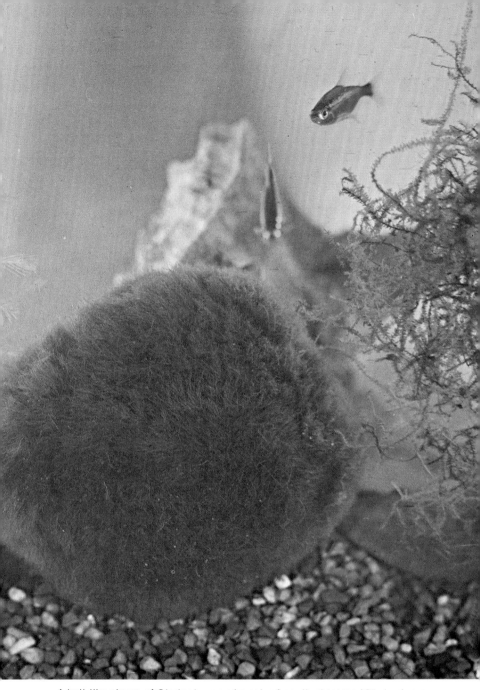

A ball-like clump of *Cladophora* and a pair of cardinal tetras (*Cheirodon axelrodi*). Photo by A. Noznov.

Tadpoles are efficient algae eaters and are easy to obtain. Photo by H. Pfletschinger.

The occurrence of green algae in the aquarium is a sign that conditions are good for the development of higher plants and fish. If kept under control by regular mechanical cleaning of excess algae, they are often a positive addition to the tank. Some species are used as food by such fish as mollies, Chinese algae eaters, many species of barbs, and many of the South American armored cat-fishes.

Complete removal of green algae from the aquarium is very difficult unless chemicals are used. The fish mentioned above will help, as will snails. Most green algae are too hard for snails, how-ever, which prefer to nibble on the more tender leaves of higher plants.

Another well known algae eater is the upside down catfish (*Synodontis nigriventris*). Photo by G.J.M. Timmerman.

BLUE-GREEN ALGAE (CYANOPHYTA)

Blue-greens form a slimy covering of thousands of cells in a gelatinous matrix. This covering not only looks bad and interferes with the leaves of higher plants, but actually smells like a swamp. Fortunately the film is seldom attached and can be removed mechanically from the substrate and plants. These algae are very dangerous in large quantities and could eventually destroy all other life in the aquarium if not controlled. They develop mainly in fresh tap water, especially if it contains a high percentage of calcium salts. They often appear in newly established aquariums or when a large proportion of the water is changed too frequently and is replaced by hard tap water.

Plenty of light and undisturbed conditions are required for the growth of these algae. If the water is in constant motion through heavy aeration or filtration, blue-greens will not thrive; nor will they increase in numbers if there are fish constantly moving through the tank and disturbing the bottom material.

Close-up view of a bubblenest together with some branches of *Riccia*. Photo by H.J. Richter.

Very young fry of a leaf fish (*Polycentrus schomburgki*) resting on a very broad leaf of *Echinodorus*. Photo by H.J. Richter.

If blue-green algae do appear in the aquarium, they should first be removed by stripping off the film which rapidly covers the plants and bottom of the tank. The remaining fragments are allowed to settle to the bottom and then siphoned out. If just these precautions are taken, the algae will appear again within a few days. At the same time the algae are manually removed, some of the water (containing fine fragments of algal film) should also be removed and replaced by soft water. The lighting should also be changed for two or three days, either by reducing the light, moving the aquarium to a shaded area, increasing the light by the addition of extra bulbs, or moving the aquarium into sunlight. As long as the light intensity changes, either up or down, the algae will be discouraged. Gro-Lux type lighting also greatly retards the growth of blue-green algae. Snails eat some species of blue-greens, as do the various algae-eating fishes, and *Corydoras* catfishes and

There are many commercial products and devices for the mechanical removal of algae. Courtesy of Eureka Products Company.

Armored catfish (*Corydoras aeneus*) photographed while stirring up the bottom in search of food.

cichlids constantly stir up the bottom and prevent formation of algal colonies.

Blue-green algae often appear toward the beginning of spring, which allows the seasonal use of frog and toad tadpoles as algae-eaters. If many tadpoles are put in the aquarium and not fed, they will soon eat virtually all the algae and prevent the remainder from forming colonies because of their constant swirling of the water during swimming.

DIATOMS (DIATOMACEAE)

The diatoms are brownish algae commonly seen in aquariums. They are unicellular and generally live attached to the substrate, the aquarium glass, and plant leaves. Shaded situations are preferred, so they tend to appear in largest numbers in poorly lighted aquariums, especially during the autumn months when

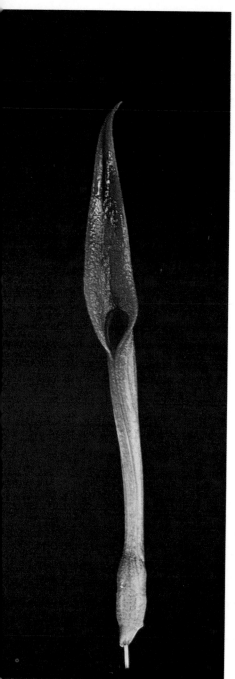

Inflorescence of *Cryptocoryne petchii.*

Inflorescence of *Cryptocoryne pontederiifolia.*

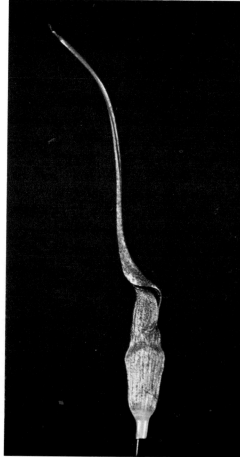

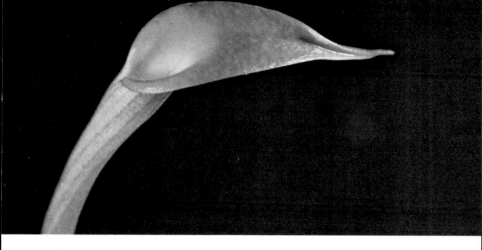

Colorful limb of the inflorescence of *Cryptocoryne siamensis* var. *ewansii.*

Cryptocoryne siamensis var. *ewansii.*

natural light is weak. Diatoms are harmful to the growth of aquarium plants and also cover the glass with a brown scum. They can be removed from the glass by a scraper or a coarse sponge, but cannot be scraped off the plant leaves. They are best controlled by increasing the light, either by repositioning the aquarium or adding extra light bulbs.

TURBIDITY CAUSED BY ALGAE

Discoloration and cloudiness of aquarium water occur most frequently in newly established aquariums. Fresh water, whether from the tap or from other sources, contains numerous microscopic algae and protozoans as well as sufficient mineral substances for their continued reproduction. Turbid water is therefore a common phenomenon in new aquariums, although this cloudiness usually disappears within 5 to 10 days and does not return. For the first few weeks the water should not be changed or added to, as the

Many fishes, like this breeding pair of *Haplochromis burtoni,* stir up and dig into the substrate in search of possible breeding sites. It would be a great mistake to put them in aquariums with delicate plants.

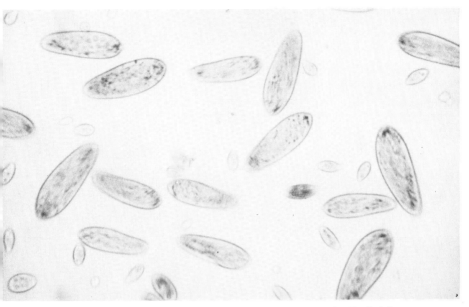

A colony of *Paramecium* and other ciliates. Photo by Dr. R. Geisler.

new water will contain more organisms and a fresh supply of nutrients. The cloudiness will thus reappear.

If the initial turbidity lasts more than a couple of weeks, the filtering can be increased. This removes the turbidity but not its causes. If the excess growth of algae and protozoans is caused by an overly rich planting medium or by excessive fertilizing of the substrate or water (whether by natural or artificial fertilizers), the turbidity immediately reappears as soon as filtration is stopped. This will continue for as long as the surplus nutrients remain in the water, which may be months. This is one more reason for using plain sand for the bottom material.

Turbidity in older aquariums is generally of a seasonal nature. Summer often brings a green coloration caused by dense growths of unicellular green algae stimulated by excess light. This turbidity is sometimes beneficial but also curtails the transparency of the water and is therefore largely disagreeable to the aquarist. This heavy growth of green algae is in fact a sign of sufficient light but at the same time indicates a superabundance of nutritional substances in the water. As soon as the algae have consumed all the available mineral nutrients, they die off *en masse* and their bodies

Rotifers occasionally appear along with protozoans and algae in a tank.
Photo by C.O. Masters.

enrich the water, providing organic substances on which protozoans can feed. When the green turbidity becomes gray or brown, it
is no longer even marginally beneficial but may be dangerous. The
turbidity is now composed of protozoans and other minute animals
which remove large quantities of oxygen from the water, possibly
causing suffocation of the fish.

In extreme cases such as this a substantial part of the water
can be changed, but it should not be replaced by water containing
additional nutrients. Only distilled water, rain water, or water
from a clean aquarium should be used. A prompt use of increased
filtering helps also, if the filter is powerful enough to remove the
cloudiness within 2 or 3 days. If turbidity caused by protozoans is
left for more than this time, it almost certainly will prove dangerous.

Cryptocoryne petchii.

Cryptocoryne pontederiifolia var. *sarawacensis.*

Enlarged photo of *Eichhornia crassipes* showing the swollen petioles of this plant.

8

Reproduction in Aquatic Plants

Most aquarium plants propagate vegetatively, putting out new plants from root stocks or runners, and seldom flower and produce viable seeds under cultivation. In spite of this generalization some species can be reproduced only from seeds (as *Aponogeton* among others), seldom or never producing vegetative offshoots. Because of the beauty and value of the flowers of aquatic plants, sexual reproduction is discussed here in some detail even though it must be remembered that many common aquarium plants will never flower in the home.

Bisexual flower of *Cabomba*. Both male and female structures are present in such flowers.

Cryptocoryne costata.

Flowers and fruit of *Echinodorus cordifolius.*

SEXUAL REPRODUCTION

In plants the flowers are termed perfect or bisexual if they have both the male (stamens) and female (pistils) organs. The ovary is at the base of the pistil, while pollen is produced toward the tip of the stamens in the anthers. Bisexuality is probably the most common condition in aquatic plants.

If the flowers are not bisexual, two other conditions can exist. The plants can be monoecious (literally, one house) and have separate male (staminate) flowers and female (pistillate) flowers on the *same* plant, or they can be dioecious (literally, two houses), having the male and female flowers on *different* plants. Typical monoecious plants include the *Sagittaria*, while examples of dioecious plants are *Vallisneria*, *Elodea*, and *Lagarosiphon* among others. Transitional forms exist.

Female flowers of *Sagittaria graminea.*

Bisexual and monoecious plants can be either self-sterile or self-fertile. Self-sterile plants must be pollinated by pollen from a different plant, while self-fertile plants can be successfully pollinated by pollen from the same or a different plant. Self-fertile plants such as *Aponogeton, Ottelia, Sagittaria,* some *Echinodorus, Nuphar,* and *Barclaya* produce seeds with relative ease in the aquarium.

It must be clearly understood that self-fertile species can be pollinated by pollen of either the same plant or a different individual of the same species; self-fertility is not an exclusive character. Almost all self-fertile plants can be cross-pollinated (fertilized with the pollen from a different plant), with the few exceptions of those species in which the flower never opens or the flower opens under water. If the flower never opens (a situation known as cleistogamy) self-fertilization is of course necessary because pollen from different flowers cannot enter. Underwater flowers have about the same problem as it is unlikely that pollen will be transmitted from one plant to another.

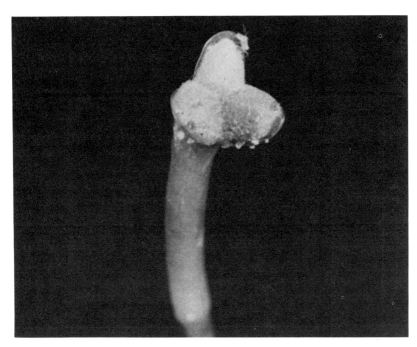

Female flower of *Vallisneria gigantea.*

Male flower of *Vallisneria gigantea.*

Echinodorus cordifolius is seen here blooming and fruiting in the emersed condition.

With self-sterile plants, self-fertility is almost impossible under normal conditions. It must be remembered that if we take two plants grown vegetatively from the same plant, they will also be self-sterile. This is because the plants have the same genetic make-up and are in reality not two different individuals, but just separate parts of the same original individual. Thus if a cutting is made from a self-sterile plant and allowed to come to flower, it cannot be used to fertilize flowers on the 'mother' plant from which the cutting was obtained; the nature of pollen from the two plants is identical. The only exception occurs when the cutting is grown under very different conditions than the 'mother' plant.

Ball-shaped fruit of *Echinodorus cordifolius* containing a large number of seeds called achenes.

Artificial pollination is usually necessary in order to ensure fertilization and viable seeds from a self-sterile plant. Pollen from a flower on one plant (never one produced as a cutting or other vegetative offspring of the other plant) is carried by a fine brush or other tool to a flower on another plant. This necessitates that ripe pollen be present on two different plants at the same time, making artificial pollination far from easy. In the cryptocorynes, for example, the sexual questions are so complicated that they are often the topic of serious scientific research.

Seeds are the product of sexual reproduction, a process termed generative as opposed to vegetative. It is rather slow and tedious and is seldom used in the cultivation of aquatic plants, with three classes of exceptions including only a few species.

1) Species not reproducing vegetatively (*Aponogeton*, among others) and annual species that die after flowering (*Ottelia*, etc.). With these species the generative reproduction from seeds is either necessary to continue the species under aquarium conditions (annuals) or necessary if we wish to increase the number of plants.

2) Species that reproduce slowly by vegetative means but flower and produce seeds easily. These are mainly large species of the genus *Echinodorus*. During one vegetative period they are able to render only 2 to 30 young plants, but in the same period may produce up to 10,000 seeds.

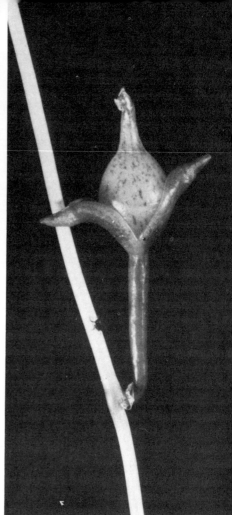

Irregular flower (left) and fruit (right) of *Utricularia.*

3) Species that do not flower in aquariums or do so only rarely yet also do not reproduce vegetatively. Such plants are raised in emersed cultures (paludariums or terrariums) and usually flower there quite easily. Seeds are sown in humid soil and the young plants can be replanted underwater into aquariums. Under these conditions generative reproduction is very laborious but extremely productive. It has one disadvantage: plants grown from seeds do not always resemble their parents in quality and appearance, as do plants produced vegetatively.

VEGETATIVE REPRODUCTION

Vegetative reproduction is well known to aquarists. Some aquatic plants (*Cryptocoryne*) reproduce by rhizomes, others (*Vallisneria, Sagittaria*) by roots. In the genus *Echinodorus* new plants arise on flower stems in the axil of the flowers. Many species of aquatic plants reproduce through large or small portions being able to root and continue growing after being removed from the parent plant. In the genera *Ludwigia, Elodea, Ammania, Alternanthera*, and *Hygrophila* new cuttings are commonly taken from the axil of the main plant. This ability to produce new roots is so strong in some species that even parts of the leaves will root (examples: *Bacopa amplexicaulis, Hygrophila polysperma*).

Many aquarium plants like *Ludwigia* develop roots very quickly and are very easy to propagate.

Rooting young *Echinodorus paniculatus* are easily.separated and replanted. When grown under the best of conditions this species can produce more growth than desired. Photo by G.J.M. Timmerman.

Another method of vegetative reproduction is use of the roots themselves. If we separate the roots from the mother plant, new rooting plants arise from the dormant buds which then become independent plants. This is an especially useful process in plants with long creeping rootstocks such as *Anubias, Lagenandra,* and *Acorus.* In perennial plants without creeping rootstocks, for example *Echinodorus,* new plants will grow from the outer edges of the round base of the root. Roots of some plants can be divided into 2 to 6 parts. This is possible with many members of the family Araceae. With some *Aponogeton* and with larger *Echinodorus* vegetative propagation usually takes place spontaneously, with exceptions. The exceptions will be mentioned under the descriptions of the individual species.

9

Practical Propagation of Aquarium Plants

There are only two major methods of propagating aquarium plants: vegetatively and generatively. The vegetative or asexual way is the most practical one for aquarists because of its simplicity. In addition, the plants obtained by vegetative reproduction are relatively mature and develop quickly. Generative propagation (from seeds) is used only for those species which cannot be reproduced vegetatively. It is also of importance where it is necessary to obtain large numbers of young plants, as in nurseries.

From the point of view of the quality of the final product, reproduction from seeds is the better method. If a species is propagated only asexually, only a single form is being systematically repeated. After a few generations there is a strong tendency for the line to deteriorate, showing decreased hardiness in unfavorable conditions, dwarfed growth, or loss of ability to produce flowers, among other problems. All the positive properties of a species can be maintained by reproduction from seeds, although a larger amount of variation than desirable may occur.

REPRODUCTION FROM SEEDS

About the same procedures are common to all flowering plants. In the first place, the aquarium or terrarium should be designed so that all conditions favor successful flowering, pollination, and setting of the seeds. The seeds should be left to mature properly. After a resting period in either a moist or dry atmosphere, the actual conditions and length of time depending on the plant, the seeds can be sown. At this time and after they develop into seedlings extra care and caution must be exercised, as the germinating seeds and young seedlings are very delicate.

Propagation from seeds is necessary in the case of plants that do not reproduce vegetatively (*Aponogeton*), annuals which die

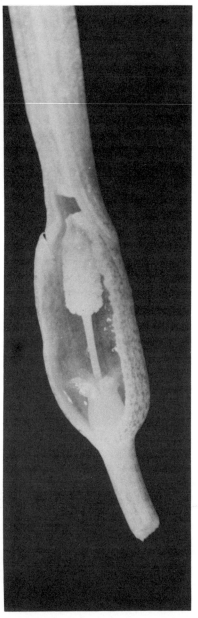

Left: The complete inflorescence of *Cryptocoryne wendtii* showing the important structures: kettle, tube, and limb.
Right: Dissected kettle with the male and female structures exposed; female organs at the base, male organs at the distal end.

each year after flowering (*Ottelia*), and species such as *Echino-dorus cordifolius* which reproduce faster and more abundantly by seed than vegetatively. A few plants, such as *Samolus valerandi*, flower well in terrariums but neither flower nor produce vegetative offspring under aquarium conditions. Such plants are allowed to flower in terrariums or paludariums and the seeds sown underwater or the seedlings transplanted to the aquarium.

In nurseries it is often more practical with such groups as *Echinodorus* to use seeds than vegetative offspring. One year of vegetative propagation might produce 1 to 30 new plants, while a pair of plants during the same time might produce over 1,000 viable seeds. To produce large numbers of new plants vegetatively would require large numbers of parent plants and correspondingly large tanks and floor space, while much less space is necessary for two or three flowering parents and their offspring. Although the plants produced from seeds may take twice as long to reach salable size, the reduced need for space makes generative reproduction economically practical.

Bifurcate spike inflorescence of *Aponogeton ulvaceus*.

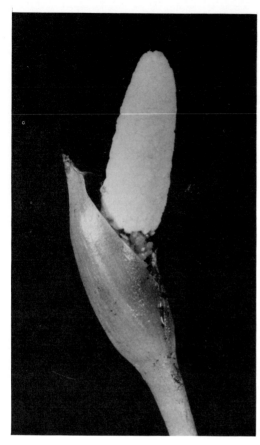

Typical inflorescence of *Anubias*. The distal part consists of male flowers only. The female flowers are situated on the more protected basal part.

The major disadvantage of depending on flowering in the aquarium is that many genera and species of aquatic plants never (*Hygrophila polysperma, Najas, Lagarosiphon*) or rarely (*Elodea, Anubias*) flower in the aquarium. Some species flower readily when cultivated emersed, yet flower only sporadically and with special attention in the aquarium, and even then do not produce viable seeds (*Cryptocoryne, Vallisneria*). For these plants we are of course still dependent on vegetative reproduction. In some species succeeding generations produced vegetatively flower more and more rarely or, after developing floral stalks, put out roots instead of flowers. Thus the floral stalk of *Echinodorus osiris* when fully developed produces either buds which never open or root shoots.

ARTIFICIAL POLLINATION

In species where self-sterility predominates, artificial pollination is necessary. Pollen must be transferred by hand from one flower to the stigma of another flower on a separate plant.

For the best chance of successful pollination, it is wise to fertilize different flowers by transferring pollen from other flowers situated as far away as possible. If possible, flowers from different floral stalks should be used. In *Aponogeton*, *Echinodorus*, and *Sagittaria* it is common for a single plant to develop 2 or 3 stalks at one time.

As a practical point it has proved useful to fertilize a flower with a mixture of pollens from both its own species and a different but closely related species. If, for example, the self-sterile *Echinodorus paniculatus* and the self-fertile *E. cordifolius* bloom at the same time, *E. paniculatus* can be pollinated by a mixture of the pollens of both species. This method is used in other branches of horticulture and experiments have shown that by this means seeds of the self-sterile species of *Echinodorus* can be readily obtained. The pollen of another species makes possible the fertilization of flowers by the proper pollen, but no hybrids will develop.

The technique of artificial pollination is not difficult to master. The pollen of one flower is transferred to another by means of a fine brush. In species that produce many flowers pollination can be accomplished by picking flowers and rubbing the mature anthers against the stigmas of other flowers or by shaking off yellowish clouds of pollen into the flowers which are to be fertilized. Pollination should take place in the morning about 10:00 or 11:00, as the pollen is not mature earlier than this and is not loose on the anthers.

We have not yet had any experience with the pollination of some popular species of aquarium plants, such as cryptocorynes, which are undoubtedly self-sterile. The pollen perhaps is transferred in these plants by small insects attracted to the spathes. Perhaps only one species of insect is able to enter the flower and carry pollen, and it has not been imported with the plants. This is also a possible reason why *Vallisneria*, although flowering readily, does not produce seeds in the aquarium.

The *Aponogeton* species are self-fertile, responding to pollen from the same or different plants. The production of seed is heavily dependent on the environment, and the complicated conditions for successful seeding are described fully in the introduction to the family Aponogetonaceae.

Close-up views of the flowers of the self-sterile *Echinodorus paniculatus* (above) and the self-fertile *Echinodorus cordifolius* (below).

78

HYBRIDIZATION

Some species of plants can be crossed only with difficulty and the possibility of new forms arising by hybridization is negligible. On the other hand, some plants can be crossed very easily so that large numbers of hybrids have been obtained. New varieties of animals and plants can be obtained either by hybridization, which is often difficult or impossible, or by selectively breeding individuals having wanted traits. Selective breeding of individuals showing unusual traits (usually mutants) has led to many showy varieties of aquarium plants (some *Vallisneria* and decorative forms of *Sagittaria*) and fishes (high- or long-finned guppies and swordtails).

Hybrid formation between known species of *Aponogeton* is not unusual. This unidentified *Aponogeton* species has very wide undulate leaves.

Relatively few successful hybrid plants have found their way into aquariums as yet, but the capacity for hybridization is found in many species of aquarium plants. In nature hybrids between some species of *Echinodorus*, such as *E. cordifolius* and *E. berteroi*, are known. Yet it is not really certain that these are true hybrids, for the possibility remains that they are merely forms or variants of the species. Artificial hybrids of these *Echinodorus* have not yet been created in the aquarium. In *Aponogeton*, however, hybridization is common. It has been proved that the Asiatic *A. crispus*, *A. echinatus*, and *A. natans* can be easily crossed. Because the subject is rather complicated, it will be treated in detail later.

GERMINATION

The seeds of such aquatic plants as *Echinodorus* and *Sagittaria* readily take up water and swell quickly because they do not possess hard and impervious outer coatings. They germinate very readily and quickly. In other genera the seeds are firm and hard, germinating only after a long immersion during which bacteria and other organisms have time to weaken or dissolve the waterproof outer coating. The seeds of *Potamogeton*, for example, require a 'fermentation' process in marshy conditions. In cultivating them, large quantities of seeds are left in small dishes of water where their surface decomposes anaerobically with the emission of foul-smelling gases. Under these conditions many will germinate successfully.

Some aquatic plants develop seeds which germinate immediately after maturing. This group includes the Pontederiaceae such as *Eichhornia* and *Heteranthera*. In other species, perhaps the majority of aquatic plants, the seeds require longer or shorter resting periods of 1 to 6 months between maturing and germinating. During this resting period the seeds can survive both dry and cold conditions.

Fully mature seeds usually are collected from the parent plants in the late summer or autumn and are sown at the beginning of spring or late winter (February or March). The seeds of almost every species of aquatic plant can withstand drying, even when the seeds ripen under water as in *Ottelia*, *Barclaya*, and the like.

If seeds are to be over-wintered they should be dried out properly after collection and then put in paper bags and stored in a dry, well ventilated room. Storing in greenhouses with a high humidity very quickly diminishes their viability. As a general rule,

A floating "islet" of *Ceratopteris* with new plantlets on the margin of the leaf blades. Photo by Dr. D. Sculthorpe.

if the seeds hibernate at average indoor temperatures above 59° F (15° C), they require a very dry medium.

If 'moist' seeds are over-wintered they should be stored at low temperatures, which will inhibit germination. Even a temporary increase of temperature, for instance above 46° F (8° C), may greatly decrease the chances of germination, especially in plants of the genus *Nuphar*. The seeds of *Nuphar* must be stored in cold surroundings, either covered with moss or buried in the sand. When dry seeds are stored, germination is inhibited by lack of moisture; with moist seeds it is by lack of warmth.

At the beginning of spring the seeds of aquatic plants from temperate and subtropical areas are sown at temperatures of 59° to 68° F (15° to 20° C), while those from the tropics are sown at temperatures of 77° to 86° F (25° to 30° C).

The seeds of typically submersed plants (*Ottelia, Barclaya, Nuphar*) are sown in water about 10 cm deep. Amphibious species are sown on the surface of moist sand; only after the seeds have germinated and the first roots have appeared are they covered by a layer of water 12 to 25 mm deep. This is suitable for *Bacopa, Limnophila, Myriophyllum, Sagittaria*, and some species of the genus *Echinodorus*.

Many plants are provided with only moist sand in their dishes even after germination and are not covered with water (and then only a few centimeters) until the seedlings reach a height of 50 to 90 mm. This procedure is followed in the case of the majority of *Echinodorus* species, such as *E. cordifolius, E. macrophyllus, E. paniculatus, E. tenellus*, and others, while it is the only suitable way of ensuring a high yield of such genera and species as *Samolus valerandi, Ammania, Ludwigia*, and *Hygrophila*.

Aponogetons are the only plants commonly transplanted after germination. The mature seeds are left in soft water (rain water is best) at temperatures around 54° to 59° F (12° to 15° C) for a period of 1 to 2 months. Then the temperature is raised to about 77° F (25° C) and the seeds are left to germinate. The seedlings, 25 to 40 mm high and with well developed leaves and roots, are then planted in sand on the bottom of a shallow, well lit aquarium and the water level is gradually raised. The seeds of the true species (not hybrids) of *Aponogeton* are left in cool water, usually for the whole winter and until the spring (which in nurseries and greenhouses may begin as early as late February).

VEGETATIVE PROPAGATION

This is the most common method of propagation used by aquarium hobbyists and is also used at the commercial level. Some species of aquatic plants are commonly reproduced by rhizome runners (*Cryptocoryne, Vallisneria*) or by root runners (*Sagittaria*). In *Echinodorus* this is relatively rare and is found only in the smallest species, *E. quadricostatus* and *E. tenellus*. Vegetative reproduction in *Echinodorus* is most commonly through the development of new plants on the floral stalk, where rooting plantlets arise in the axil of the flower petioles. The same process is found in the "viviparous" species of *Aponogeton*.

Numerous species of aquatic plants can be propagated by cuttings or by fragments of the plant body that can take root and continue growing. This is common in plants of the genera *Ludwigia*, *Elodea*, *Ammania*, *Alternanthera*, and many others which sprout new branches from the axillary buds at each separate internode of the stem. In some plants this ability is so strongly developed that even torn leaves or their fragments may take root, as in *Hygrophila polysperma* and *Bacopa amplexicaulis*.

A further source of vegetative reproduction lies in the rhizomes of numerous species. If they are separated from the parent plant, new plants will develop from the dormant buds on them and become separated in the course of time. This is most useful in plants with a cylindrical rhizome that is long and creeping, such as *Anubias*, *Acorus*, and some *Echinodorus* (*E. osiris*).

In perennial plants without the typical cylindrical rhizome new plants will develop around the perimeter of a globular woody rhizome if it has been plucked out of the sand and left underwater in the light. This method is useful with *Echinodorus berteroi*, among others.

The rhizomes of some perennial plants can also be divided into 2 to 6 parts, each of which is able to continue growing independently. This is possible with most of the plants in the family Araceae, with *Aponogeton* species, and with all larger species of *Echinodorus*. In some perennial water plants the rhizome cannot be divided, for either the plant is entirely destroyed or only a single part of the divided rhizome will grow, that on which the single growing point has remained. *Nuphar* and *Nymphaea* are this way.

Since with few exceptions vegetative reproduction does not require any special professional knowledge and often occurs spontaneously without intervention of the aquarist, the few problems encountered occasionally will be discussed only with the descriptions of the exceptional species.

10

Characteristics of Tropical Floral Areas

Conditions for the growth of water plants vary considerably in different parts of the world. For this reason it is useful to describe briefly the principal ecology of the aquatic and marsh vegetation in the more interesting parts of the world from the aquarist's viewpoint: the tropics of Asia and South America.

THE TROPICS OF SOUTH AMERICA

The Amazon basin, measuring over 2½ million sq. mi., is for the most part a great plain, especially in the middle and lower reaches of the river. The South American forests, to which we turn because of an interest in *Echinodorus* species, do not have marshy characteristics but resemble temporary water reservoirs. It is true that the deep forests are moist, but they are entirely without permanent standing water. Where any great water surfaces are found, they are mainly concentrated in the vicinity of large rivers which during the rainy period overflow their banks and inundate the surrounding countryside. After the water has drained back into the main stream, a system of still backwaters and pools arises, often very extensive, which during the dry period gradually changes into marsh or dries out entirely.

There are two rainy periods in this area (January to April and November to December). Between these two periods there is a dry stage which is not so conspicuous as it is in the areas where there is only one rainy period and where, consequently, the dry period is longer.

Rainfall in the Amazon area reaches 20 to 25 meters a year, and it tends to rain more often in the upstream direction. As everywhere in the tropics, the rainfall is distributed unevenly so that during the rainy period the daily downpours cause floods. At this

This photo shows the typical marshy conditions of the natural habitat of *Sagittaria montevidensis* in the Amazon. Photo by H. Schulz.

time the water level of the Amazon rises by anything up to 15 meters (on the average, 3 to 6 meters) and the force of the flooding river destroys the vegetation. Only a few plants grow successfully year after year either in the river or on its immediate banks. In the vicinity of the river no trees grow and an open landscape arises, with the result that fluctuations of temperature during the day and over the course of the year are much greater than, for instance, in the jungles of southern Asia. In the main stream of the river only a very small number of annual species grow, and these are propagated by seeds or spores (examples are *Victoria*, the giant water-lily, *Pistia*, water lettuce, and *Azolla*, a fern).

Plant communities in the vicinity of the Amazon arise in accordance with the undulations of the terrain. In the lowest-lying places, which are flooded at any slight rise in the water level, no trees grow. During the rainy period the whole area is inundated

Note the scarcity of vegetation in this almost dry marshy terrain near Rio Araguaia, Brazil. Photo by Dr. H.R. Axelrod.

and later (during the dry period) becomes muddy and quite impassable. Yet even here annual plants prevail to grow and during the short dry period produce seeds. Perennial plants do badly at this level and seldom survive to produce seeds.

From the point of view of the aquarist, the most interesting habitats are situated 6 to 9 meters above the normal level of the river and are flooded only during the highest waters of the rainy season. After the waters recede, extensive lagoons and marshes are formed as the ground gradually dries out. These provide suitable habitats for the amphibious species of *Echinodorus*. In the lagoons where the water remains all year, both amphibious and typically submersed plants are found, such as *Echinodorus amazonicus, Cabomba, Heteranthera, Myriophyllum*, and others.

The average annual temperature of the Amazon area is 77° to 79° F (25° to 26° C), but during the year the temperatures may vary from 57° F to as much as 104° F (14° to 40° C). The fluctuation in temperature is therefore considerable, explaining why the South American species of aquatic plants are generally very resis-

A river bank scene along the Rio Negro, a tributary of the Amazon River. Note the low vegetation in the background of the picture. Such vegetation is under water during the rainy season. Photo by Dr. H.R. Axelrod.

tant to temperature changes, the majority of them able to be cultivated successfully even in unheated indoor aquariums. The temperature of the river water in the Amazon basin varies from 65° to 86° F (18° to 30° C) in quiet areas of still water. It reaches an average of 83° to 86° F (28° to 30° C) in lagoons during the vegetative (dry) period, but during unusually warm periods shallow lagoons can reach as high as 104° F (40° C).

In the tropics of the Amazon we find variable habitat conditions that produce what is sometimes called a cycle of development in plants. During the rainy period there is a stage of inconspicuous vegetative rest caused by the mechanical effects of fast moving water and movement of soil driven by flood waters. In addition there is a lowered temperature and a lack of light because the muddy water transmits little sunlight. When the floods are over the submersed plants start to flower; with the development of leaves such plants as *Echinodorus* also sprout flower stalks reaching above the water surface or, as in *Cabomba*, develop both floating leaves and flowers. Amphibious plants develop leaves now but do not yet flower.

By the time the water level falls to 20 to 40 cm most submersed plants have finished flowering and the floral stalks of some types begin to take root after maturing. A period of vegetative propagation follows. On the contrary, amphibious species develop only floriferous stalks. This means that in one and the same place various kinds of plants grow in stages, one after the other, also flowering in sequence, a definite cycle of development.

Other changes in the composition of vegetation can be observed on the fringes of lagoons and still waters where the treeless formations of the savannas pass into marshes and on to the shallows of the river. Here the development of the plants is extraordinarily varied. The specific composition of the plant growth varies continually, the number of some species is increased, and others disappear temporarily or permanently. The plants very often change their shape and the size of their leaves (the so-called "leaf multiformity"). On the fringes of the waters, on the banks and in the shallows, are found such plants as *Echinodorus quadricostatus*, *E. tenellus*, and various species of *Eleocharis*. Toward the savanna zone are found various marsh plants of the Araceae family which are not capable of withstanding permanent inundation. Toward the lagoons, even in shallow water, plants of the genera *Myriophyllum* and *Heteranthera* grow, while everywhere on the surface of both shallow and deep still waters are many floating plants.

This picture illustrates the variety and density of vegetation in the back-waters of Rio Negro, Brazil. Photo by Dr. H.R. Axelrod.

The aquatic and marsh plants of the Amazon area are thus characterized by a relatively great ability to withstand fluctuations of temperature. They tolerate ordinary indoor conditions and are not damaged by even a fall of temperature to 54° or 59° F (12° or 15° C). The species are mainly amphibious and can be cultivated in both paludariums and aquariums. Distinctly submersed plants are very rare, and even these can grow emersed for a short time (*Heteranthera, Cabomba*). The South American plants of the genus *Myriophyllum* are better adapted to an emergent life than are species from all other continents except Australia.

The aquatic and marsh plants of tropical South America have no distinct resting period, growth ceasing only during those floods in which their leaves and more delicate stems are destroyed. That is why they can grow indoors all the year around and are content with a temperature of about 68° F (20° C). Illumination for about 12 hours a day suits them well at all seasons. Of the conditions in their environment, it is the depth of the water that mainly influences their development. Since they are characterized by a high resistance to external conditions, the South American plants are most suitable for the aquarium. In indoor aquariums we can prepare much better and more stable conditions than are offered in their natural habitat.

It should not be forgotten that a number of very decorative aquarium plants from South America do not grow in the tropical area proper, but in the subtropical and temperate zones of southern Brazil, Paraguay, Uruguay, and Argentina. Here are found the exquisite novelties of our aquariums, such as *Echinodorus osiris*, *E. horemanii*, *E. opacus*, *E. longiscapus*, and many others. These species, growing permanently under water, are found in relatively cool conditions with temperatures about 58° to 67° F (14° to 19° C). This of course does not mean that they could not do well at the ordinary aquarium temperature of about 72° F (22° C).

THE TROPICS OF THE INDO-MALAYAN AREA

Together with the South American tropics, this area produces more aquarium plants than any other area. Most aquarium plants (and fish) from the Indo-Malayan area originate from the Malayan peninsula and Indonesia (especially the larger islands of Java and Sumatra), Borneo, the Celebes, and New Guinea. A great number of species also come from Ceylon (Sri Lanka).

The most conspicuous feature of the area is the absence of large rivers. In the places where, because of thorough drainage, no rice fields have been cleared, the whole country is covered with impenetrable jungle interspaced with small lakes, rivers, and marshes. Two factors, the land being covered by dense vegetation plus the proximity of the sea, influence the nearly constant temperature which varies only slightly from 77° to 81° F (25° to 27° C). During the changing seasons of the year as well as during the day, the temperature varies so slightly that an almost constant annual temperature may be said to reach a substantially higher value than the temperature of tropical aquariums in the home.

The greater part of the Indo-Malayan area is very rainy (25 to 40 meters rainfall per year). Though the rains are distributed over two periods, no distinct dry period occurs (except in the eastern

A typical rural scene in Thailand. In this kind of habitat the environmental conditions do not change very much throughout the year. Photo by Dr. H.R. Axelrod.

part of Indonesia), so the waters have no periodic variations in conditions and in the jungle there are many permanent water reservoirs of large and small size. Only in very shallow pools and in marsh formations does the depth of water vary sufficiently to be able to influence the composition of both aquatic and amphibious vegetation.

The flooding in this tropical area is not caused simply by rising river waters, but during the rainy periods an excess of water is present everywhere and increases evenly. Afterward the height of the water level decreases evenly. The aquatic vegetation is therefore not damaged by a wild current and the cycle of development is distinct in the numerous species of amphibious plants.

Although a great number of species of water plants come from the Indo-Malayan area, the most typical of them are the Araceae, particularly the cryptocorynes. The typically submersed species (*Cryptocoryne affinis*, *C. siamensis*, *C. cordata*, etc.) grow in

A typical site in a rubber plantation in Indo-Malaysia where *Cryptocoryne cordata* is found growing in the irrigation canals.

permanent, often very deep, waters and can flower throughout the year, although in waters deeper than 30 to 40 cm they do not flower but are propagated vegetatively. In such cases the cycle of development is not typical.

Amphibious species (*C. becketii, C. walkeri, C. nevillii, C. lucens*) are submersed during the rainy period, when there is a stage of vegetative propagation by runners from the rhizome. If the water level falls they pass into the emersed way of life, when they flower and produce seeds. These species are typically plants of the jungle formations. They grow in semi-shaded conditions under several layers of luxuriant forest growth, often in water where the surface is quite covered with floating plants.

Other aquatic Indo-Malayan plants such as *Limnophila, Ceratopteris*, and *Bacopa* are found in artificial and natural channels which connect the lagoons and small lakes.

In summary, the Indo-Malayan species of plants are characterized by a medium which offers them an unvarying and relatively high temperature, about 79° to 83° F (26° to 28° C), for both air and water. The aquatic vegetation consists of amphibious spe-

A mass of amphibious vegetation growing along a river bank in Bangkok, Thailand. These plants are rarely completely inundated except, perhaps, during extreme high water as a result of a typhoon. Photo by Dr. H.R. Axelrod.

cies (*Lagenandra*, some *Cryptocoryne* species, *Limnophila*) as well as typically submersed species (some *Cryptocoryne* species, *Myriophyllum*). They have no period of vegetative rest, but some amphibious species, in accordance with the period, are capable of vegetative growth and propagation as well as a flowering stage with the consequent production of seeds.

The plants of this area are, therefore, more exacting in their requirements. They are sensitive to fluctuation in temperature, especially to serious drops which for extraordinarily delicate species may be deadly even at 65° F (18° C). Other plants may succumb at about 59° F (15° C). It is essential to give Indo-Malayan plants temperatures of 77° to 80° F (25° to 27° C) throughout the year.

Some cryptocorynes can be induced to flower only with great difficulty. Even though a sufficient number of experiments has not yet been undertaken along this line, it can be presumed that in artificial cultures it is necessary to adhere to the normal cycle of development if blossoming is to be encouraged: the change from emersed to submersed growth and back again must be duplicated by a regular fluctuation of the water level.

According to notes on herbarium sheets and detailed observations by Prof. Schulze (1967 and 1971), aquatic plants in the Indo-Malayan area (particularly *Cryptocoryne*) grow within three main biotopes.

1) Banks of strong rivers up to 10 to 100 km from the mouth. The cryptocorynes grow in well lit or only slightly shaded areas up to 50 meters above sea level. Under these conditions are found all the species preferring the terrestrial way of life. They are nearly always found in shallow waters, the leaves and inflorescences growing above the level of the water, as in the case of *C. ciliata*. These species are often found along strong streams penetrating deep into the woods, but wider streams may have more vegetation on their banks because of increased illumination. These species do not grow in association with *Lagenandra* and *Hygrophila* because they do not occur in river beds. Other species of the genus *Cryptocoryne* also are not found in river beds with such a biotope. The aquatic vegetation is represented chiefly by *Aponogeton rigidifolius, Myriophyllum* spp., *Hydrilla verticillata, Blyxa*, and *Potamogeton* species. The submersed form of *Crinum thaianum* joins this typically Malayan flora in Thailand. In Sarawak *C. ciliata* occurs with *C. lingua* and *C. pontederiifolia* var. *sarawacensis*; these species often descend right into the beds of rivers together with *Barclaya mottleyi*. In spite of the nearness to the sea, *C. ciliata* grows mostly in the areas with fresh water. It is rarely found in areas with brackish water.

2) Small streams up to 2 to 10 meters wide and under normal circumstances quite shallow (10 to 30 cm), with the surface rising to 1 or 2 meters after heavy rains. These brooks are found in thickly wooded and shaded areas, usually in elevations of 50 to 100 meters in Ceylon (rarely to 500 meters) and 1200 meters in northeastern India. The main characteristic of these biotopes is crystal clear water with a pH of about 6 to 6.5, and mainly soft rainwater. The bed of the brooks is rocky or stony and covered with a sand-silt mixture brought down by running water from higher elevations. The cryptocorynes occur mainly in cultures of single species on overgrown river beds and are exposed to the conditions of amphibious life. Depending on the rainfall, the depth of the water often

A newly collected *Cryptocoryne* plant from its natural habitat in Thailand.
Photo by Dr. H.R. Axelrod.

varies within a few days from 1 to 2 meters to a few centimeters. In
such conditions *C. balansae* grows in Thailand, *C. wendtii* and *C.
axelrodii* in Ceylon, and *C. bullosa* in Sarawak. In the case of lowland species living at 25 to 100 meters above sea level, *C. nevillii*
and *C. becketii* ascend to the limit of 500 meters in Ceylon, and *C.
crispatula* was found up to the height of 1200 meters in northeastern India.

3) Marshes of primeval forests, tidal mangroves, irrigation
canals of rubber plantations, and stagnant waters. The beds of
these localities are usually soft, either muddy or of sandy clay. The
water is crystal clear and slow moving, usually neutral or a little
acid. Only during rainfall are these areas flooded with thick layers
of mud and the water becomes tinted brown, which temporarily
lowers the pH. *Cryptocoryne cordata* as well as *C. lingua, C. gracilis*, and other species grow mainly under these conditions.

Plants in nature are exposed to some environmental conditions
which can be duplicated in the aquarium only with difficulty. An
aquarium is only a small water reservoir into which only a few
plant species can be planted. These species may come from diverse

parts of the world and are quite unrelated to each other. Yet the dissimilarity of plants in natural locations is nullified by the fact that there is the same depth of water all year, and usually also the same temperature and other physical and chemical conditions. As a rule only the duration and intensity of the light vary.

In the aquarium other changing conditions appear, conditions that are unknown in nature. In nature the least variable part of the habitat is the soil, while in the aquarium it is very variable. If the bottom is enriched with organic substances (peat, humus, etc.) they will influence the composition of the water and may themselves undergo anaerobic decomposition. Consequently poisonous gases arise to adversely affect the medium. Thus the advantage of using clean sand which is gradually enriched from normal decomposition of plant and animal wastes.

In natural aquatic plant communities there is generally a characteristic biological balance. In accordance with the depth of the water, the temperature, illumination, etc., some species develop only in certain seasons of the year, later to die and give place to others. The species composition therefore changes with the period of vegetative growth and the period of flowering. This does not occur in the aquarium.

The main reason for the disturbance of the biological balance is the fact that conditions in the aquarium change but little during the year. The community is not subject to the proper cycle of development, but the species for which the conditions of a certain aquarium are most favorable thrive to the detriment of plants not so favored. The species which propagate vegetatively repress the plants propagated only by seeds. In darker aquariums the members of the genus *Cryptocoryne* will prevail and make the growth of *Echinodorus* and *Vallisneria* impossible; in lighter aquariums the reverse occurs.

The interaction between the separate species of plants is therefore much stronger in the aquarium than in nature. After a while it is generally necessary to make certain changes in the aquarium such as thinning out the overly abundant species, removing shade plants, and regulating the amount of floating vegetation.

The facts that the amount of water in the aquarium is relatively small and that changes take place (although slowly) mean that various species of plant influence each other chemically by acting upon the properties of the water. For example, *Cryptocoryne* species tend to acidify water while *Vallisneria* species tend to alkalize it. This causes a mutual intolerance between some spe-

Enormous amounts of silt from surrounding higher ground account for the brown color of this tributary of the Amazon River at Tefe, Brazil. Photo by Dr. Herbert R. Axelrod.

A great mass of water plants growing under water in the very clear waters of the Paranajuba River, Upper Xingu, Brazil. Photo by Harald Schultz.

Vallisneria is best maintained with those plant species that tolerate alkaline conditions. It can also be utilized alone as seen in this set-up. Photo by Dr. Herbert R. Axelrod.

cies of aquarium plants, which sometimes becomes much more evident in the aquarium than in nature.

It goes without saying that this intolerance does not arise where the aquarium is planted with a greater number of species. It may, however, appear in those aquariums where *Cryptocoryne* plus *Vallisneria* or *Cryptocoryne* plus *Sagittaria* combinations form a substantial part of the vegetation. In darker aquariums the growth of *Cryptocoryne* species will predominate, which will influence the reaction of the water because they will acidify it and thereby further inhibit the development of the *Sagittaria* or *Vallisneria*, eventually arresting their growth. In brightly lighted aquariums there are better initial conditions for the development of the latter two genera, which will regulate the reaction of the water toward the neutral point or will alkalize it slightly, inhibiting any further development of cryptocorynes.

In summary, we have seen that the aquarium is mainly a sector of shallow to moderately deep bankside waters and cannot support the diverse forms of vegetation that are present in various depths and on bankside fringes in nature. Thus it is ideal to complement an indoor aquarium with appropriate containers of various sizes in which shallows covered with floating vegetation can be maintained and where a number of marsh and amphibious flowering and non-flowering plants can be cultivated.

In this aquarium set-up the tall and more robust plants are confined to the background, while the low vegetation is limited to the front part. The bushy-leaved plants provide some contrast to the broad-leaved forms.

Terrestrial plants (trees) and aquatic plants (floating and emersed) are seen growing together in this area of the Amazon River at Tefe, Brazil. Photo by Dr. Herbert R. Axelrod.

Glossadelphus zollengeri is an aquatic moss from Java and Celebes. The small black and white photo shows a part of the plant in detail. Photo by Dr. D. Terver.

11

AQUATIC AND AMPHIBIOUS PLANTS SUITABLE FOR THE AQUARIUM
Non-Flowering Plants (Cryptogams)

Cryptogams are non-flowering plants that are not capable of forming seeds and are propagated by microscopic spores. Such spores seldom develop in aquariums, so these plants are propagated vegetatively. The Bryophyta (mosses and liverworts) and Pteridophyta (ferns) belong to this primitive group of plants.

HEPATICEAE
(Leafy Liverworts)

Liverworts are minute green plants that can be propagated by spores enclosed in pods, but they are usually propagated vegetatively. Most liverworts live in moist places and in water.

RICCIACEAE (Thallose Liverworts)

This is a family of minute liverworts with a flat thallus. The thallus is the undifferentiated body of these plants, in this group disc-shaped or stellate in form. They live for the most part on moist soil, but some have adapted entirely to life in the water, where they float on the surface or live submersed, attached to other plants or to the bottom.

RICCIA (FLOATING LIVERWORT) (III. 53) *

The thallus is lobate and forked, with the ventral surface finely scaled. Altogether there are four similar species known from the tropics and the temperate zones.

RICCIA FLUITANS L. (III. 104)

R. *fluitans* is probably a cosmopolitan species. The thallus is ribbon-shaped (with 2-5 prongs), 15 mm long and up to 1 mm wide. This widely distributed species is found on the surface of backwaters and ponds. It develops submersed as well as floating and terrestrial forms. Submersed forms are usually disc-shaped, light green, and attached to the ground or in tangles of underwater plants. Floating forms are very varied in shape; under optimal conditions a conspicuously grassy green globular form develops. Land forms with developed roots appear on disturbed moist ground and on banksides.

This species is not exacting with respect to light and soil composition, but disappears in tanks with a high nutrient content. It is a good spawning medium, but it is necessary to inhibit its growth, which can be abundant. In the aquarium it hibernates regularly.

RICCIOCARPUS

This genus is represented by a single species, *Ricciocarpus natans* (L.) Corda, which is distributed almost throughout the globe. The cordate thallus is an ashy gray-green, 5 to 15 cm long, and 5 to 10 mm wide. On the lower surface of the thallus purple ribbon-like scales can be seen against the brownish purple background.

Ricciocarpus natans is a very decorative species which grows on the surface of peaty pools, ponds, and still backwaters. It is found as both a fully-floating form or as a land form. A winter resting stage is less common in this species than in R. *fluitans*.

MUSCI (Mosses)

Mosses are minute plants living in the most varied places, from dry rock to water. These plants propagate by spores. Very little attention has been paid to mosses in aquariums and terrariums. In spite of importation difficulties, a great number of amphibious

---

* In order to facilitate the location of illustrations, each apropos reference has been noted alongside the homologous description, in small type. Thus, for example, "Ill. 75" means "See page 75 for an illustration of this plant."

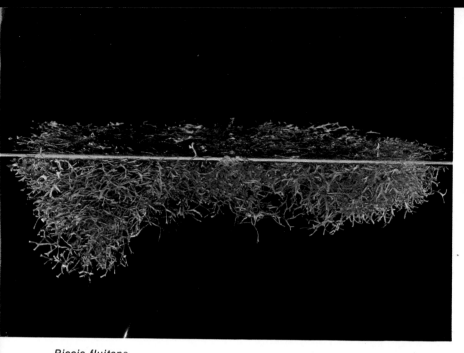

Riccia fluitans.

Vesicularia dubyana.

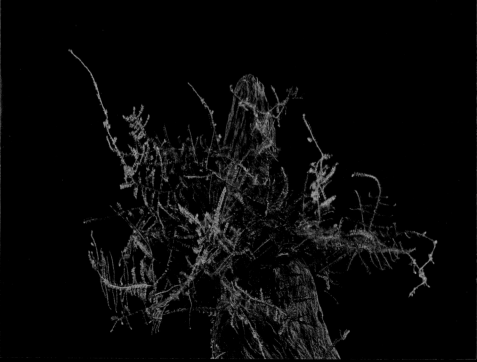

Salvinia minima.

Isoetes malinverniana.

and aquatic species do quite well as very decorative additions to the list of aquarium plants. There are many beautiful forms for both terrariums and aquariums. They grow like curtains of fine leafy lace which, combined with carpets of other plants, can add a strange charm to the tanks. Only those examples that are known to do well in aquariums are treated here.

VESICULARIA DUBYANA (C. Mull.) Broth (III. 104)

This plant belongs to the family Hypnaceae (of the 30 genera only the genus *Vesicularia* contains aquatic representatives). There are about 135 *Vesicularia* species coming from the warmer regions of the world, with a few species from Southeast Asia and Africa submersed plants. Only *V. dubyana* is frequently cultivated as a decorative aquarium plant.

In its original home, tropical Southeast Asia, it grows amphibiously in moist jungles, covering fallen trees, stones, or the soil. The small stems are irregularly branched, with the leaves arranged in two rows. The lanceolate emerald green leaves are 10 to 15 mm long and 5 to 7 mm wide. In land forms they are wider and a glossy dark green or sometimes olive yellow-green.

In the aquarium *V. dubyana* is cultivated in rather shady conditions attached to stones and other objects. It requires soft, clear water and temperatures about 68° to 77° F (20° to 25° C). Initially it grows very slowly, but once attached it grows faster and spreads over rocks or other decorations, increasing the natural look of the aquarium. It blooms even under water. In paludariums *V. dubyana* grows more rapidly than when fully submersed, covering the surface of stumps, branches, and stones with a beautiful green carpet.

DREPANOCLADUS ADUNCUS (Hedw.) Moenkem

D. aduncus belongs to the family Amblystegiaceae, which contains about 16 genera with aquatic members. This plant occurs in temperate to cold climates, but it is exceptionally adaptable and able to withstand temperatures from 10° to 28° C. In nature it often appears in masses in moist places and in water. Typically amphibious, it occurs in rivers and peat bogs from the lowlands up to the mountains in Europe, Asia, North America, and New Zealand. Like *V. dubyana* it extends over stones and submersed wood, forming a green or yellow-green to brownish cover of plants. *D. aduncus* can be used successfully even as a spawning plant and is able to exist in very hard water. Light conditions are not critical; the plant does not die even during long periods of darkness or in

Fontinalis antipyretica. Photo by Dr. D. Sculthorpe.

high temperatures of spawning tanks and also winters well.

In spite of all these features we prefer *V. dubyana* for the tropical aquarium. With *Drepanocladus* it is possible that your success as a grower will depend very much on the geographical origin of the plants.

FONTINALIS   (Ill. 107)

Fontinalis belongs to the family Fontinalaceae, which comprises water mosses with floating and rooted forms. They grow in running streams as well as in stagnant water of ponds, backwaters, and wells. The firm glossy green water mosses with ovate to lanceolate leaves belong to the genus *Fontinalis*. These plants rarely produce spores but propagate vegetatively. The family has 3 genera: *Fontinalis*, *Brachelyma*, and *Dichelyma*, but only *Fontinalis antipyretica* is commonly cultivated in aquariums.

This species is distributed throughout Europe, northern Asia, North America, and northern Africa. The leaves on the stem and branches are trihedral ovately lanceolate.

Isoetes species
collected in Brazil. In
nature the stems of this
plant provide food for
water birds. Photo by
T.J. Horeman.

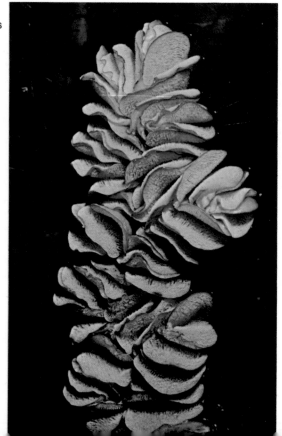

Close-up view of
Salvinia auriculata.
Photo by T.J. Horeman.

Regnellidium diphyllum. Photo by T.J. Horeman.

Dense clumps of *Salvinia auriculata* in Brazil growing like a carpet. Photo by T.J. Horeman.

In the running water of clear brooks and small rivers the plant grows attached to stones or develops submersed to amphibious forms; in stagnant waters it becomes attached to the substrate. In lakes the rooted forms may appear at a depth of 2 to 3 meters. As a land form it appears only temporarily, for in the summer it dries out quickly. It has been found that in acid water *Fontinalis* develops short but densely leaved forms, has normal growth in a neutral medium, and in alkaline water has branches which are elongated but with very minute leaflets.

In the aquarium *F. antipyretica* requires a rather cool temperature (68° F, 20° C), slightly acid to neutral water, a sand or gravel base, and somewhat shaded tanks. Smaller plants are best placed in tanks together with the stones on which they are growing. Larger examples are found in stagnant waters. As a decorative species it is suitable in either form and can be used for spawning.

PTERIDOPHYTA (Ferns)

Pteridophytes are vascular cryptogams propagated partly vegetatively and partly by spores which are dispersed by wind or water. The technique of propagation by spores is lengthy and requires considerable knowledge. For this reason aquatic ferns are generally propagated vegetatively either by dividing the rhizomes and stems or by separating new plantlets developing directly on the leaves of parent plants.

ISOETACEAE   (Quillwort Family)

This family contains two genera and is represented by perennial plants living either submersed or amphibiously (the latter is especially the case with the species from the Mediterranean area). There are also species with land forms that live on wet soils. The subterranean rhizome is generally short, the narrow leaves forming a dense rosette. The lower surface of the leaf is usually ovate and the upper surface is awl-shaped. Roots are fibrillar and branched.

ISOETES   (III. 108)

The genus *Isoetes* has about 75 species distributed in the warm areas of the northern hemisphere. Only a small number of species are found in the southern temperate zone or in the tropics. Water birds and rodents like to eat the stems of *Isoetes.*

Sterile plants can be determined only with difficulty. Some plants of this genus are imported occasionally for aquariums, but identification is difficult or impossible. Most often they belong to the following species.

ISOETES LACUSTRIS L.

I. lacustris is found in Europe, Siberia, and North America. The rhizome is 20 to 30 mm long, globular; leaves are dark green, stiff, cylindrical in cross section, 8 to 28 cm long, and 8 to 30 mm in diameter.

It grows in clear water with a sandy substrate, mainly in lakes (rarely in ponds) at a depth of 30 cm to 3 meters. When the water is silted or frequently disturbed, it disappears quickly.

In spite of growing in cold lakes in nature, *I. lacustris* does well in temperatures above 68° F (20° C). It requires soft water and some shade. The plant is propagated by dividing older tufts or by spores; growth is very slow.

ISOETES ECHINOSPORA Durieu

This slow-growing species from Europe differs from *I. lacustris* by its thicker rhizome (10 cm long) and fine, short-pointed leaves. Both species grow under the same conditions in nature. It requires very cool water and soon dies in aquariums.

ISOETES MALINVERNIANA Cesti et de Notaris   (Ill. 105)

The habitat of this species is the Po River basin in Italy, where it grows in local brooks. It is the largest of European species, has light green leaves 30 cm to 1 meter long and 1 to 2.2 mm thick.

This is a well known species in the aquarium, requiring water with temperatures from 68° to 77° F (20° to 25° C) and reasonably deep tanks where its size can be best displayed. It can be propagated not only vegetatively but also by spores sown in the sand where, with sufficient heat and moisture, they germinate readily. When the plants are about 10 mm high they are transplanted and set out at intervals of about 30 mm. Before reaching a height of about 10 cm they are replanted several times; later they can be transplanted into a tank. Great care and attention should be given during transplantation as the plants are very fragile.

AZOLLACEAE (Azolla Family)

The family consists of minute aquatic ferns floating on the surface or growing in a moist medium as terrestrial forms. The plants have a very short, branching stem. *Azolla*, with six species distributed from the tropics to the temperate zone of both hemispheres, is the only genus in the family.

Marsilea quadrifolia, cultivated emersed.

Pilularia globulifera.

Cryptocoryne parva from Ceylon with inflorescence. Photo by T.J. Horeman.

Close-up photograph of the inflorescence of *Cryptocoryne parva*. Photo by T.J. Horeman.

A small group of floating *Azolla filiculoides*. Photo by Dr. D. Sculthorpe.

These are not desirable plants in aquariums because they can grow too profusely, like a weed. Under different situations in nature *Azolla* is regarded to be an undesirable weed or a very beneficial plant. The *Azolla* - blue-green alga combination fixes atmospheric nitrogen and is widely used as fertilizer and as forage. *Azolla* is best suited for terrariums and paludariums; it can provide small shallow pools with a decorative growth or cover the surface of moist sand with a varied red-green mosaic carpet. The following species of *Azolla* (water-velvet) are cultivated.

AZOLLA CAROLINIANA Willd.

This species is distributed throughout North and South America and the West Indies. It was introduced to Europe and is now found in many places (Germany, Netherlands, Czechoslovakia), often only temporarily. The plants hardly reach a length of 5 to 12 mm and are round in outline. The stem as well as the leaves are often intensely reddish or green with red margins.

AZOLLA FILICULOIDES Lam. (III. 114)

This plant, a native of South America, was brought to Europe and now grows in the same areas as the preceding species plus France and Italy. Compared to *A. caroliniana*, the plants are larger (10 to 25 mm). Both species float on the water with the greater part of the plant being above the surface, so with intensive vegetative propagation it does not take long to cover the surface of the aquarium.

SALVINIACEAE (Salvinia Family)

The Salviniaceae is represented by annual to perennial rootless plants floating on the surface of the water. The leaves grow on short stalks; two leaves are green and very hairy, while the third is finely divided and submersed, acting as a root. *Salvinia* is the only genus of the family. It includes 12 species which are found mostly in the tropics of America and Africa (*S. natans* reaches the temperate zone). Due to introduction the family is almost cosmopolitan. *Salvinia* has become a very serious pest in southeastern Africa, Ceylon, and southern India.

These are suitable plants for shading the surface of the water. Propagation is fast. The majority of *Salvinia* species (floating moss), especially those that have well developed root hairs, form a favorable medium for the spawning of fish.

SALVINIA AURICULATA Aublet (III. 108, 109)

This species comes from tropical America. It differs from *S. natans* in having round to ovate leaves. In the aquarium it requires water with temperatures from 66° to 77° F (18° to 25° C) and a bright situation. As in the majority of floating plants, it is recommended that the aquarium be covered with a sheet of glass to retain the humid conditions.

SALVINIA NATANS (L.) All.

S. natans is found in the warmer areas of Europe and in eastern Asia. The leaves are elliptical to ovate and 5 to 15 mm·long, their surface covered with short, stiff cilia (hair-like processes).

In nature this species grows in quiet backwaters, pools, and canals with slow moving water where during the summer it often forms a very dense growth on the surface of the water, dying off in autumn. In the aquarium it requires a great deal of light; in rooms heated by gas it becomes pale green and often does not last long. Propagation is by runners.

Hygrophila difformis. Photo by Dr. D. Terver.

Inflorescence of *Hygrophila corymbosa*. Photo by T.J. Horeman.

SALVINIA ROTUNDIFOLIA Willd.

S. rotundifolia comes from South and Central America. The leaves are round, 10 mm long, and densely covered with cilia. It grows in pools and ponds and requires warmer water.

SALVINIA MINIMA Bak. (III. 105)

This species is probably the most convenient for aquariums. It grows well at temperatures from 20° to 32° C, winters well, and endures oscillation of the pH. Although it comes from South America (from Santa Catarina, southern Brazil), it can be used together with cryptocorynes. Its rounded, nearly sessile leaves are only 6 to 9 mm long. Submersed leaves are divided into 5 to 6 segments (each 25 to 76 mm long) and look like roots. In the water they form a thick network of greyish white or pinkish "rootlets" in which young viviparous fish like to live. Islets of floating plants serve as spawning plants to many species of fish and are used for building bubblenests by fightingfish and gouramis.

MARSILEACEAE (Marsilea Family)

This family is comprised of amphibious ferns that are rooted on the bottom with submersed, floating, and aerial leaves as well. Some species develop terrestrial forms. This family of perennial plants includes three genera: *Marsilea* (about 65 species), *Pilularia* (6 species), and *Regnellidium* (1 species). They have a creeping rhizome with developed roots at the base. The leaves are of various shapes and arranged mostly in two rows on the rhizome; young leaves are rolled. The plants live mainly in a marshy environment and are propagated by division of the rhizome.

MARSILEA (PEPPERWORT) (III. 30)

The leaf stalk is long, terminating in four leaflets which are arranged symmetrically cross-wise; the plant is submersed, floating, or emersed. Its distribution ranges from the tropics to the warmer areas of the temperate zone of both hemispheres. Only two species are fit for the aquarium: the European *M. quadrifolia* and the Australian *M. browni*. All the other species are suitable only for paludariums and terrariums, as they do not grow under water. In nature *Marsilea* is found in ponds, ditches, swamps, rice paddies, and other areas with standing water. Several species are regarded as troublesome weeds in rice fields and irrigation ditches.

MARSILEA BROWNII R. Br.

This species comes from Australia, growing there in marshes as an amphibious plant. The smallest of the imported species, in its terrestrial form it has petioles that are not more than 80 mm long. The leaves are smaller than in the other species. Juvenile foliage is glossy, but later develops a soft downy or ciliate covering. This species forms sporocarps more readily than others. Under water only simple to 2-parted leaflets are formed on the petioles. The plants reach a maximum height of 25 to 50 mm.

This plant propagates as speedily in deep water as in a marshy habitat, the thin rhizomes taking root quickly. During summer a dense green or olive carpet is formed on the bottom. It is best cultivated in soft, moderately acid or neutral water and is the most suitable species for aquariums and terrariums. It hibernates in all forms.

MARSILEA QUADRIFOLIA L. (III. 112)

M. quadrifolia is found in central and southern Europe, Caucasia, western Siberia, Afghanistan, southwestern India, China, Japan, and North America. It has a long creeping rhizome from which leaves similar to a four-leaf clover develop in two rows.

In the aquarium this species should be cultivated in sand and in the shade. Only in this way will it prosper under water, the petioles growing to a length of 10 to 15 cm. In bright situations the petioles become elongated and the leaves reach the surface and emerge from the water. It is less suitable for paludariums and terrariums as in these situations the plant develops petioles that are up to 20 cm long and become prostrate.

PILULARIA (PILLWORT) (III. 112)

This genus contains minute plants with narrow cylindrical leaves; the juvenile foliage is coiled as in other ferns. They are generally found on the banks of shallow waters. Only *P. globulifera* is cultivated.

The rhizome is 20 to 50 cm long (in submersed forms it can grow to 2 meters), creeping, pilose or bare, and densely covered with cylindrical leaves which are 2.5 to 10 cm long in land forms and 30 cm long in submersed forms.

It grows in shallow water in pools and ponds, most frequently on substrates ranging from sand to fine silt. The plant is sensitive to alkaline conditions and prefers cool waters but temporarily withstands higher temperatures. Under water it usually dies at the approach of winter, a disadvantage which makes it more suitable for terrariums, where it can form an attractive carpet.

REGNELLIDIUM (III. 109)

Except for having only two leaflets this genus is like *Marsilea*.

Ceratopteris thalicroides. Photo by Dr. D. Terver.

Bolbitis heudelotii. Photo by Dr. D. Terver, Nancy Aquarium.

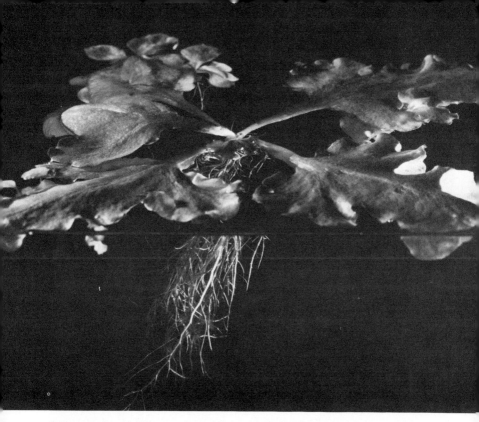

Ceratopteris pteroides is an appropriate plant for spawning fish. Newly hatched fry can seek protection in its fine root system.

The unique *R. diphyllum* Lindm. is endemic to southern Brazil and northern Argentina. Although regarded as an aquarium plant, this species does not grow under water permanently and is suitable only for paludariums.

CERATOPTERIDACEAE (Parkeriaceae) (Ceratopteris Family)

This family (with the single genus *Ceratopteris*) consists of annual floating or rooted ferns living in water or marshes. The leaves are of various shapes and sporangia are formed on their lower surface. *Ceratopteris* (6 species) grows in the tropics and subtropics and is mainly confined to shallow waters. The plants are propagated partly by axillary buds on the leaf margins and partly (during maturity) by generative reproduction from spores which germinate readily. Propagation in the aquarium is similar to that of *Isoetes*. (III. 81)

Ceratopteris thalicroides.

All cultivated species are usually regarded in existing aquarium literature as forms or varieties of a single species, *C. thalicroides*. Plants with wide leaf blades are labeled as *C. thalicroides*, plants with deeply indented leaves as *C. thalicroides* var. *javanicus*, and floating plants as *C. thalicroides* form *cornuta*. The identity of floating plants of *C. cornuta* (P. Beauv.) Lepr. coming from Africa is doubtful. They often represent the following three species:

Hygrophila difformis. Photo by T.J. Horeman.

Hygrophila corymbosa.

Inflorescence of *Echinodorus berteroi.*

Echinodorus berteroi.

CERATOPTERIS PTEROIDES (Hooker) Hieron (Ill. 122)
(FLOATING WATER SPRITE)

C. pteroides extends to tropical Asia and America. Rosettes of four to six leaves are formed. The petioles are flat, green, 25 to 75 mm long, and widen into lance-shaped or heart-shaped blades. The leaves are sometimes nearly entire, but their sides are usually incised and resemble oak leaves. On the margins or on the ribs new plantlets arise that separate (in this way become islets). The widely branched roots form an ideal hiding place for viviparous fish. At the same time they serve as a suitable spawning medium for many species of aquarium fish. Gouramis like to build their bubblenests among them.

C. pteroides is grown on the surface of water that is acid and soft and has a minimum temperature of about 18° C, although it grows best with 25° to 30° C. Sometimes it propagates too rapidly, but the number of plants can be reduced. This plant dislikes hard and alkaline water but does not mind plenty of light or half-shade.

CERATOPTERIS THALICROIDES (L.) Copel (Ill. 120, 123)
(WATER SPRITE)

The leaves (50 to 80 cm long) have petioles that are three to seven times shorter than the blade, which is green, flat, and very fragile. The blades are deeply incised, but the indentation does not reach as far into the petiole, so the rib is 12 to 25 mm wide. The blades are typically odd-pinnate and the leaf segments are 25 to 75 mm wide. In older literature it is characterized as a broadleaved fern.

This species prefers acid waters (pH 5-6.5) and deeply shaded places. Its bright green color and incised leaves serve as a most suitable complement to cryptocorynes. Having a rather poor root system, it gets nutriment mainly from the water. It is an annual plant. To keep it alive during winter the light has to be prolonged to 12 hours a day or it will die. Some of the youngest spirally twisted leaves can be saved and will develop in the spring. *Ceratopteris* is tasty food for aquarium snails. During the period of retarded growth (especially in winter), the number of snails has to be reduced; only smaller individuals up to 12 mm can be kept.

CERATOPTERIS SILIQUOSA (L.) Copel (Ill. 127)
Incorrect name: *C. thalicroides* var. *javanicus*

The leaves are 25 to 113 cm long, with petioles narrower than in the preceding species; deep incisions reach to the petioles so they are typically odd-pinnate. The individual segments of the leaves grow on the petioles in pairs standing against each other as well—thus a double odd-pinnate leaf. The leaves are much more ragged, the individual segments only 2.5 to 7.5 mm. It is cultivated in the same conditions as *C. thalicroides*, but is more decorative and grows easily. It is amphibious and often forms emersed leaves, so it can be grown as a terrestrial form in paludariums, where it reproduces quite easily also.

Ceratopteris siliquosa.

Microsorium pteropus (broad-leaved plant in background). Photo by Dr. D. Terver.

Microsorium pteropus.

POLYPODIACEAE (Polypody Family)

The Polypodiaceae is the largest family of ferns and contains perennial plants with a prostrate rhizome. Juvenile foliage is spirally coiled. The blades are copiously divided or only lobate, rarely smooth-edged. Many species grow on moist, periodically flooded soil. Only two species are cultivated in aquariums.

MICROSORIUM PTEROPUS (Blume) Ching (JAVA FERN)

M. pteropus comes from India, southern China, and the Indo-Malayan area as far as the Philippine Islands, where it is found as an amphibious plant attached to old tree trunks, stones, or the ground.

The plant has a creeping rhizome from which dark brown plume-like petioles develop with leaf blades that are 10 to 25 cm long and 25 to 75 mm wide. The blades are wide, lanceolate, smooth-edged, and green to brownish green with a distinct nervation; leaf margins are undulate.

This is one of the most beautiful aquarium plants. It is not exacting with respect to the composition of the water and grows well in a good light as well as in more shaded positions. Reproduction is by the separation of daughter plants which arise on the leaf margins of fully developed specimens and take root readily.

To cultivate this fern it is necessary to attach it to submersed branches or fasten it to the rocks used as decorations in the tank. After some time the roots become firmly attached. It should never be planted in sand. *M. pteropus* requires temperatures of about 68° to 77° F (20° to 25° C). Very suitable for paludariums, it grows over rocks, stumps, or branches but requires artificial illumination.

BOLBITIS HEUDELOTH (Bory ex Fee) Alston (III. 121)

The interesting water fern *B. heudelotii* comes from Guinea in tropical Africa. Its leaves are 25 to 37.5 cm long, odd-pinnate, with five to seven incisions on both sides of the blades, which are dark olive green, bottle green, or brownish. Cultivation is slightly more difficult than with the preceding species. *Bolbitis* is not planted in the bottom, but the plants can be fastened to stones or roots used as decorations in the aquarium. It demands a clear, soft to medium hard water and temperatures from 72° to 82° F (22° to 28° C). It does not do well in thickly planted tanks. This plant likes moving water and grows well when placed next to the filtering system, which enhances their normally slow growth. Sometimes algae can stop the development and growth of these plants, nor should there be too many fish in the tank. Successful aquarists often cultivate this species on decorative roots together with fish of the genus *Aphyosemion*.

Other species like *Bolbitis fluviatilis* (Hook.) Ching from tropical West Africa, *B. hydrophylla* (Copel) from the Philippines, and *B. lonchospora* (Ktze.) C. Chr. from Polynesia should also be considered for the aquarium. Even their names (*fluviatilis, hydrophylla*) indicate that they are water ferns.

Flowering Plants (Spermatophyta)

This group includes those plants with a perfectly developed body generally possessing roots, stem, leaves, flowers and fruit—in the botanical sense. They are divided into gymnosperms (conifers, cycads, etc.) and angiosperms (all flowering plants). The angiosperms are separated into two important divisions: monocotyledonous plants and dicotyledonous plants. The dicotyledons (Dicotyledonaceae) germinate from seeds with two flat, usually horizontal leaves; the monocotyledons (Monocotyledonaceae) germinate with only one, usually vertical, leaf. These differences are not important to the aquarist, so all the flowering plants presented here are arranged in alphabetical order by their family names.

ACANTHACEAE (Acanthus Family)

These are herbs or shrubs, rarely trees. They are mainly species of the tropics and subtropics, but some of them grow in warm areas of the temperate zone; they are found in forests, steppes (prairies), meadows, and marshes, as well as on inaccessible rocks and on the borders of deserts; some grow high in the Himalayas and Bolivian Cordilleras. Some species of this family have a very limited distribution. The family is large and contains about 250 genera with 2,650 species. Only a limited number grow submersed, but probably many of these will become aquarium plants in the future. In addition all are very suitable for planting in shallow containers.

Recently there have been many important changes in the nomenclature of the family. The genera *Asteracantha*, *Nomaphila*, and *Synnema* are no longer regarded as independent genera but are now all placed in the genus *Hygrophila*. Today the family Acanthacea includes only two aquatic genera, *Justicia* and *Hygrophila*.

The genus *Justicia* (about 300 species) is tropical and subtropical. Many species are marsh plants. *J. americana* (L.) Vahl. is aquatic and the cause of some concern in southeastern North America. Dense stands of this plant are the favorable breeding places for malarial mosquitos. It is not a very attractive plant and is not cultivated in aquariums.

The genus *Hygrophila* has an erect or ascending stem. The leaves are opposite, entire, lanceolate to obovate, with many species heteromorphic, having very variable emersed or submersed plants. Flowers arise in the leaf axil and are minute, with a deep two-lipped corolla, white or blue to purple. Emersed plants are usually finely pilose; submersed plants are naked. About 80 species grow in the tropical areas of the world.

The plants can be cultivated emersed as well as submersed. Although growing well under water, they adapt to normal soil conditions and can be cultivated in flowerpots as indoor plants. They flower abundantly and produce seeds. Some larger species grow very slowly under water, so they are propagated in tanks with water to a height of 10 to 15 cm, allowing them to grow quickly and form profusely branching stems. If the tips are cut off and planted in deeper water, they take root fast and within a week the stems and leaves lose the typical short soft hairs and the appearance of emersed plant growth is changed to that of submersed growth.

Hygrophila plants when cultivated in water require a moderately rich sand and soft or moderately hard water that is slightly acid to slightly alkaline. Some species require generous light, but others tolerate a certain amount of shade. Species from the tropics are usually the ones that are cultivated in aquariums.

HYGROPHILA ANGUSTIFOLIA R. Br.   (Ill. 133, 134)
Syn: *Hygrophila salicifolia* Nees.

This species comes from tropical eastern Asia, Indonesia, Australia, and New Zealand. The stem is often 10 mm thick, with leaves that are opposite, lanceolate with indistinct veins, 12 to 15 cm long, and 10 to 15 mm wide. The leaves are straight, have entire margins, are naked, and are light green above and whitish green below. Submersed leaves are only 7.5 to 10 cm long and 5 to 10 mm wide and richly branched. The plant blooms only in the emersed form. In marshy conditions they can form a densely branching bush 1 to 1.5 meters high, resembling the willow (*Salix* spp.). Tips cut from the emersed plants and transferred into water take root very readily, developing a stalk with long decorative

Hygrophila angustifolia.

Inflorescence of.*Hygrophila angustifolia.*

leaves. The tips of these plants (when well-rooted) are cut off to make them spread further and form profusely branching tufts 40 to 50 cm high.

    H. angustifolia is best cultivated in a medium rich soil with soft or moderately hard water in a lighted situation. The plant is thermophilic (68° to 77° F (20° to 25° C)); lower temperatures will do no harm even though the lower leaves often are lost. The acclimatization of emersed plants into an aquarium environment is sometimes very lengthy or unsuccessful.

HYGROPHILA CORYMBOSA (Blume) Lindau   (III. 117, 124)
Syn: *Nomaphila stricta* (Vahl.) Nees.

    This *Hygrophila* species is from the Malayan area, where it grows as a robust marsh plant with both emersed and submersed leaves. Above water it forms stems up to 10 mm thick with opposite leaves that are about 10 cm long and 50 mm wide, very broadly lanceolate, nearly cordate, tapering into an extended apex, and with serrate margins. The whole plant (especially the stem) is pilose, brownish green to reddish green.

134

The growing points transferred to underwater conditions take root very quickly and become naked. Within ten to twenty days the leaves change to a light green, but do not grow to be as broad as those of emersed plants. They are 25 mm long and are not too distinctly serrated. The now green stem becomes swollen at the nodes rather like bamboo. The upper leaves keep the reddish coloration. It is one of the most beautiful plants.

This plant is cultivated in aquariums with a fairly rich planting material and with any type of water. It requires a well illuminated situation but is content with artificial light; grows very quickly in temperatures above 68° F (20° C).

In winter the plant should be given artificial light, otherwise the bottom leaves are lost; in such a case at the beginning of spring the heavy part of the stem has to be cut off and replanted. Propagation is by planting pieces detached from the stem. These pieces can also be cultivated in flowerpots where they develop very well if lighted properly. They need to be watered well every day.

HYGROPHILA DIFFORMIS (L. fil.) Blume   (III. 116, 124)
(WATER WISTERIA)
Syn: *Synemma triflorum* (Roxb. ex Nees.) O. Kuntze

H. difformis can be found as an erect or prostrate plant in the Indo-Malayan area. The stem is thin and rooted. The leaves are opposite, light green in color, the lower submersed leaves divided or deeply incised and 7.5 to 10 cm long and 25 to 50 mm wide. The upper leaves are at first nearly smooth-edged, later changing and featuring the same form as the lower leaves. Aerial leaves are smooth-edged, not more than 50 to 65 mm long, and finely pilose. Roots usually appear at the nodes.

This plant is cultivated in soft to medium hard water in diffused light; it requires less light than the other species of the family. Artificial light suits it very well, but in indirect sunlight it sometimes becomes pale. It is a thermophilic plant that requires 68° to 77° F (20° to 25° C); although it grows below 68° F (28° C), submersed leaves are then smooth-edged and less ornamental. Growth ceases at 59° F (15° C).

H. difformis is a very beautiful aquarium plant which under favorable conditions is propagated very quickly by planting fragments of the stem. With its light green leaves it is a suitable complement to darker brownish green plants. By cutting off the tips of the stems some profusely branching plants can be obtained whose shape and size may be freely arranged as desired or needed.

Hygrophila lacustris.

HYGROPHILA LACUSTRIS (Schlect.) Nees. (III. 136)

This is among the latest novelties of the genus *Hygrophila*, being imported as recently as 1971 and 1972 from Thailand. Emersed plants resemble *H. angustifolia* but are always quite naked and the leaves are longer and wider. *H. lacustris* in comparison to *H. angustifolia* is more easily acclimated. Emersed plants transplanted under water root very quickly and without exceptions grow immediately. Submersed leaves are usually shorter at the base of the plant, prolonged upward to a length of 10 to 12.5 cm, and can be up to 25 mm wide though usually only 10 mm.

In any case *H. lacustris* is much more suitable for indoor aquariums than *H. angustifolia*. It grows well in slightly alkaline water in light and half-shade. It is one of the most resistant aquarium plants and should become very popular.

HYGROPHILA LANCEA (Thunb.) Miq.

H. lancea is native to Japan and Taiwan and is one of the lesser known but very suitable aquarium plants. It reaches a height of 50 to 60 cm, with a stem 8 mm in thickness and leaves that are opposite, lanceolate, and 50 to 75 mm long and 10 to 20 mm wide. The veins are elevated and conspicuous. The whole leaf blade is moderately curved with curled margins. It grows very quickly in the emersed form, and its stems and leaves are almost naked. In the submersed form it grows more slowly and in appearance does not differ very much from plants grown out of the water. The plant is light green and very decorative.

This species, cultivated in a bright place at temperatures around 68° F (20° C), requires neutral water. After being transplanted it as a rule grows toward the surface. If the tip above the second or third pair of leaves is cut off, the axillary buds begin to grow and a very decorative little shrub develops.

HYGROPHILA POLYSPERMA (Roxb.) T. And. (III. 138)

This marsh plant originated in India. Among all the cultivated species of *Hygrophila* it is the one best adapted to submersed existence.

Specimens cultivated under this name for some forty to fifty years have never flowered. Their identity is therefore uncertain. Among the imported plants of the last few years have appeared plants similar in the submersed form, but in the emersed form with top leaves clearly hairy; the plants flower easily and regularly. These flowering plants have been reliably determined without doubt to be *H. polysperma*. Is the plant cultivated for so many

Hygrophila polysperma.

years in aquariums under the name *H. polysperma* only a non-flowering form of this species? Or is it a question of another species? This problem cannot be solved until we are able to make the sterile plants flower.

The stem is delicate, seldom branching, prostrate, and rooting as a marsh plant. The light green leaves with darker veins are 25 to 50 mm long and 10 to 15 mm wide. Aerial leaves are darker than the submersed ones, sometimes green, sometimes brownish green.

This species is the most common representative of the genus and thrives under normal aquarium conditions, tolerating even quite hard water. Low temperatures are not dangerous, but they limit the growth. The plant develops best at temperatures of 68° to 77° F (20° to 25° C) and requires generous illumination, but the leaves become pale in direct sunshine. It is propagated vegetatively by planting detached sections of the stem.

ALISMATACEAE (Water Plantain Family)

The family Alismataceae is not too large (about 11 genera with 100 species). It is distributed in the tropical, subtropical, and temperate zones of the world. The plants develop subterranean rhizomes or tubercles from which more or less petiolate leaves arise. The leaf blades are lanceolate, ovate, round, or arrow-shaped. Some genera are unisexual, but the majority are bisexual. With few exceptions the members of this family are perennials.

They grow in places which are periodically flooded or permanently under water. A substantial number of them can grow submersed, therefore this is one of the most important of the aquarium plant groups. They fit large as well as small aquariums and are not exacting as to their environment; they are suitable for all aspects of the hobby.

Small species reaching a height of only 25 to 75 mm are useful for planting in the foreground of the aquarium, but this family also provides some of the tallest aquarium plants with tough, ornamental leaves. Some species develop floating leaves.

The majority of the genera are limited to certain continents. The genus *Sagittaria* grows mainly in North America, with only a few species known from South America and the Old World. The most important genus, *Echinodorus*, is found only in the American area, mainly in South America, but some species have penetrated the Central American countries and even to the southern states of the U.S.A. Other important genera are *Ranalisma* from Africa and tropical Asia (only the African species is cultivated) and *Baldellia* from Europe and North Africa.

The genus *Alisma* (water plantain) is the most widely distributed and grows in all the continents. Only *Alisma gramineum* Gmel. is found in a permanently submersed form, and this is also a native species in parts of Europe. In summer the plant develops ribbon-like submersed leaves up to 60 cm long and about 20 to 25 mm wide (distinctly resembling *Vallisneria gigantea*). In the late summer, however, the leaves disappear and the plant does not resume growth until the beginning of spring. The other species of *Alisma* grow under water only temporarily. Their leaves push above the water from a depth of more than 40 cm.

Further genera, such as *Caldesia*, *Burnatia*, *Damasonium*, and *Enneandra*, are of no importance in aquariums. The genus *Luronium* is rarely cultivated. *Wisneria filifolia* Hooker f. from tropical Africa is interesting, but not yet imported to Europe.

BALDELLIA RANUNCULOIDES (Engelm.) Parl.   (III. 141)
Syn: *Echinodorus ranunculoides* Engelm.

B. ranunculoides comes from northern Africa and from Europe, where it grows relatively far to the north but is absent in some places. It is a perennial aquatic or marsh plant, usually 20 to 30 cm tall. Emersed, its leaves have long petioles and the blade is extended and narrowly lanceolate, 2.5 to 10 cm long. The floral stalk is nearly as long as the leaves, erect, and bears flowers which are about 10 mm in diameter and pinkish purple (rarely almost white). Seeds are formed readily and germinate satisfactorily.

In submersed plants the leaves form a rosette. They are without petioles, narrow at the base, taper slowly toward the apex, and are 20 to 25 cm long and not more than 10 to 15 mm wide.

This is a very peculiar but decorative plant which in submersed form differs conspicuously from the other members of the family. Its roots are short but very dense, forming a rich white tuft. Plants cultivated under water neither flower nor form aerial leaves.

B. ranunculoides is a valuable aquarium plant that is not particularly exacting with respect to cultivation but is little known to aquarists. It is not known to be propagated vegetatively at all and can only be reproduced from seeds. Sown in clean sand and shallow water at room temperature, the seedlings at a height of 50 mm are then transplanted to the aquarium. At first they resemble a small *Sagittaria* but are easily identified; if a piece of the leaf is broken off and crushed between the fingers, a strong but pleasant scent is given off.

ECHINODORUS (Burhead)

Echinodorus plants are widely distributed and are beautiful plants in well lit aquariums. There are 53 species found from tropical America (especially from Brazil) and to the southern part of the U.S.A. These plants are not found anywhere in the Old World.

Nearly all of the species are marsh plants which also grow on the banks of still as well as moving waters. In the period of regular floods the whole plant is covered with water and develops submersed leaves which are sometimes very different from the emersed types. Only a few species (*E. amazonicus, E. parviflorus*) are typically aquatic and grow permanently under water. If they grow on dry land they develop dwarf leaves and live poorly.

The leaves of particular species of *Echinodorus* are highly variable, from small and narrowly lanceolate to broadly lanceo-

A flowering *Baldellia ranunculoides* growing in a small garden pool. Photo by Dr. D. Sculthorpe.

Seldom growing more than 10 cm tall, *Echinodorus tenellus* is a good choice for planting in the front part of the tank.

late, cordate, elliptical, or round and oblongly ovate. There are species that are only a few inches tall, but others grow from one to four meters high.

The leaves are usually of a light green color, although in some species they may be dark green to greenish black or even reddish brown. Veins may be thin or very thick and elevated and are generally lighter in color than the blade.

The plants produce bisexual flowers and, unlike *Sagittaria*, have anthers and stamens in each flower. The flowers are white and measure in the smallest species 2.5 to 10 cm across, yet in tall and decorative plants are 2.5 to 5 cm across. On the floral stalk the blooms are arranged racemosely in whorls, less frequently in panicles, and rarely umbellate.

In the genus *Echinodorus* there are distinct groups of self-fertile and self-sterile species differing in the leaf petioles. It can be said that, in general, the species with round leaf petioles (for example *E. cordifolius*) are self-sterile, whereas those with triangular petioles (such as *E. paniculatus*) are distinctly self-fertile. To obtain seeds in every case is therefore not so simple as it might be supposed.

Plants of this genus produce minute nutlets (about 2.5 to 3 mm long) that are elongated and beak-shaped in the majority of the species. Before maturing they are set up in a globular or ovate compound fruit out of which the beaks of the individual nutlets protrude, so that the whole structure can be said to resemble a hedgehog (echinate). After maturing the fruit breaks up; in some species the nutlets disperse readily on being touched directly, but in others the nutlets stick firmly to the point of attachment.

All the species of *Echinodorus* are easily cultivated and there are no species known that are exceptionally sensitive to external conditions as are, for example, the cryptocorynes. They require a good depth of sand and either neutral, slightly acid, or slightly alkaline water which should be soft to medium hard (yet plants can live in very hard water). For smaller species the planting medium may be supplied with a fair amount of nutrients; for larger species a poorer medium is more appropriate to prevent the plants from growing out above the water. The only important prerequisite is that there must be light: they do not thrive in dark tanks. Give them a good illumination and a few hours of sunlight every day.

During winter, prolongation of daytime by artificial illumination is useful if the plants are to be kept in full growth all year long. This is not really essential because *Echinodorus* species are steady perennial plants and survive the winter in a very good condition even without additional light. In fact, by shortening the daylight period their growth is stopped and in this way a period of vegetative rest is created. Then in the beginning of spring they grow faster and better. In tanks without additional artificial light a high temperature should not be maintained in winter because plenty of heat accompanied by lack of light can upset the probability of a temporary cessation of growth. The most suitable temperature in winter is about 63° to 67° F (17° to 19° C) and in summer 72° to 82° F (22° to 28° C).

The majority of *Echinodorus* species are propagated very easily by one or more of five methods of reproduction:

1) From rhizome runners. This method of propagation is well known to aquarists (used for *Vallisneria*). Among the *Echinodorus* species only a few of the smaller species are propagated in this way, like *E. quadricostatus* and *E. tenellus.*

2) By rooting the floral stalks. The plant develops a floral stalk on the nodes from which, at the same time as the buds or flowers, leaves develop to take root and grow into a new plant. From one node two to three new plants may arise. On the parent plant six to seven racemose- or panicle-like floral stalks can develop each year, and in some species 30 to 150 new individuals can arise in this manner.

3) By dividing the rhizome. Some species, such as *E. maior* and *E. osiris*, develop a robust rhizome. The parent plant is taken out of the water and the rhizome cut off; be sure that some of the younger roots remain on the plant close to the place where the first leaves arose. Then it is replanted and the rhizome is left to float in the tank (snails should not be present). In a short time the rhizome is covered with small groups of leaves. Up to 15 new plants may arise from a rhizome with a length of 10 cm.

4) From the rhizome (undivided). Species forming a short globular rhizome are pulled up and left floating in a well lighted tank. From the dormant buds on the rhizome five or six new plants will arise and become detached as soon as they have developed separate roots. This is the only vegetative method of propagation in some species (such as *E. berteroi*) which otherwise can be propagated only from seeds because the floral stalks do not take root.

5) Sexual reproduction from seeds. This is the most difficult method as far as the aquarist is concerned. In the aquarium *E. cordifolius* often develops seeds; other species require a greenhouse if

the seeds are to mature, but popular species such as *E. amazonicus, E. parviflorus*, and *E. bleheri* develop seeds only with difficulty even in the greenhouse. The seeds are sown first in flat dishes with clean sand and then immersed in water (10 cm deep) at a minimum temperature of 68° F (20° C), preferably 81° to 83° F (27° to 28° C). Amphibious species will not develop easily from seeds placed under water, so in this case it is advisable to immerse the dishes in water that is only about 10 mm deep. The seedlings then develop emersed and are planted in a tank when the leaves are 5 to 10 cm long.

ECHINODORUS AMAZONICUS (III. 145)
(SMALL-LEAVED AMAZON SWORDPLANT)
Incorrect name: *E. brevipedicellatus* (O. Kuntze) Bunch

A Brazilian species from the river basin of the middle and lower reaches of the Amazon, *E. amazonicus* is a typically submersed plant and is exceptional because it grows in the emersed state.

The blades are long, lanceolate, and acute at both extremities, merging with the petiole at the base. The first pair of lateral veins issue from the central rib shortly above the base of the blade. The petioles are usually very short (about 50 mm), rarely longer—up to 15 cm, so the whole blade is substantially longer than the petiole. The leaves are numerous, green, and arched.

A thin floral stalk projects above the surface of the water, where between four and nine white flowers are formed; each flower is about 10 mm in diameter and has six to nine stamens. In the aquarium generally only the buds develop and at the same time two to three new plants arise at the nodes of the floral stalk. The flowers do not open and consequently no seeds are produced. By separating the young plants from the floral stalk speedy reproduction is encouraged. Within a year as many as 60 new plants can develop from four to ten such inflorescences. Seeds are obtained only from sturdy plants cultivated in the greenhouse at temperatures of 77° to 86° F (25° to 30° C) in water about 30 cm deep. The floral stalk should be led above the water before the buds develop. *E. amazonicus* is best cultivated in large tanks with medium hard water at temperatures around 68° F (20° C). In nature this plant grows under water and is one of the few species which have no particular lighting needs; it grows well even in diffused artificial light. It is not fit for terrariums and paludariums.

Echinodorus amazonicus.

ECHINODORUS ANGUSTIFOLIUS Rataj　　　　(Ill. 146)
　　This species was discovered only recently in southern Brazil, in the state of Mato Grosso. The emersed form develops leaves 10 to 15 cm long with narrowly lanceolate blades, thus resembling other small species such as *E. tenellus* and *E. latifolius*. The submersed form differs from these two species quite distinctly; the narrowly lanceolate or ribbon-shaped light green leaves reach a length of 30 to 40 cm and a width of only about 10 mm. Each plant possesses as many as 20 leaves.

Echinodorus angustifolius.

E. angustifolia is propagated by rhizome runners on which a large number of plants arise which take root easily. As a non-tropical species it does well in low temperatures of unheated aquariums, and yet it thrives equally well when cultivated in tropical aquariums.

ECHINODORUS ARGENTINENSIS Rataj   (III. 148, 149)
Incorrect name: *E. longistyllis* Buch.

Coming from the subtropical zone of South America (southern Brazil, Paraguay, Uruguay), *E. argentinensis* penetrates into the temperate zone (Argentina). It appears in several forms and is related to *E. grandiflorus* and *E. longiscapus*, with which it is easily crossed; hybrids with very varied characters are produced.

In the emersed state this species develops leaves that are 1.2 meters long. The blades are lanceolate, 10 to 15 cm long and 50 to 75 mm wide in the narrow-leaved form; ovate to oval, 10 to 20 cm long and 5 to 10 cm wide in the broad-leaved form. These differences are evident even in the submersed plants that have blades of the same shape and size but with much shorter petioles usually as long as the blades. The broad-leaved form has been cultivated for a long time but not identified correctly; usually it is offered in the trade under the name *E. longistylus* or *E. longistyllis*. The narrow-leaved form was first imported only a short time ago.

Both forms are suitable for aquarium use; they have grass-green to greenish brown blades, the broad-leaved form having leaf margins that are moderately undulate. Veins are often dark reddish brown and the blade somewhat ornamented by reddish brown irregular spots.

E. argentinensis withstands great fluctuation of the temperature and can be cultivated in warm as well as cold water.

ECHINODORUS BERTEROI (Spreng.) Fassett   (III. 125)
Syn: *E. rostratus* Engelm.
Incorrect name: *E. nymphaeifolius*

E. berteroi is found in the southern parts of the U.S.A., Central America, and the West Indies. Apart from *E. cordifolius* this is the only large species penetrating to the edge of the temperate zone. During the summer it thrives even in garden ponds.

From the rhizome submersed leaves of the most varied shape arise first; they are either linear, lanceolate, or ovate to broadly cordate. Later broadly ovate (cordate at the base) floating leaves are formed which resemble those that have already emerged above the surface. The base of the leaf is distinctly cordate or in others

Echinodorus argentinensis.

Inflorescence of
*Echinodorus
argentinensis.*

truncate. Both floating and emersed leaves are distinctly green, fragile, and with a translucent membrane.

E. berteroi grows very easily in all conditions; plants are known to grow on dry soil, producing leaves that are only 30 to 40 mm long but developing flowers and seeds. Submersed plants put forth from a depth of 30 to 50 cm a paniculate floral stalk up to a meter long, with a great number of self-fertile flowers that are about 10 mm in diameter. All such flowers produce fruits that are strongly echinate and contain viable seeds. "Bud plants" are never formed at the inflorescence.

The plant can be reproduced by obtaining bud plants from dormant buds on the rhizome, but reproduction is usually from seeds. These are sown in shallow water and, as soon as they have developed submersed leaves about 25 mm long, are transplanted into well lit tanks about 20 to 50 cm deep.

E. berteroi, with its green leaves, is one of the most beautiful aquarium plants; nearly every leaf is of a different shape and there are about ten to thirty leaves on each submersed plant. The only disadvantage is that it readily grows out of the water; this can be prevented by breaking up the roots as indicated in the section for *E. cordifolius.*

Plants are best cultivated in a poor medium in a well lit to bright situation. It is an exception among the species of *Echinodorus* by being sensitive to hard water to which it reacts by a discharge of minute crystals of limy salts on the surface of the submersed leaves. In emersed form the plant can be cultivated only in paludariums.

ECHINODORUS BLEHERI Rataj (AMAZON SWORDPLANT)
Incorrect names: *E. paniculatus, E. rangeri, E. tocatins.* (III. 169)

This species is one of the most beautiful and most popular swordplants. *E. bleheri* has been cultivated for a relatively long time but studied scientifically only recently. Its origin is not known.

E. bleheri resembles the small-leaved *E. amazonicus* (incorrectly called *E. brevipedicellatus*), but its leaves are much broader and the blades are not always curved. Each plant develops a very nice tuft with twenty to thirty leaves reaching a length of 20 to 40 cm and a width of 40 to 60 mm. The floral stems develop under water and in their whorls young plants arise which are separated and transplanted after the roots have been formed. It is cultivated under conditions similar to those for *E. amazonicus.*

ECHINODORUS CORDIFOLIUS (L.) Griseb.
Syn: *E. radicans* (Nutt.) Engelm. (III. 65, 68, 78, 188)

E. cordifolius is from the warm areas of the southern U.S.A., penetrating to Mexico. It is one of the few non-tropical species growing to the edges of the temperate zone; thus it can even be cultivated in garden ponds.

The plants develop a thick rhizome with a dense root system. On the roots oblong tubercles which are obviously reserve organs are formed. In more northern areas this plant drops its leaves for the winter. From the rhizome a few leaves that are 40 to 70 cm long grow up above the surface of the water. The petiole is substantially shorter than the blade that is 15 to 20 cm long and 10 to 15 cm wide, ovately cordate, about half as long as it is wide, and usually with seven (rarely nine) lateral veins lying at an acute angle with the midrib. The base of the blade is broadly cordate.

The floral stalk is racemose, at first erect and then creeping, with flowers 20 to 25 mm across growing on petioles with a length of 25 to 50 mm. Flowers are white and self-sterile, readily forming seeds in a globular, moderately echinate fruit. The seeds are capable of germination immediately. The leaves and roots develop in the nodes of the floral stalk at the same time as the flowers appear.

In the aquarium the submersed plants differ substantially from those growing out of the water in a natural environment. The petioles of the submersed leaves are much shorter and about as long as the blade, which is moderately undulate at the margins and has an apex which is more rounded than that of the emersed leaves. The submersed leaves are cordately incised at the base. Before the emersed leaves have developed, floating leaves are formed and may cover the whole tank; they are sometimes rounded, sometimes blunt at the apex, up to 20 cm long and 15 cm wide.

E. cordifolius should be cultivated in a moderate indirect light in an aquarium with a poor planting medium in order to keep the plant permanently in a condition of submersed growth. The temperature of the water is not important; the plant will grow in temperatures ranging from 59° to 86° F (15° to 30° C). Submersed plants usually have four or five well developed light green leaves. They are very popular with aquarists who know it by the old name (now invalid) E. radicans.

When these plants begin to develop floating or emersed leaves, the bundle of petioles should be gripped near the base and the plant pulled out from the substrate at a distance of 10 to 20 mm. In this manner a part of the root system is broken and the plant stops growing. The submersed leaves are not lost and the transition of the plant to the emersed life is inhibited. Submersed plants develop floral stalks very rarely.

This Echinodorus is grown from seeds or propagated vegetatively from the bud plants arising on the floral stalks. The seedlings are raised in shallow dishes in an emersed culture; their development is much faster than if they stay in deep water after germinating. This species is fit to use in paludariums.

ECHINODORUS GRANDIFLORUS Micheli (III. 197)

This plant is found throughout tropical South America and penetrates to southern Brazil. In nature the leaves reach a length of 1.5 to 2.7 meters and the branching stems are up to 4 meters long. It is the largest Echinodorus, with large cordate leaves and typically with discernible pellucid dots on the blades. Although mentioned very often in aquarium literature, E. grandiflorus does not thrive under water and can not be cultivated in the aquarium; it is thus erroneously cited. Submersed plants with large cordate leaves offered in the trade under the name E. grandiflorus are always E. macrophyllus or E. scaber.

*Echinodorus
horizontalis* being
collected in
Brazil. The emersed
plants grow to two feet
high. Photo by
T.J. Horeman.

ECHINODORUS HOREMANII Rataj   (Ill. 189)

The most beautiful novelty introduced in recent years, *E. horemani* comes from the state of Parana, southern Brazil. Only the submersed form is currently known; emersed leaves and inflorescence have not yet been observed. Submersed leaves somewhat resemble those of *E. maior* (= *E. martii*). They are 30 to 50 cm long, with petioles shorter than the blade, which is 20 to 35 cm long and 25 to 50 mm wide. The surface of the blade is dark olive green, very glossy, with undulate margins. The midrib at the base of the blade is very strong; lateral veins are at first closely parallel to the central rib and then diverge so the leaf is pseudopenninerved (has the appearance of having many veins diverging from along the course of the midrib). All the veins are lighter than the surface of the blade.

E. horemanii is a very decorative and at the same time unexacting plant. It requires clear water and a poor planting medium supplied with detritus and can stand any normal aquarium temperature from 57° to 81° F (14° to 27° C). In nature it often grows in very cool water.

ECHINODORUS HORIZONTALIS Rataj (III. 152, 196)

This species is distributed over the entire Amazon basin and is found in Peru, Bolivia, and Brazil as far as Belem. It is a recently imported decorative novelty that is offered in the trade by the names *E. guyanensis* Hort., *E. dewittii*, or by the incorrect name *E. tunicatus*, to which it is related.

Emersed and submersed plants closely resemble each other. The leaves are 40 to 50 cm long, though in the aquarium they are usually shorter, reaching a length of only 20 to 30 cm. The leaf blades are dark green, distinctly cordate, and taper into an acute apex; they are arranged on the petioles at an obtuse angle so that they are situated almost horizontally (hence the name *E. horizontalis*). The stem is a little longer than the leaves. Flowers are white; after flowering, the fruit is quite covered by the broadened calyx. In the whorls of the inflorescence a few juvenile plantlets develop which root readily. Seeds germinate very well, especially at higher temperatures, about 82° F (28° C).

Rather more exacting with respect to cultivation than the other species, *E. horizontalis* requires tropical temperatures and clear, very soft water.

ECHINODORUS INTERMEDIUS (Mart.) Grisebach (III. 197)

E. intermedius has not been cultivated in the aquarium up to now and has been introduced in the literature erroneously. It is a native of Brazil. The plants offered in the trade by this name are usually *E. quadricostatus*.

ECHINODORUS LATIFOLIUS (Seubert) Rataj (III. 154-156)

E. latifolius comes from Central America (Costa Rica, Panama). It has been previously cultivated in the aquarium under the incorrect name of *E. magdalensis*.

In submersed form it develops rosettes of leaves 10 to 25 cm long and 5 to 10 mm wide. *E. latifolius* resembles *E. quadricostatus* but its leaves are longer and narrower. *E. quadricostatus* in the emersed form has horizontal, lanceolate leaves about 55 mm long and 15 mm wide, while *E. latifolius* develops leaves that are narrowly lanceolate, erect, and about 10 cm long and 5 to 9 mm wide. It resembles the emersed form of *E. tenellus* except that on the leaf-

Emersed form of *Echinodorus latifolius* with indistinct inflorescence.

Enlarged photograph of the inflorescence of *Echinodorus latifolius*.

Echinodorus latifolius, submersed form.

less creeping or erect floral stalk the small flowers are usually arranged in two rows, one above the other; achenes (fruit with a single seed) are larger; the flowers of *E. latifolius* are about 15 mm in diameter, those of *E. tenellus* only 7.5 mm in diameter.

E. *latifolius* is resistant, grows in the same conditions as those for *E. quadricostatus*, and is propagated from rhizome runners. It forms dense growths that are short in bright situations but taller in half-shade.

ECHINDORUS LONGISCAPUS Arechavaleta (Ill. 157, 196)

E. *longiscapus* comes from the subtropical to temperate zone of South America and it grows in southern Brazil, Paraguay, and Uruguay, to central Argentina. It is imported under the commercial name *E. heikoiana* Hort.

Emersed leaves are 50 to 90 cm long, the blades are ovate or oval and 10 to 15 cm long. The inflorescence is longer than the leaves and not branching. In submersed form the plant develops a rosette of leaves that are cordate to rounded, bright green, and 20 to 40 cm long; blades are 10 cm long and 50 to 75 mm wide. The surface of the blade has reddish brown spots, especially in the juvenile leaves. It differs from the similar *E. macrophyllus* in its smaller, more rounded leaves and the leaf margins not being undulate.

This plant is propagated by developing solitary young plants in the whorls of the inflorescence, by dividing the rhizomes, or from seeds which germinate readily even at temperatures around 68° F (20° C); it withstands both cold and warm water and is not difficult to cultivate.

Inflorescence of *Echinodorus longiscapus.*

ECHINODORUS MACROPHYLLUS (Kunth) Micheli (III. 168, 200)

This *Echinodorus* is found over the whole of eastern Brazil and even penetrates to the temperate zone in Argentina. It is most frequently found in southern states of Brazil (Sao Paulo, Sta. Catarina). This plant has been cultivated in aquariums for a long time, often under the incorrect names *E. grandiflorus* or *E. muricatus*. Emersed leaves are up to 120 cm long, with blades triangularly cordate or ovate, 30 to 40 cm long and of about the same width. The branching inflorescence bears white or yellow flowers.

In submersed growth the plant develops leaves with a length of 30 to 40 cm and dark green blades; there are sometimes red-spotted blades that are only 20 cm long and 20 cm wide with undulate margins, thereby differing from the similar *E. longiscapus*. For exact determination the pellucid markings in the leaves can be used. *E. grandiflorus* has pellucid dots on emersed leaves, *E. longiscapus* has long pellucid lines, and in *E. macrophyllus* any pellucid markings are lacking.

E. macrophyllus is cultivated in clear water with a poor substrate. It is not exacting with regard to temperature and is suitable for tropical as well as cold-water aquariums.

ECHINODORUS MAIOR (Micheli) Rataj (III. 328)

This Brazilian species is known among aquarists by the incorrect names *E. martii* or *E. leopoldina*. The plant develops a firm rhizome from which light green leaves (with much lighter veins) arise. The lateral veins are not tapering to the base of the blade, but one to two pairs end a short distance above the base, sometimes in the lower third of the leaf. The leaves (30 to 50 cm long) have as a rule very short petioles; leaf blade is 20 to 40 cm long, width varying greatly from 25 to 75 mm.

Plants cultivated in half-shade have very narrow leaves and resemble some species of *Aponogeton*. In reasonable light the leaves are broad and very ornamental, making this species among the most valuable aquarium plants.

E. maior is always submersed and lives poorly as an emersed form. From a depth of 30 to 50 cm it develops an erect floral stalk 30 to 70 cm long (according to the depth of the water) with a paniculate inflorescence at the end. Flowers are white, about 10 mm in diameter, with small petals. It is self-fertile, developing seeds easily, so this method of propagation is most frequently used. It is propagated neither from root runners nor by forming young plants on floral stalks. Besides being propagated from seeds, new plants can be obtained from dormant buds on the rhizome.

This species should be cultivated in spacious tanks with soft to medium-hard water at temperatures of 68° to 77° F (20° to 25° C), but it is indifferent to lower temperatures. The substrate may be richer than usual for the genus because this plant grows out of the water. It often flowers several times a year. It is not suitable for paludariums and terrariums.

ECHINODORUS NYMPHAEFOLIUS Buchenau

This plant, coming from Cuba and sometimes from Central American countries, has not been brought to Europe and has never been cultivated in aquariums. The plants offered by this name belong to the species *E. berteroi.*

ECHINODORUS OPACUS Rataj (III. 168)

The emersed form and inflorescence of this plant are not known. In the submersed form the leaves are 20 to 40 cm long, with leaf blades that are distinctly cordate, lobate at the base, moderately elongated, and pointed at the apex. The surface is olive green with lighter colored veins.

This species is relatively little known at the present time. It requires clear water and withstands temperatures of about 57° F (14° C) as well as warm water in the tropical aquarium. Since the inflorescence is not yet known, the plant is propagated only from dormant buds on the rhizome.

ECHINODORUS OSIRIS Rataj (III. 213)

E. osiris is a native of southern Brazil and is one of the most beautiful aquarium plants. It has been offered in the trade under the commercial names *E. osiris rubra, E. special, E. aureobrunneus, "Echinodorus* from Sweden," and the like.

This marsh plant has a robust rhizome from which long petiolate leaves sprout and grow above the surface of the water. These leaves are a meter long or longer, with the petiole sharing about three-fifths of the length so that the blade of the leaf (regular oval shape) is generally 20 cm long. The floral stalk (70 to 80 cm long) is at first erect, then becomes creeping with the flower bud groups of rooting leaves beginning to appear on it. The buds do not develop in greenhouse conditions; nutlets in this species are not yet known.

If the plants that have arisen on the floral stalk are transplanted under water, leaves with short petioles (50 to 75 mm) and robust blades develop from them. The blade is 20 to 30 cm long and 50 to 75 mm wide, oval with strong, elevated veins. The leaves are green, most often red-green or brown-green, with the two youngest leaves being brown-red to gold-brown; leaf margins are moderately but distinctly undulate. Floral stalks grow above the water or close to the surface and form bud plants.

An extraordinary characteristic of this plant is the absolute permanence of the submersed way of life: plants cultivated under water never sprout leaves above the water surface. If transplanted to shallow water the submersed plants develop leaves (with short petioles) pressed against the ground and live very poorly. On the other hand, if transplanted in deep water (30 to 50 cm) the formerly emersed plants form further aerial leaves and do not form new submersed ones. Only but cutting off all mature leaves and by transplanting the rhizome to deeper water can such a plant be made to grow submersed.

E. osiris is best cultivated in spacious tanks (the tuft has a diameter of 50 cm). The plant requires medium-hard water, and approximately neutral pH, a moderate to rich substrate, and temperatures about 68° to 77° F (20° to 25° C). In cooler waters, however, it does not come to harm; on the contrary, the red coloring of the leaves becomes more intense. It is propagated by dividing the rhizome on which plants from dormant buds are easily formed and by plants that arise on the floral stalks. This species is not recommended for use in paludariums.

ECHINODORUS PANICULATUS Micheli   III. 72, 78

This species inhabits a large area from Central America to Argentina. It was first imported in 1965 by the commercial name *E. bleheri.*

E. paniculatus usually grows emersed in nature, its leaves reaching a length of 1.5 meters. The leaf petioles are always triangular in cross section and can be easily distinguished. The leaf blades are lanceolate to broadly lanceolate and the inflorescence is branching.

When maintained in submersed condition only young plants that have developed from seeds can be cultivated for a period of one to two years. The leaves are lanceolate with triangular petioles and light green blades with darker veins. In the second year plants drop the submersed leaves and grow above the surface of the water. This is why the species is not too suitable for the aquarium.

E. paniculatus is propagated by separating young plants from the whorls of the inflorescence or by seeds. The plant is not particular about the temperature but requires a very poor planting medium which can inhibit the growth of the leaves which might emerge above the surface of the water.

Echinodorus paniculatus.

ECHINODORUS PARVIFLORUS Rataj (III. 201)

E. *parviflorus* is now known from Peru and is believed to be distributed over the Pacific side of South America. The plant originally reached our tanks through importers without any indication of its origin. It is sold under the name *E. peruense* or *E. peruensis*.

E. parviflorus is a typically submersed plant related to *E. amazonicus*. On land the plant develops dwarf leaves growing well at almost 100 % humidity. Under water it forms two types of leaves on short petioles. Their blades are either long, broadly lanceolate and narrowed at both ends, or are of the same size but distinctly cordate at the base. The leaves are 20 to 25 cm long and 35 to 50 mm wide with conspicuously dark red-brown veins. This is why this plant is sometimes called "the black *Echinodorus*."

Submersed leaves produce floral stalks similar to those of *E. amazonicus*. Flowers are smaller however, only about 5 mm in diameter. Seeds are rarely produced; in spite of this they can be obtained in aquariums if the floral stalk is prevented from being immersed. Bud plants arise on the stalks during this time.

It is cultivated under the same conditions as *E. amazonicus*. The plant is very decorative with its dark-veined leaves. On one mature plant there are forty to sixty leaves in a rosette so that a robust, very attractive plant is formed.

ECHINODORUS PELLUCIDUS Rataj (III. 164)

This plant comes from southern Brazil and is closely related to *E. argentinensis*. Unlike the latter, however, when *E. pellucidus* is cultivated in emersed conditions it develops leaves that are 50 to 60 cm long, with blades 10 cm long and 30 to 40 mm wide which are lanceolate to ovate. In submersed form it differs from *E. argentinensis* by its smaller growth. Leaves are then 25 cm long and 40 to 50 mm wide and dark green with distinct darker venation; juvenile leaves are varied with red-brown dots.

It is a very decorative novelty of our tanks and withstands cold as well as warm water.

ECHINODORUS QUADRICOSTATUS Fassett (III. 165)
(DWARF AMAZON SWORDPLANT)

Although long known to aquarists by the incorrect name *E. intermedius*, this species was not described scientifically until 1955 from specimens from Colombia. The plant takes the form of any of three varieties known. The main form (var. *quadricostatus*) produces seeds with a very long beak, as does var. *magdalenensis* which differs from the main form by the absence of ribs on the seeds. Both of these varieties come from Peru and Colombia and are not cultivated in the aquarium. Only the variety coming (probably) from the middle reaches of the Amazon is cultivated in the aquarium, *E. quadricostatus* var. *xinguensis* Rataj, known as the dwarf Amazon swordplant.

From the indistinct rhizome a rosette of leaves develops; the leaves are without petioles, narrowly lanceolate, bright green, and 10 to 15 cm long. In the aquarium leaves commonly grow only to a length of 5 to 15 cm and a width of 10 mm. The plant develops larger leaves only under excellent conditions in moderate diffused light; the leaves are erect and considerably elongated. In good illumination the majority of the leaves are spread obliquely to the sides.

The leaves of plants grown in the emersed state are similar to those under water, but they are shorter and somewhat wider, measuring 50 mm long and 12 to 15 mm wide. The thin floral stalks bear 6 to 10 white flowers, 10 to 12 mm in diameter. Seeds are very rarely produced.

E. quadricostatus is best cultivated in a medium rich bottom with fair to good light and a temperature of 77° to 86° F (25° to 30° C), but the plant is not harmed by a drop in temperature to as low as 59° F (15° C) or even less; it grows in any aquarium water. Propagation is exclusively by separating young plants which are formed on the long root runners in the same way as in *Vallisneria*. This unexacting plant is very suitable for foreground planting in the aquarium and terrarium; both are soon covered by its dense growth.

ECHINODORUS SCABER Rataj (III. 167)

E. scaber is found throughout tropical South America, but mainly in the eastern part of Brazil. Until now this plant has been known incorrectly as *E. muricatus*, which is in fact a synonym of *E. grandiflorus*.

It closely resembles *E. macrophyllus* and like the latter has no pellucid markings in the leaf blades. The blades of emersed plants are unlike those of *E. macrophyllus*, being ovate and incised at the apex. Both species differ also in their achenes and bracts.

Cultivation methods are the same as those with *E. macrophyllus*.

ECHINODORUS TENELLUS (Mart.) Buchenau (III. 141, 172)

This species comes from the area lying between the southern part of the U.S.A. and Paraguay, between the boundaries of the

Echinodorus pellucidus.

Inflorescence of
*Echinodorus
quadricostatus.*

Echinodorus quadricostatus.

Flowers of
Echinodorus scaber.

Echinodorus scaber.

northern temperate zone and the subtropical region of the southern hemisphere. With respect to the large distribution this plant is very variable; a few forms have been described, differing in the shape of the achenes and the size of the leaves.

E. tenellus is the smallest species of the genus *Echinodorus*, reaching a height of 30 to 40 mm; only a few rare forms may be 10 cm tall. The leaves are usually only a few millimeters wide, very narrowly lanceolate to linear, and almost without petioles.

The dry land plants, suitable for paludariums and terrariums, have leaves distinctly divided into the petiole and narrowly lanceolate blades. They develop a floral stalk at the tip of which there is one single umbel of several flowers about 3.5 mm in diameter.

Under water as well as on dry land *E. tenellus* is propagated vegetatively from the root runners. In good conditions it soon covers the bottom with fine, fresh growth. This plant is not particular in cultivation but requires sandy soil and plenty of light; although it develops best at a temperature of 68° F (20° C), lower temperatures do not harm the plant.

ECHINODORUS URUGUAYENSIS Arechavaleta   (III. 169)

E. uruguayensis is a native of the subtropical to temperate zone of South America, sporadically recorded in Uruguay, Paraguay, and Argentina. It resembles *E. maior* but differs in the size, color of the submersed leaves, and shape of the emersed leaves. Under water *E. maior* reaches a height of up to 50 cm; its leaves are green, the submersed leaves resembling the emersed ones. Under water the species *E. uruguayensis* is 30 cm high; the emersed leaves bear ovately lanceolate blades, about 10 cm long, on long petioles. The plant belongs to the most decorative species of the genus. Its submersed leaves are 20 to 30 cm long and 15 to 30 mm wide, with undulate to curled margins, dark olive green-brown to red-black. This is the species of *Echinodorus* possessing the darkest and most colored leaves.

This plant has been known for 60 years but has not yet been cultivated extensively in the aquarium. It is usually propagated by dividing the rhizome; this is a slow process, so this species is still uncommon in cultivation. The plant is quite unexacting and is grown in the same way as *E. horemanii*; like the latter this species also tolerates even very cold water. The junior author has recently succeeded in cultivating *E. uruguayensis* in his greenhouses and has had successful flowering.

Echinodorus macrophyllus thriving in the center of plants that have been sprayed with insecticides. Photo by T.J. Horeman.

Echinodorus opacus. Photo by T.J. Horeman.

Close-up view of a flower of *Echinodorus uruguayensis*. Photo by T.J. Horeman.

Echinodorus bleheri.

KEY TO THE IDENTIFICATION OF THE SPECIES
OF THE GENUS ECHINODORUS

This key has been developed from information gained over many years of study of the plants of the genus *Echinodorus*. It is sometimes impossible to identify submersed plants without the flowers and achenes, so that it is necessary to cultivate the plants in emersed form in order to have at hand not only leaves but also the inflorescence and fruits. Moreover, some species have so varied a character in accordance with the environmental conditions (water temperature, illumination, depth of water) that the same species will appear to have distinctly different characteristics when kept by different aquarists. When cultivated in the emersed state the flowering plants exhibit standard characters, and only in this way are exact identifications possible.

It should be explained, for the benefit of any readers who may not be familiar with the use of dichotomous keys, that the key consists of a series of paired contrasted characters (to which additional information has been added here and there); in endeavoring to establish the identification of a specimen it is merely necessary to follow the characteristics of the plant through the stages of the key. For example, in the first instance one decides whether or not the plant has "ribbon-like" leaves, etc.; if the answer is YES, one is led to couplet 2, whereas if the answer is NO, one is led to couplet 5, and so on.

Key to Echinodorus Species

1a Leaves ribbon-like, several times longer than wide, but not more than 20 mm wide; flowers with 6 to 9 stamens, propagated by root runners 2

1b Leaves not ribbon-like, blades wider than 20 mm, the flowers with more than 9 stamens 5

2a Submersed leaves lanceolate, generally wider than 15 mm, 5 to 10 times longer than wide . . . .*E. quadricostatus*

2b Submersed leaves narrower than 15 mm, usually 10 to 30 times longer than wide 3

3a Leaves usually only 25 to 50 mm long, not more than 75 mm long . . . .*E. tenellus*

3b Leaves more than 5 cm long 4

4a Leaves 5 to 15 cm long, about 10 mm wide . . . . . .*E. latifolius*

4b Leaves 20 to 40 cm long, not more than 10 mm wide . . . .
. . . .*E. angustifolius*

5a Plants develop only submersed leaves and do not grow out above the surface of the water; leaf blades much longer than wide, lateral veins connected with midrib some inches above the blade base. 6

5b The plant develops, in a good light, floating or emergent leaves, as well as submersed leaves; blades not more than twice as long as wide; all main veins directed towards the blade base. 12

6a Leaf margin undulate, blade apex blunt or rounded 9

6b Leaf margin flat, blade tapered 7

7a Leaves not more than 3 or 4 times longer than wide, base sometimes cordately incised or truncate . . . .*E. parviflorus*

7b Leaves at least 6 times longer than wide, the base tapering to the petiole, blades arched, recurved, not more than 30 mm wide 8

8a Blades arch-like recurved, max. 30 mm wide . .*E. amazonicus*

8b Blades not curved, 30 to 50 mm wide . . . .*E. bleheri*

9a Leaves green. 10

9b Leaves reddish, red-brown to black-brown. 11

10a Leaves light green, dull; usually narrower in the lower third, widening towards the apex . . . .*E. maior*

10b Leaves dark olive-green, very glossy; regularly tapering towards base and apex, widest in the middle . . .*E. horemanii*

11a Leaf blades 40 to 50 mm wide; young leaves bright red, older leaves dark brown-green . . . .*E. osiris*

11b Leaf blades not more than 30 mm wide; young leaves red-black, older leaves red-brown . . . .*E. uruguayensis*

12a Submersed leaves may take many shapes (multiform), some ribbon-like, others narrowly to broadly lanceolate or cordate to rounded; floating, emersed leaves ovate, cordately incised . . . .*E. berteroi*

12b Submersed leaves uniform 13

13a Leaf blade heart-shaped, pointed at the apex 14

13b Leaf blade not pointed, blunt at the apex 15

14a Leaf blades at an obtuse angle to the petiole, almost horizontal . . . .*E. horizontalis*

14b Leaf blades not at an angle to the petiole but continue in the same direction as the petiole . . . .*E. opacus*

Inflorescence of *Echinodorus tenellus.*

Echinodorus tenellus.

Sagittaria graminea.

Inflorescence of *Sagittaria graminea* with a close-up view of a male flower.

15a Blades ovate, tapering to the petiole, 2 or 3 times longer than wide, eventually tapering to the apex as well as to the base 16

15b Blades cordate, lobate at the base, usually only a little longer than wide 17

16a Blades 15 to 30 cm long, usually broadly oval ....*E. argentinensis*

16b Blades not more than 10 cm long, lanceolate, often spotted red-brown ....*E. pellucidus*

17a Leaf margins not undulate, leaves nearly rounded ....*E. longiscapus*

17b Leaf margins undulate, leaves cordate with blunt apex 18

18a No pellucid markings on the leaf blades (there being two species, distinguishable only in the emersed form) 19

18b Discernible, long pellucid lines in the blades of emersed as submersed leaves ....*E. cordifolius*

19a Blades of emersed plants cordate to triangular, with short points; achenes with a large number of glandules (i.e., visible organs of secretion) ....*E. macrophyllus*

19b Blades of emersed plants ovate, incised at the apex; achenes with 3 glandules ....*E. scaber*

LURONIUM (= ELISMA)

The interesting genus *Luronium* is a transitional form between the genera *Alisma* and *Damasonium*. Outwardly the plant resembles the small species of the submersed *Sagittaria*. The genus contains only a single species.

LURONIUM NATANS (L.) Buchen
Syn: *Elisma natans*

A European species, *Luronium natans* is found only occasionally in the Atlantic area. It is a typical aquatic plant with a very short rhizome; stems are very thin, rooting or floating in water. Lower (submersed) leaves are linear; upper leaves are floating, with long petioles. The ovate blades have three veins and are 30 mm long and 10 to 15 mm wide. Both leaves and flowers float on the surface. The flowers are 10 mm in diameter, on long pedicels; petals are white, yellow at the base.

In the emersed form the stem is creeping; leaves are petiolate and not linear, but narrowly oval, sometimes cordate at the base.

An unexacting plant, *L. natans* grows in cold as well as warm water; it hibernates well in tanks but requires more light. Propagation is by planting the stem cuttings. It is not very decorative and is of limited importance to aquarists.

RANALISMA

Ranalisma is represented by two species formerly classified as members of the genus *Echinodorus*. One of these is *R. rostrata* Stapf., found in southern Asia (Malacca). Living plants have never been imported to Europe, and consequently there are no records of its cultivation. This perennial plant has leaves resembling those of some *Cryptocoryne* species. It grows well under water and could be a valuable contribution to the hobby. It is alleged, however, that *R. rostrata* is rare even in its native habitat. The second species, *R. humilis*, has been imported and is cultivated in aquariums and terrariums.

RANALISMA HUMILIS (Kunth) Buch.

Syn: *Echinodorus humilis* Kunth

R. humilis originates in tropical Africa, distributed from Senegal to the Nile area. It is a low, stemless plant, 30 to 60 mm, and an annual (perennial under water). The broadly lanceolate leaves are 20 to 60 mm long and 10 to 20 mm wide. In the submersed form this plant cannot be distinguished from *Echinodorus quadricostatus*. In an emersed culture the blades are of the same length as those recorded above, but much wider and tapering to a visible petiole. Seeds are produced readily.

After bearing seeds the emergent forms generally die. In the submersed form *R. humilis* is a perennial plant cultivated and reproduced as *E. quadricostatus*.

SAGITTARIA (ARROWHEAD, DUCK POTATO) (III. 26)

Sagittaria is distributed almost all over the world, and about 30 species are known. The majority of the species come from North America, with a few from Central and South America and Australia, while in Africa the genus is represented only by some introduced species. In the Euro-Asiatic area, three species are found: *S. pygmaea* (from southern and eastern Asia), *S. natans* Pallas (northern Europe and from Siberia to the Far East), and *S. sagittifolia* L., which is found throughout Europe. It has white flowers with a purple spot. The variety *S. sagittifolia* subsp. *leucopetala*, from Asia, produces clear white flowers. Its horticultural form develops tubercles that grow to 50 mm in diameter and are utilized as common food in China and Japan. It often becomes barren and is

Fruits of *Sagittaria graminea*. Each fruit consists of numerous achenes.

Sagittaria subulata var. *gracillima* (left) and its male inflorescence with a male flower (right).

found freely in nature, being called *S. sagittifolia* subsp. *leucopetala* var. *edulis*. This is the so-called "Chinese arrowhead;" like all other species coming from the Old World, it is quite unsuitable for aquariums. The use of the name Chinese arrowhead (*S. chinensis* or *S. sinensis*) for the so-called "broad-leaved arrowhead" of our aquariums is evidently in error.

Most *Sagittaria* species come from the American continent. Many of them have gotten into aquarium literature, although they cannot be cultivated in the aquarium. In this group the following species may be found:

Sagittaria latifolia Willd., the most common species of North America, reaches a height of 1 meter and has arrow-shaped leaves. Submersed, ribbon-shaped leaves (the phyllodes or flat petioles without blades) develop seedlings only in the first year and only for a short period. It can not be cultivated in the aquarium.

Sagittaria engelmanniana J.G. Sm., together with the variety *brevirostra* (Mack. et Busch.) Bogin and variety *longirostra* (Micheli) Bogin, grow under water only for a short period, and all are quite unfit for the aquarium.

Sagittaria longiloba Engelm. is found in the southern states of the U.S.A., in Mexico, and in Venezuela. It too has arrow-shaped leaves and cannot be cultivated in aquariums.

Sagittaria montevidensis Cham. et Schl. is a South American species and has several forms. The basic form grows in eastern South America; var. *chilensis* (Cham. et Schl.) Bogin grows in Chile, and var. *calycina* (Engelm.) Bogin and var. *spongiosa* (Engelm.) Bogin have spread to Central and North America. None of them can be cultivated in the aquarium. (III. 85, 180)

Sagittaria lancifolia L. is from tropical and subtropical areas: the southern states of the U.S.A., the West Indies, and Central and South America. It is a robust plant up to 1.8 meters tall; it has lanceolate leaves and is quite unfit for the aquarium.

Only two American species are useful: *S. graminea* Michx. and *S. subulata* (L.) Buch., each of which has several varieties.

SAGITTARIA GRAMINEA Michx. (III. 66, 173, 176)

S. graminea is distributed in the eastern United States and Canada. Of the seven varieties, three or four have been found to be useful to the hobbyist and are usually known by the incorrect name "Chinese arrowhead."

S. graminea var. *graminea* Michx. is the basic variety and is distributed over a relatively large area. Emersed leaves are lanceolate, narrowed at both extremities, rounded at the apex, generally

40 cm long; the achenes are smooth with a very short beak. Submersed leaves (phyllodes) are ribbon-like, moderately curved, green or green-brown, 40 cm long and usually 10 mm wide. It is best cultivated in a medium that is not too rich, but with adequate illumination; it thrives at temperatures of 59° to 86° F (15° to 30° C). In water that is not more than 30 cm deep it rarely grows above the surface and is thus very useful in aquariums. It also grows well in soft as well as medium hard water.

This variety is propagated from root runners which develop throughout the summer. During winter, coincident with the shortening of the day, tubercles arise on the roots from which new plants develop at the beginning of spring. It is one of the most suitable plants for the beginner.

Sagittaria graminea var. *platyphylla* Engelm. was formerly held to be a separate species, i.e. *S. platyphylla* Engelm. J.G. Sm. It differs from the preceding variety in that the emersed leaves are pointed at the apex and are generally larger. The achenes have a beak longer than 0.3 mm; the submersed leaves (which are important to aquarists) are wider and more ornamental and measure up to 45 cm long and 15 mm wide. It is the most robust variety, but readily grows above the water surface even in the aquarium.

Sagittaria graminea var. *weatherbiana* (Fernald) Bogin is found on the Atlantic coast of the U.S.A., mainly in the southern states. It differs from the preceding varieties by having a more robust growth. The pedicels of the female flowers are very long (40 mm), and the submersed leaves are up to 50 cm long and 25 mm wide. This larger variety of the species is sometimes offered in the trade under the commercial name *Sagittaria gigantea* Hort.

Sagittaria graminea var. *teres* (S. Wats.) Bogin grows in the narrow coastal strip of the eastern states of the U.S.A. from Massachusetts to Florida. This variety was formerly considered to be a separate species (*S. teres* S. Wats., *S. isoetiformis* J.G. Sm.). In the first year the seedlings grow only up to 5 to 10 cm long and have round leaves; in the second year they reach a length of about 10 to 30 cm and have round, spongy petioles with narrowly lanceolate blades. It is suitable for aquariums but practically never cultivated.

SAGITTARIA SUBULATA (L.) Buch.   (III. 177)
Incorrect name: *S. natans*

This species is native to the eastern states of the U.S.A., being found in marshes and shallow waters. It is a submersed plant that is fully adapted to life under water; submersed leaves are ribbon-

Sagittaria montevidensis found growing submersed in a fast flowing river near Ponta-Grossa, Brazil. Photo by T.J. Horeman.

Sagittaria montevidensis growing emersed in Porto Alegre, Brazil. Note the characteristic arrow-shaped leaves of emersed plants. Photo by T.J. Horeman.

Crinum thaianum. Photo by T.J. Horeman.

like, not differentiated into petiole and blade. Before flowering the floating leaves appear on thin petioles with blades that are ovate, oval, or rarely cordately arrow-shaped. The flowers develop on very thin, long, light-green stalks; there are usually two to five male and one to two female flowers on each stalk. Flowers are white, about 10 mm in diameter. The fruit resembles a green raspberry and contains a great number of minute achenes, moderately dentate on the front as well as on the back. When the water dries out S. *subulata* develops land forms with ovate blades that are 25 to 50 mm long and with petioles that are equally as long or perhaps up to three times longer than the blade.

All varieties of this species withstand hard water as well as water with a surplus of organic substances. They are fit for any tank and, not being sensitive even to temperature variations, are suitable plants for beginners. Plants thrive with a very poor planting medium but require a generous light; they appear very beautiful in a good, diffused light. In sunlit places all varieties of S. *subulata* adopt a dwarf form and develop as a very low carpet (25 to 50 mm) formed by the grass-green, ribbon-shaped, recurved leaves. In a diffused light of sufficient intensity the same varieties form exquisite growth of long bright green leaves. This plant is propagated very easily by development of new plants from root runners.

Sagittaria subulata (L.) Buch. var. *subulata* develops submersed leaves that are usually only 5 to 10 cm long, rarely up to 30 cm, and 1 to 7 mm wide. Leaves are generally stiff, short, and recurved. Flowers rarely develop in the aquarium. This variety is suitable for foreground planting. It is offered in the trade under the name S. *pusilla* or S. *natans*.

Sagittaria subulata var. *gracillima* (S. Wats.) J.G. Sm.. Syn: S. *lorata* Small. This variety develops submersed leaves (phyllodes), 30 to 90 cm long and 1 to 6 mm wide, forming dense clusters in the tank. When the leaves have reached the water level they wind about below the surface and become dense tangles. This variety is especially useful for planting in the corners of an aquarium, where it provides a shelter for refuge-seeking fishes.

Sagittaria subulata var. *kurziana* (Gluck.) Bogin is the most decorative plant of the species. Submersed phyllodes are 10 to 90 cm long and 7 to 15 mm wide. This variety comes to the shops under the commercial name S. *japonica* Hort.; it resembles some species of *Vallisneria*. It is very useful for the same purpose as the preceding variety, but is more decorative.

It is possible that the genus *Sagittaria* will offer further suitable aquarium plants in the future. There are, for example, *S. demersa* J.G. Sm., a very rare plant from Mexico, until now unknown in artificial surroundings; *S. ambigua* J.G. Sm. from the states of Kansas, Missouri, and Oklahoma; and *S. pseudohermaphroditica* Rataj, an exquisite but extremely rare species from Brazil, with submersed broadly cordate leaves. Also worth mentioning are the newly described *S. planitiana* Agostini, which has been imported in recent years under the commercial name *"Echinodorus lophotocarpi latifolia,"* and *S. rhombifolia* Cham., which is imported as *"Echinodorus lophotocarpi angustifolia."* Both these species, however, seem mostly to develop emersed forms that have decorative leaves.

The members of the genus *Sagittaria* are monoecious; on a single plant there are both male flowers (containing only anthers) and female flowers (in which the seeds arise). They are self-fertile and self-sterile as well. The inflorescence is racemose. The male flowers open first in the top part of the inflorescence, and only then do the lower whorls of female flowers open. The achenes of *Sagittaria* species differ from those of *Echinodorus* species by not being ribbed.

Species of *Sagittaria* are cultivated in a way similar to that adopted for the members of the genus *Echinodorus*, but they are less exacting growing in all conditions that are likely to be met in the aquarium, and they do not require high temperatures. With few exceptions they are light-loving plants.

AMARANTHACEAE

This family is represented by perennial herbs, shrubs, or trees with alternate or opposite leaves. They are found all over the world except in the cool areas of the temperate zones. About 60 genera with 850 species, for the most part growing in America and Africa, are included in the family.

Many species are marsh plants which have not yet been tested for use in the aquarium. Two genera are aquatic. *Centrostachys aquatica* (R. Br.) Wall is found from tropical Africa to Southeast Asia in swampy localities, but has not yet been imported to Europe. The genus *Alternanthera* with about 170 species contains only very few aquatics. Recently three very decorative species have been imported from tropical South America under the commercial names *A. lilacina*, *A. rubra*, and *A. osiris*. The last species, *A. os-*

Alternanthera sessilis var. *lilacina.*

Alternanthera reineckii with sessile flowers.

Hydrocotyle vulgaris, cultivated emersed.

iris, was identified as *A. reineckii* whereas the other two species are probably varieties of *A. sessilis*.

ALTERNANTHERA REINECKII Briquet (III. 185)
Incorrect name: *Alternanthera (Telanthera) osiris* Hort.

A plant from southern Brazil, where it occurs as a marsh plant permanently accustomed to a submersed life. As a member of the genus *Alternanthera*, *A. reineckii* prefers to be under water. It is easily cultivated and is certainly going to remain a colorful decoration for the aquarium.

Submersed stems that are green or reddish point upwards to the surface. The leaves are arranged so that each pair is situated perpendicular to the axis of the preceding leaves. Leaves are nearly sessile, long and elliptical, 25 to 35 cm long and 5 to 15 mm wide; the upper surface is green, while the lower surface is pink or reddish. A most beautifully colored plant, *A. reineckii* grows in the shade; in good light, the green color prevails. It withstands slightly acid water and slightly alkaline conditions and grows well with *Cryptocoryne* and *Echinodorus*. Stems reach to the surface; the plant has to be pruned regularly or it will grow above the water.

As with other underwater species, *A. reineckii* is kept only in groups of five to seven stems. In smaller tanks it is useful in corners and in larger tanks as a center piece. It resembles some species of *Ludwigia*. This plant can withstand shady conditions and will hibernate (winter) well.

ALTERNANTHERA SESSILIS (L.) DC. var. *LILACINA* Hort.

The leaves are olive green on the upper surface, dark red to violet on the lower surface, sometimes red on both sides, and about twice as large as those of *A. reineckii*. They vary greatly in the shape and color. Aquarists have little experience in the keeping of *A. sessilis*; for some it will grow admirably under water, for others only a little or not at all. The main prerequisite for success is old, clean water. *A. sessilis* does not grow well in newly established tanks. *A. sessilis* var. *lilacina* does well with sufficient light as well as in shady conditions. A neutral pH is ideal. Propagation is by rooting parts of the stems. (III. 184)

ALTERNANTHERA SESSILIS var. *RUBRA* Hort.

The emersed form of var. *rubra* develops creeping stems that are branching just above the ground. The leaves are 25 to 50 cm long and 7.5 to 14 mm wide. The stem and both sides of the leaves are ruby red. The plant will root easily even at the base of each leaf and propagates only in the emersed state. The tips of the long stems with many leaves can be pinched out (to a length of 10 to 15 cm) and put into the aquarium in groups. Under water they root in about ten days, but they usually grow very slowly and stay in a nice decorative form for two to six months. When the lower leaves begin to die the plants have to be replaced by new ones. Although not a true aquatic plant, it is the only plant able to decorate our tank with ruby red color, even if only temporarily.

AMARYLLIDACEAE (Amaryllis Family)

Representatives of this family are found, for the most part, in the steppes of southeastern Europe and Asia Minor, in the savannahs of the Capetown area and in tropical Africa, in Western Australia, in Brazil, on the islands of the Caribbean, and in the region of the Andes in South America. In total, 85 genera with 860 species are known. They are plants of the most varied appearance, and they also possess either a bulb or tubercle. Many are known for their beautiful flowers, often being plants of early spring, such as *Leucojum* (snowflake), *Galanthus* (snowdrop), and *Narcissus* (daffodil). The three genera named are the main representatives of the family in the temperate zone; most other plants in the family are tropical or subtropical.

Although many species of the family Amaryllidaceae grow in very moist, marshy conditions, only the genus *Crinum* (with well-known aquatic species) can be cultivated under water.

CRINUM

Plants of the genus *Crinum* form a short stalk with a great number of ribbon-like leaves that are flat or channeled, sometimes curved upwards. They are found mainly in the tropics of eastern Asia, and many of them are cultivated as indoor or greenhouse plants. Some species, such as *C. gigantéum*, reach the size of a tree. The bulbs of other species are used as a curative. It is interesting that most of the species are capable of permanent or at least long-term growth under water, even though they are found only in moderately moist soil in their native habitat. More than 110 species are known to grow in the maritime areas of the tropics and subtropics.

CRINUM NATANS Baker   (III. 190)

This species is found in the African tropics (Liberia, Ghana, Nigeria, etc.) and in India, where it grows in rather deep water. Bulbs (25 to 50 mm long) protrude halfway out of the ground. The leaves on a short stalk are ribbon-like, longitudinally veined, 10 to 15 mm wide and 1.5 meters long. They grow vertically toward the

Inflorescence of *Echinodorus cordifolius*.

Echinodorus cordifolius.

Echinodorus horemanii.

Inflorescence of *Echinodorus horemanii.*

Crinum natans.

Crinum thaianum.

surface and then float under it, in a fashion similar to that of tall *Vallisneria* plants.

    C. natans is cultivated at temperatures of 68° to 86° F (20° to 30° C) in a not-too-nutritious soil in a well-lit situation. The plant is propagated by way of small bulbs which develop on the main bulb from time to time. Propagation in the aquarium is very slow and rare. One of the most decorative but also rare plants in the aquarium trade, *C. natans* seems to be very rare even in nature.

CRINUM THAIANUM Schulze (Ill. 181, 190)

A species incorrectly called *"Crinum natans"* has been regularly imported in recent years from the Indo-Malayan area along with specimens of the genus *Cryptocoryne*. It was presumed incorrectly on the basis of these imports that this species appears in Africa and in tropical Asia as well, but plants growing in Asia were described some time ago under the name *C. thaianum* Schulze.

C. thaianum differs from *C. natans* by having much broader leaves. They are strap-like, 1.5 to 2 meters long and 25 to 50 mm wide, with strikingly undulate margins; the surface is usually bullate. This species is extremely attractive but suitable only for large tanks where the leaves coil decoratively under water. Large lily-like flowers are developed very rarely in the aquarium. *C. thaianum* requires old clean water, is not troublesome in general, and is among the most hardy of aquarium plants.

APIACEAE (= Umbelliferae) (Parsley Family)

Members of this big family are distributed all over the world. A number of cultivated plants, i.e. parsley, carrot, cumin, fennel, etc., belong to this family, and many of them (about 15 genera) grow amphibiously. These plants develop distinct finely divided submersed leaves and smooth-edged aerial leaves. All are cold-water plants that are not truly fit for aquariums; the only really suitable representatives of the family are the genera *Hydrocotyle*, with about 100 species, and *Lilaeopsis*, with 10 to 40 species.

HYDROCOTYLE (WATER PENNYWORT)

The stem is floating or creeping, rooting at most nodes. Leaves are distinctly stalked, peltate or cordate at the base, orbicular to reniform, with smooth, toothed, or lobed edges. The only species fit for the aquarium are one European species (*H. vulgaris*) and two from South America (*H. verticillata* and *H. leucopetala*).

HYDROCOTYLE VULGARIS L. (Ill. 185)

H. vulgaris grows in the Mediterranean area and nearly all over Europe, being found in the still waters of ditches, marshes, and ponds. It is a minute, very decorative herb with a thin and creeping rooting system. The leaves (up to 10 cm long) have long petioles leading into the center of the round blade; margins are finely notched. It flowers readily in the emersed form; the small whitish flowers are in racemes.

Relatively little known, but its shield-shaped leaves make *H. vulgaris* a very interesting plant. It is usually planted in the foreground of aquariums and paludariums, forming a dense growth; it

Inflorescence and fruits of
Hydrocotyle leucopetala.

Hydrocotyle leucopetala.

Inflorescence of *Aponogeton madagascariensis.* Photo by T.J. Horeman.

Liliaeopsis novae-zelandiae.

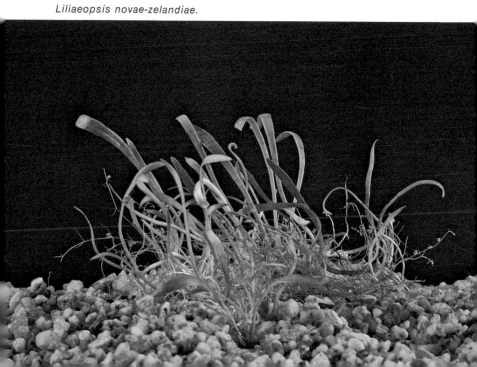

is propagated by runners from the creeping stem. This species is cultivated in a sandy medium, with any kind of water, in a generously lighted situation; it tolerates low as well as high temperatures. Growth is inhibited in the winter, but hibernation takes place even in well lit tanks.

HYDROCOTYLE LEUCOPETALA Cham. et Schlecht. (III. 192)

H. leucopetala (from South America), unlike *H. vulgaris*, has petioles that do not lead into the middle of a shield-shaped blade; instead the blade is deeply cut from the edge to the center so that the petiole runs into the deepest point of this cut. Stems are usually under water or float on the surface, where they flower easily and reproduce. The dimension of blades is variable, from 25 to 75 mm. If the plants are used in their floating form (not rooted) the blades are usually small. It is better to plant them into the medium and cut off the tips as soon as the stems reach the water surface. *H. leucopetala* demands plenty of light but is not particular as to the quality of water and other external conditions.

Occasionally one will come across the species *H. verticillata* Thunb. from tropical South America, together with *H. leucopetala*. They differ in the shape of the blades; the leaf edges in *H. leucopetala* are nearly entire or only shallowly cut, while those of *H. verticillata* have deep cuts sometimes consisting of five nearly symmetrical lobules.

LILAEOPSIS (III. 193)

Lilaeopsis includes 14 to 20 species distributed in North America and South America, Australia and New Zealand. Most of the species are found on the shores of brooks or submersed in rivers and lakes; some are found in brackish water. Others, like *L. lacustris* A.W. Hill, are found deeply submersed in water as deep as 4 meters in New Zealand. The stems are creeping or floating, rooting mostly at the nodes. Leaves are erect, reduced to simple septate leaf stalks, entire, subulate, linear or spathulate.

Only *Lilaeopsis novae-zelandiae* A.W. Hill is commonly cultivated. It is a tiny plantlet, about 25 to 50 mm tall, of a bright green color, especially suitable for planting in the front of an aquarium. Its creeping stock branches very quickly and rapidly make a thick green carpet completely covering the bottom of the tank. Each plant has only one to three leaves. Being so delicate, it is not available in large quantities commercially. It is difficult to find for sale, and aquarists help each other by way of exchange. This is one reason why *L. novae-zelandiae* is little known as an aquarium plant. It grows exceptionally well and is not particular about the quality of the water or the light; it is just as beautiful in the aquarium during summer as in winter.

APONOGETONACEAE

Aponogeton, the only genus in the family Aponogetonaceae, is distributed in the tropical and subtropical areas of the Old World. It is absent in the New World (except for the introduced *A. distachyus*). About 45 species are known.

The plants commonly cultivated in aquariums come mainly from tropical Asia. They grow in India and farther to the east; on the eastern coast of Asia they extend well to the north, as far as South Korea; they are found even on some islands of the Indo-Malayan area. From these parts come the most popular and most resistant species, i.e. *A. crispus*, *A. undulatus*, and *A. natans*. Recently some new species propagated vegetatively have been imported from Asia.

In Australia it is mainly *A. elongatus*, a species that is very suitable for aquariums, that is recorded.

Aponogeton is found throughout the African continent, but no African species is suitable for use in the aquarium. They are usually plants requiring a rather long resting period and should be taken from the aquarium and put into a moderately moist sand over winter (e.g. *A. leptostachyus*). Other species are not amphibious and cannot withstand permanent underwater conditions (e.g. *A. junceus*). Some species (*A. distachyus*) are robust, up to 1 meter tall, and develop large, floating leaves; on account of this, they are unsuitable for aquariums. They are best used for planting in garden pools and the like. *A. distachyus* is very resistant and hibernates even in low temperatures. It has been brought to Europe (to southern France) and to South America (Peru). It flowers abundantly and forms seeds easily. There are horticultural varieties with pink or white flowers.

Very interesting and decorative too are the species found in Madagascar. The exquisite *A. ulvaceus* has long been useful in the aquarium.

Aponogeton species are principally submersed plants, those from Asia, Australia, and Madagascar being typically submersed representatives. Species from the African continent are generally submersed only during the rainy period; they drop their leaves later and survive the dry period with the help of starchy tubercles.

Echinodorus horizontalis. Photo by T.J. Horeman.

Echinodorus longiscapus.

Echinodorus intermedius collected in Paraguay. Photo by T.J. Horeman.

Echinodorus grandiflorus found in swamps near Mage, Brazil. Photo by T.J. Horeman.

Some species, such as A. *junceus*, have become adapted still further and can develop emersed leaves. They can withstand water up to 10 cm deep and live, though poorly, in this submersed state.

In nature plants of this genus are propagated mainly from the seeds. This is also true for plants cultivated in the aquarium, except those species forming rhizomes. The rhizomes can be divided, and two to four new plants will develop from a single plant. This is possible, for instance, with well-developed individuals of A. *madagascariensis*. Only two species are propagated vegetatively: A. *undulatus* (= *stachyosporus*), which develops tubercles on the floral stalks from which leaves and roots grow, and A. *rigidifolius*, which forms a horizontal rhizome on which new plants arise.

The species of *Aponogeton* are practically the only aquarium plants that must be virtually propagated from seeds. Above water these plants develop spicate inflorescences consisting of a great number of minute white, yellow, bluish, or pink flowers. The Asiatic and Australian species form one single spike on the floral stalk, and the African (including Madagascar) species exhibit a forked inflorescence with two to five spikes.

The pollen is usually transferred by tiny insects visiting the sweet and colored flowers where these plants are cultivated. In greenhouses the pollen is transferred in the same way, but in the aquarium it is necessary to pollinate the flowers artificially. *Aponogeton* flowers are self-sterile as well as self-fertile, i.e. they can be pollinated by both the pollen of the same individual plant and by pollen of another plant of the same or a different species. That is why hybrids are formed easily.

In artificial pollination either a fine brush or a piece of soft cloth or gauze wound on a small stick, etc., is used. If several flowers in one or more plants mature at the same time, they are best pollinated by holding one flowering spike above the other and giving it a moderate shake; clouds of yellow pollen then fall upon the lower spike and the grains stick to the stigmas.

We are of the opinion that the success or failure of artificial pollination of *Aponogeton* species is not dependent upon the method of pollination, but upon the conditions the plants have during their development. Our thinking is based on the fact that in certain years the seeds of *Aponogeton* mature in indoor aquariums for some people, whereas in other years the seeds do not develop in spite of being pollinated artificially.

It is certain that the members of the genus *Aponogeton* develop better and form seeds readily only when the illumination is from above—in ponds, in tanks placed near the floor, below the window, etc. Also of great importance are the composition of the medium and water and the number and kinds of fish in the tank. The common Asiatic species and their hybrids develop seeds regularly in greenhouses and ponds.

The seeds are relatively large (50 to 75 mm) and are enveloped in follicles filled with air so that mature seeds float and are transported by water; thus new plants can be distributed far from the parent plants. After about 24 hours the seed coating splits open and the seed sinks to the bottom. It usually germinates at once, and within a few days little roots develop and allow it to take hold. Mature seeds can be separated easily from the axis of the spike. They are collected before they fall off naturally, because if left to separate spontaneously many of them get lost in the dark corners of the tank or pond, where they cannot develop.

The seeds are sown on the surface of washed sand and then transferred into tanks some months later. Development is better if the seeds are kept in a bottle of clear water for a period of four to eight weeks and are transplanted (to tanks without fish) only when their leaves are about 25 mm long and the roots about 50 mm long.

The propagation of *Aponogeton* from seeds is elaborate and slow and requires special tanks without fish. As a rule neither the seeds nor the young plants develop if put into tanks holding fish. It will be more advantageous for the aquarist to acquire pre-cultivated seedlings or fully developed plants from aquatic plant shops. In species propagated vegetatively, the young plants developing on the floral stalks are separated only after some short rootlets have been formed. One parent plant can provide up to twenty new ones from four to five stalks during the vegetative period.

True species of *Aponogeton* (i.e., those which are not hybrids) are difficult to cultivate. They require generous overhead light. A customary error committed by aquarists is to cling to the opinion that the *Aponogeton* species do not require a rich soil. This belief arose from the fact that a mature plant with a good tubercle can live in clean, washed sand without further nourishment for four to eight months and that it continues forming new well developed leaves and flowers as well. A plant like this grows from food reserves stored in the tubercles, so it needs only a small amount of nutrients drawn from the water. But in due course the supply of energy will be exhausted and the plant will stop growing or possibly die. Its tubercle is then to be found shrunken, half-empty, or starting to rot.

A part of the inflorescence of *Echinodorus macrophyllus.*

Echinodorus macrophyllus.

A part of the
inflorescence of
*Echinodorus
parviflorus*.

E. parviflorus, submersed plant with dark veins.

The plants obtained from imported tubercles should be cultivated therefore in tanks with a planting medium supplied with nutrients. In older tanks where the bottom is enriched by detritus, they all do well except for certain kinds with gauze-like leaves. The soil should not contain lime, nor should the water be too hard.

Genuine *Aponogeton* species should be given conditions which maintain their natural rhythm of development, *viz.* a period of vegetative growth (March to May), flowering period (May to June), maturation of seeds (June to July), and a period for building up reserves in the tubercle (August to October); they then should be given a resting period. This task is achieved by not heating the tank in winter, letting the temperature fall to between 46° to 50° F (8° to 10° C) from November to January. During this period of dormancy the plant as a rule drops all its leaves. In February or in March the temperature is raised to 64° to 68° F (18° to 20° C). Within a few days the tubercles react to this temperature by starting to develop leaves, which can reach a length of up to 20 cm within a fortnight (*A. ulvaceus* is an example). The growth of the plants from tubercles treated in this manner is then very fast. They produce abundant flowers and develop seeds readily by self-pollination. This system is not possible in a tank with fish, and it is recommended only in the case of parent plants from which one wants particularly to obtain young plants.

The situation is different in the case of hybrids, which form the great majority of *Aponogeton* plants in aquariums. These hybrids have been developing over a long period, and natural selection under aquarium conditions has made itself felt, so they are adapted to life in tanks and grow well all the year round. Since they live in warm water all the time, they do not develop the typical tubercles, or they form small ones that appear only as thickened rhizomes hidden in the tangle of roots. They can flower any time, often in winter. The hybrids designated as *Aponogeton hybridus* Hort. and developed by the inter-crossing of *A. echinatus* and *A. natans* are therefore ideal aquarium plants. They withstand artificial illumination well not only from above but also from the sides and are indifferent to moderately hard water. The utilization of these hybrids rather than the genuine species of *Aponogeton* is recommended to those aquarists who do not want to occupy themselves with special cultivation of aquarium plants. Even the multiple hybrids of Asiatic species of *Aponogeton* are fertile and in good conditions develop seeds capable of germinating.

APONOGETON CRISPUS Thunb.

A. crispus is native to Ceylon, where it is found in rivers, lakes, and pools from sea level to 1000 to 2300 meters. Most plants in our aquariums identified as *A. crispus* are actually hybrids that were produced in nature or under artificial conditions. A genuine *A. crispus* is distinguishable by its leaves, which are always red or reddish and never float on the surface.

Plants with leaves of a shape similar to those of this species except that they are of uniform green color are hybrids (usually *A. crispus* X *A. natans*). *A. crispus* has an oblong horizontal rhizome up to 25 mm thick from which only submersed leaves develop. The young leaves are usually reddish, seldom light green. The basic coloration of older leaves is always brown-green to purple. The petiole is much shorter than the blade. The form of the blade is very variable; strap-like, about 25 mm wide and up to 25 to 30 cm long, or elliptical up to 50 mm wide and 20 to 25 cm long. Isolated areas among nerves are usually unevenly colored; some are transparent, so that the whole surface looks like a design in mosaic. Blade margins are thickly curled. The floral stalks are 50 to 80 cm long (a single ear 15 to 17.5 cm long); flowers are white or light violet. Relatively large seeds germinate immediately after ripening.

A. crispus requires a bright tank and prefers an illumination coming from above. Seeds are easily obtained from imported tubercles. In the winter cultivated plants should be left in water at about 59° F (15° C). Under these conditions they may lose all their leaves, but as soon as the temperature is raised at the beginning of spring the growth will be resumed; plants will develop well and be able to produce seeds.

The plant can be maintained under normal aquarium conditions, tolerates old water, and requires a medium rich planting medium without lime.

APONOGETON ECHINATUS Roxb.   (III. 205, 210)

In southern and central India this species grows in large quantities in lakes and ponds between sea level and 1300 meters. It flowers throughout the year. *A. echinatus* was known under the names *A. natans* and *A. undulatus*. *Aponogeton natans* (L.) Engler et Krause is not cultivated in our aquariums. It has submersed leaves up to 5 to 7.5 cm long and 15 mm wide and forms mainly floating leaves which are not suitable for aquariums. *Aponogeton undulatus* Roxb. is the most widely distributed viviparous species

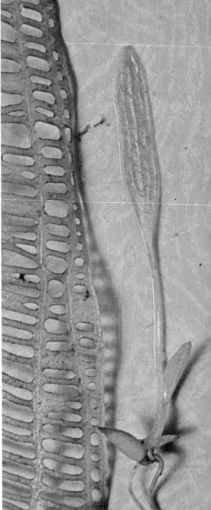

Ripe fruit on the
inflorescence of
*Aponogeton
madagascariensis.*
Photo by T.J. Horeman.

Close-up view of the leaf
structure and seedling
of *Aponogeton
madagascariensis.*
Photo by T.J. Horeman.

Aponogeton echinatus.

and is known in our aquariums under the name (synonym) *A. sta-chyosporus* De Wit.

The rhizome (tuber) of *A echinatus* is ovoid, 25 to 50 mm in diameter. Submersed leaves are variable, on long or short petioles; the blade is fragile, transparent, 15 to 40 cm long and 50 to 65 mm wide, with moderately undulate margins. The base is cuneate or truncate, the top is usually rounded. The floating leaves are oval, sometimes narrowed at the top, 20 cm long and 20 to 40 mm wide. The inflorescence is on a single spike; it has minute flowers that are white, mostly bluish, or light purple. In good conditions one plant can develop up to twenty floral stalks in a year. Fruits (10 to 15 mm long) germinate instantaneously.

This species is very variable; with the imported plants we find forms with submersed leaves on long petioles and with many floating blades, or forming numerous decorative submersed leaves on short petioles and without any floating blades. The last mentioned form is suitable for indoor aquariums.

A. echinatus is best cultivated in older tanks where the bottom is enriched with detritus. The soil should not contain lime, and the water should not be too hard. This plant is cultivated in half-shade; in this way the development of floating leaves can be avoided.

APONOGETON ELONGATUS F. Muller

A. elongatus from Australia resembles *A. echinatus* more than it does *A. crispus*, because the leaf margins are only slightly undulate and are not curled. But unlike the leaves of *A. echinatus* the leaves of *A. elongatus* are 20 to 40 cm long and often colored olive green or red-brown. Besides submersed leaves it develops floating leaves that are usually oval, glossy green, 10 to 15 cm long and 20 to 30 mm wide. After the floating leaves have developed, then the floral stalk is quickly formed. The floral stalk grows up to 12.5 cm in one day. The spike is shorter than in the other Asiatic species (5 to 8 cm), flowers are yellow. In each follicle there are only about four to six seeds (4 mm long).

As to the requirements and methods of cultivation, *A. elongatus* resembles *A. crispus;* however, it can withstand much lower temperatures (to below 46° F, 8° C) without any harm.

APONOGETON HYBRIDUS Hort.

This name covers a group of *Aponogeton* plants forming the great majority of aquarium representatives of this genus. This group includes the plants which have arisen through inadvertent crossings among the original species cultivated together in nur-

Aponogeton madagascariensis.

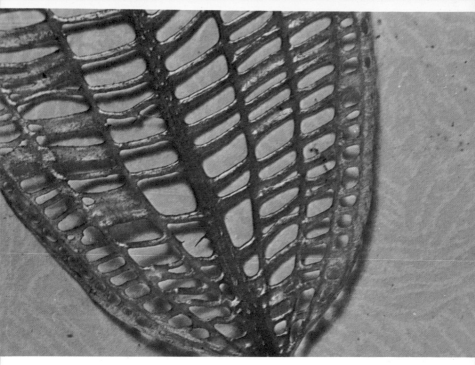

Enlarged section of a leaf of *Aponogeton madagascariensis*. Photo by T.J. Horeman.

Aponogeton rigidifolius. Photo by T.J. Horeman.

Aponogeton ulvaceus from Madagascar showing the characteristic twin inflorescence. Photo by T.J. Horeman.

Enlarged distal
end of the spike
inflorescence of
*Aponogeton
echinatus.*

series and in the tanks of aquarists. The original species are *A. crispus*, *A. echinatus* and *A. natans*.

As stated earlier, these species from natural environments are rather exacting and do not thrive well in aquariums. A natural law of biology prevails here, namely "hybrid vigor." Some of the hybrids are more resistant to adverse external conditions than either of the parent plants; less resistant hybrids died off while the more resistant plants developed and were further propagated. In this manner, i.e., by natural selection, *Aponogeton* spp. have arisen that are fully adapted to aquarium conditions and are now ideal for community tanks. They have no special requirements with regard to the composition of the substratum, water, or light and do not require a resting period. They usually flower all year round, independently of the season, and if the conditions are good they produce plenty of fertile seeds.

Because these hybrids are propagated further by seeds and continue to hybridize, several forms exist. Where a definite selection has been made, plants have been improved and possess special properties derived from all the original natural species. They have leaves 30 to 40 cm long which are probably inherited from *A. crispus* or *A. natans*, leaf margins which are only moderately undulate (from *A. echinatus*), and flowers which are generally blue or light purple (from *A. natans*).

In general there are two groups of hybrids:

1. *A. crispus* X *A. echinatus*. These plants usually have a long leaf, winding under the surface of the water (after *A. crispus*). The leaf margin is only moderately undulate (after *A. echinatus*). They are ideal plants for the aquarium. Flowers are generally white. Floating leaves are rarely formed.

2. (a) *A. crispus* X *A. natans*, (b) *A. echinatus* X *A. natans*, and (c) multiple hybrids such as (*A. crispus* X *A. echinatus*) X *A. natans*. In general it can be said that this second group is less suitable for the aquarium. The submersed leaves keep the characteristics of *A. crispus* and *A. echinatus*, i.e., a long and moderately undulate leaf, but in good light they form floating leaves which are usually undesirable in aquariums. Flowers are mostly blue or purple.

All hybrids of these Asiatic species are fertile and multiply well if the steps presented in the introductory section to this family are followed.

APONOGETON MADAGASCARIENSIS (Mirbel) van Bruggen
Syn: *A. fenestralis* (Poir.) Hook.
(Madagascar Lace Plant)   (Ill. 193, 204, 207, 208)

Aquarium literature usually mentions three species of *Aponogeton* from Madagascar which are noted for lace-like leaves formed only by the veins. These are *A. fenestralis* (Poir.) Hook., *A. henkelianus* (Falk.) Baum., and *A. bernierianus* (Descaisne) Hook. It seems that the specific differences are insignificant and that at least two of these plants (*A. fenestralis* and *A. henkelianus*) belong to the species *A. madagascariensis*. *A. bernierianus* does not have fenestrate leaves.

The rhizome is cylindrical, ovate or round, 2.5 to 10 cm long. Leaves measure up to 40 cm long; the leaf blades are oval elliptical, somewhat blunt or moderately acute at the apex, obtuse at the base, sometimes slightly cordately lobed. Blade is 10 to 20 cm long and 25 to 75 mm wide. The interstices between the cross veins are not filled with tissue, and the whole blade is lace-like; this charac-

Aponogeton ulvaceus.

Aglaonema, cultivated under water.

Echinodorus osiris.

New plants are forming on the floral stalk of this *Echinodorus osiris* plant.

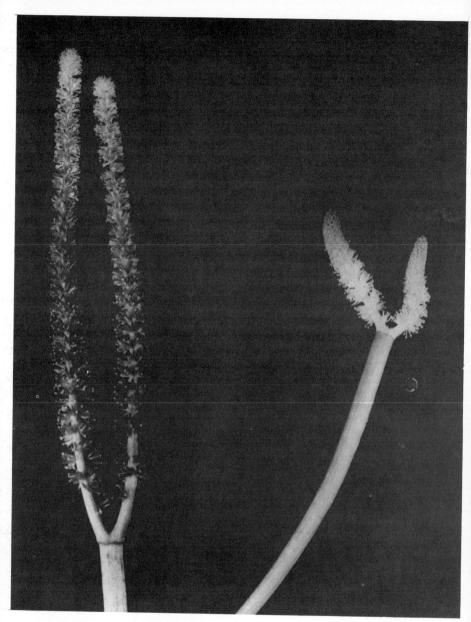

Inflorescence of *Aponogeton ulvaceus*. As many as five spikes can develop in this species of *Aponogeton*.

teristic is rarely absent. The white or yellowish inflorescence consists of two to five spikes. After fertilization the flowers turn to pink to red-purple.

This species requires frequent change of water. It can be used in the tank for a single vegetation period. For this purpose only those plants obtained from well developed tubercles are used. They live in the tank for one season and then die off.

To cultivate A. *madagascariensis*, one should put the plants in an isolated tank of a small capacity (7 to 12 gallons, 30 to 50 liters), with rinsed (not properly washed) sand, a medium amount of loam, and a very small quantity of calcium and magnesium salts. It should be located in a bright place, but out of direct sunlight. A part of the water (one-third at least) is changed not less than once a month in winter and every week or two in summer. No new rainwater is used. Under these conditions A. *madagascariensis* flowers well in some years and produces fertile seeds.

Recently two forms have been regularly imported: one has a long, broad leaf (25 to 50 mm) and is sold as A. *henkelianus*; the second has a much broader leaf (5 to 10 cm), the top usually blunt, and is sold as A. *fenestralis*. The narrow-leaved form is much more resistant and does not require a change of water. It flowers and reproduces easily. The seeds are very small (hardly 2 mm long) and the seedlings are difficult to cultivate.

APONOGETON RIGIDIFOLIUS van Bruggen (III. 208)

The rhizome of this species from Ceylon is different from that of other aponogetons. It is cylindrical, horizontal, 1 cm thick and 15 to 20 cm long, and creeping. Young plants arise from the rhizome; five to ten plants can develop from one rhizome.

The leaves are submersed and the petiole is usually distinctly shorter than the blades, which are leather-like, firm, 20 to 60 cm long and 25 to 40 mm wide, with flat or distinctly undulate margins. The color of the leaves is variable; some are dark dull green, others are dark red-brown. The midrib is distinct, wide with three to four parallel nerves on each side. The leaf is narrowly cuneate on both sides and usually blunt at the top.

The inflorescence is 50 to 90 cm long; the unique spike is usually 10 to 15 cm long, with minute white flowers. Fruits are 5 to 12 mm.

In nature A. *rigidifolius* grows in deep water (10 to 50 cm), with temperatures of 68° to 77° F (20° to 25° C), and a 7.2 pH in the sandy soil.

Inflorescence of
Anubias afzelii.

Anubias afzelii.

Anubias congensis.

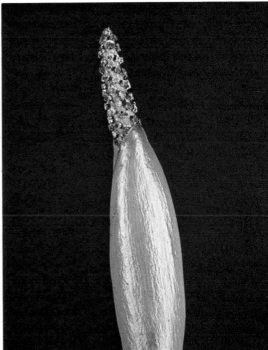

Inflorescence of
Anubias congensis.

Very suitable for the aquarium, it does not form floating leaves; the submersed leaves are very firm and rigid. The brown-red leaves are very attractive. Propagation from the rhizome buds is easy, i.e., young plants can be obtained vegetatively. This plant rarely flowers in the aquarium. As with the other common *Aponogeton* species, propagation by seeds is not so simple.

APONOGETON ULVACEUS Baker (Ill. 75, 209, 212, 214)

A. ulvaceus originates from Madagascar. It has a globular tubercle (up to 30 mm in diameter). The blades have a short or a long petiole, the base tapering gradually. They are light green, almost translucent; oblong, rounded at the upper end; 20 to 35 cm long and 40 to 80 mm wide, with moderately undulate margins. Well-developed leaves are spirally coiled.

The flowers are yellow, the inflorescence with two to five spikes. This species is propagated by seeds produced usually by plants which have been given a minimum of two to three months of dormancy at temperatures of 46° to 50° F (8° to 10° C). Such plants drop their leaves and only the tubercles remain; in the beginning of spring (after a rise in temperature) the tubercles develop leaves (up to 25 cm long) within ten to fifteen days. They begin flowering in April. For the parent plants, the temperature is decreased as early as September—from September to November at 54° to 59° F (12° to 15° C), then down to 46° to 50° F (8° to 10° C) in order to prevent their blossoming a second time, which would occur about fourteen days after the autumnal equinox (i.e., by the end of September in the Northern Hemisphere). The seeds from the autumn flowers do not usually mature; the plants use up the food supply before the winter period.

This is one of the most beautiful aquarium plants, although it is difficult to propagate. Its ordinary cultivation is not exacting, but if the plant is kept at a temperature of about 68° F (20° C) it stops growing and may die.

APONOGETON UNDULATUS Roxb.
Syn: *A. stachyosporus* de Wit

This species from Malaya has some patches in the leaves filled only by clear tissue; in other places it is light to dark green, giving the appearance of a mosaic. It is a very decorative plant. The leaves reach a length of 40 cm and a width of 40 mm. The leaf margins are undulate to curled; floating leaves are broad and oval, cordately lobed at the base.

A. *undulatus* is an unexacting plant; it can withstand even water that is rich in organic substances (i.e., it can be cultivated in aquariums with many fish), but it requires adequate light.

A. *undulatus* is a viviparous species; on the floral stalk, instead of flowers, globular tubercles usually arise on which leaves, roots and branches grow, and young plants develop at the tip of these tubercles. On each inflorescence up to twelve new plants arise and a single plant develops five to ten floral stalks during a season.

Key to Aponogeton Species

1a Leaf blade consisting only of veins, having a gauze-like appearance . . . . *A. madagascariensis*

1b Leaf blade fully formed, all tissues present **2**

2a Rhizome horizontal, leaves leather-like . . . . *A. rigidifolius*

2b Rhizome rounded or absent, leaves membranous **3**

3a Inflorescence compound from 2 or more spikes . . . . *A. ulvaceus*

3b Inflorescence simple, formed by unique spike **4**

4a Inflorescence yellow . . . . *A. elongatus*

4b Inflorescence white, bluish or violet. **5**

5a Leaves densely curled, usually reddish, plants without floating leaves . . . . *A. crispus*

5b Leaves not curled, at most undulate, floating leaves present . . **6**

6a Leaf blade with vari-colored tissue between the veins, new plants arise on the floral stalk . . . . *A. undulatus*

6b Leaf blades unicolor, without new plants on the stalk **7**

7a Mature fruits elongated in sharp, long beaks . . . . . *A. echinatus*

7b Mature fruits blunt or the beak is very short . . . . . . *A. hybridus*

ARACEAE

Most plants of this large family are moisture-loving, marshy or (more rarely) aquatic plants. Many of them are cultivated in greenhouses and as indoor plants. They are of the most varied size, from the size of herbs to the size of bushes and trees.

The leaves are of diverse shapes, simple to compound, differentiated into petiole and blade. Very minute flowers are arranged in a pulpy inflorescence (spadix) surrounded by a large bract that is often differently colored (the spathe).

The seeds of plants of the family Araceae are capable of germinating for only a relatively short time; on account of this, most

Anubias lanceolata (left) and its inflorescence (right).

220

Anubias nana. Photo by Dr. D. Terver.

species are limited to small areas, and most are propagated either by the formation of root runners or by the division of the rhizome.

Most members of the family are tropical and subtropical plants; only a few penetrate into the temperate zone. The habitat of many genera is strictly limited either to the New or Old World. Exceptions are, for example, the floating *Pistia, Arisaema*, and some other genera. The warm areas of the Old World, mainly Malaya and tropical Africa, are richer in members of the Araceae than tropical and subtropical America. Most New World species grow as forest plants at the foot of the Andes. All together 110 genera containing 1800 species are known.

ACORUS (SWEET FLAG)

This small genus contains only two species.

ACORUS CALAMUS L.

A. calamus comes from Southeast Asia; it has been gradually introduced into Europe by way of the United States. It is not suitable for indoor aquariums.

ACORUS GRAMINEUS Soland (JAPANESE RUSH) <small>(Ill. 223)</small>

A. gramineus originates in eastern Asia (China, Taiwan, and Japan). The Japanese rush is a marsh plant that can be adapted to life under water.

The rhizome is 10 to 20 mm thick and 10 to 15 cm long, from which ten to fifteen fan-shaped leaves develop. The margins are at first parallel, then prolonged acuminate (resembling the shape of the leaves of the iris (genus *Iris*) . In nature the plant reaches a height of up to 50 cm but in aquariums not more than 15 to 20 cm, with leaves that are 2.5 to 8 mm wide.

A. gramineus var. *pusillus* Engl. is a dwarf form with much shorter leaves. In nature the leaves are up to 10 cm long; in the aquarium they are generally only 50 mm long. The fan of leaves is broad, about the same width as the length of the leaves. This variety is native to China (Japanese dwarf rush).

A. gramineus forma *decoratus* Hort., known as the striped Japanese rush, is a horticultural form with yellow-striped leaves. The gay coloring is more distinct in aerial leaves than in plants cultivated under water, in which the variegations sometimes disappear completely. <small>(Ill. 223)</small>

All three forms have the same requirements. If one wishes to propagate them it is best to grow them emersed in dishes or in flowerpots immersed in water; the water should not go higher than 10 to 20 mm above the root collar. If watered regularly they grow

Acorus gramineus.

Acorus gramineus var. *pusillus.*

Ripe fruits of *Aglaonema*.

Inflorescence and close-up view of the leaf blade of *Aglaonema*.

well as indoor plants. Within one or two years a long rhizome is formed; this is then taken out of the earth, washed, and left to float freely on the surface of the water either in the aquarium or in an outdoor pond in the summer. Within ten to thirty days between twenty to fifty new plants begin to develop from the dormant buds on the rhizome. As soon as the leaves are about 25 mm long, the rhizome is cut and the leafed cuttings are planted.

Acorus should be planted in rich soil. Growth in the aquarium is very slow; in the first year it usually shows no increase. A comparatively rare plant, *Acorus* is propagated with difficulty but it is a very decorative plant when used in aquariums.

AGLAODORUM GRIFFITHII Schott

A. griffithii is an aquatic plant found in the swamps and rivers of Malaysia, Sumatra, and Borneo. It is a suitable aquarium plant, but still not imported. The rhizome is creeping; leaves are erect, glabrous, fleshy, linear to oblong; petiole is a little longer than the blade. The leaves are 20 to 50 cm long. *Aglaodorum* is closely related to *Aglaonema*.

AGLAONEMA   (Ill. 212, 224, 364)

The submersed cultivation of these well-known indoor and greenhouse plants is something rather new. A few representatives of the genus (about 45 species are known) originate in the same area as the genus *Cryptocoryne*, i.e., Malaya and eastern India.

These plants have a strong and firm rhizome from which a very short stalk bearing four to seven leaves develops. The leaf petioles are approximately the same length as the blades; the latter are broadly lanceolate, rather acute at the apex, usually cordate at the base. Leaves are stiff and thick, light to dark green, and crossed by yellow stripes in some species.

We have tested six species of *Aglaonema* (these not having been identified reliably) and found that all of them can be kept all the year without dropping any of their leaves. First they should be planted emersed, then transferred to the aquarium, where they are planted with whole and undamaged roots. Plants obtained by being cut off from the rhizome are set under water only after several weeks of pre-cultivation in the emersed state. After being transferred to submersed conditions the growth normally ceases; the plant loses its resistance, and decay spreads from the wound throughout the whole rhizome.

It is best to transfer the plants into the aquarium with the container in which they have been grown and transplant them into the aquarium substratum after sometime; they do not tolerate being transplanted into a newly furnished aquarium. Commonly cultivated species can be obtained easily in florist shops. The most common species are: A. *modestum* Schott with green, marbled leaves with silver veins; and A. *treubii* Engl. with dark green leaves decorated with light green and yellow spots. Some hybrids are extremely decorative. They are often labeled as A. *longibracteata*, A. *marmoratum*, or A. *roebelinii*. Their petioles are almost white; leaf blades are irregularly decorated with green, yellow-green, and white spots. All species mentioned reach a height of about 30 to 40 cm and are fit only for large aquariums. The most suitable species is A. *costata*. Its leaves are generally 10 to 15 cm long; the petioles are shorter than the blades, which are egg-shaped, dark green, and trimmed with light yellow round spots (5 to 10 mm diameter) irregularly distributed over the surface. It is one of the most beautiful plants.

ANUBIAS

Anubias is found in tropical West Africa and contains about twelve species growing along shady banks. During the rainy periods they survive under water in the flooded areas for several months and will withstand a permanently submersed environment. They are suitable aquarium plants and are cultivated like *Cryptocoryne* species in a medium-rich substratum and water that is not too acid. Forming a robust rhizome, the plants need sand with a depth of at least 10 to 15 cm. They are shade-loving plants.

The leaves are broadly lanceolate, ovate or elliptical, with an acuminate or rounded tip, tapering below into a petiole which is as long as the blade (though sometimes shorter) and sheathed below. The upper leaf surface is smooth and grass-green; the lower surface is lighter, a yellow-green, with distinct veins. The leaves are very strong and stiff.

Anubias plants are very decorative. They are propagated by rhizome cuttings. A mature rhizome is separated from the parent plant and either divided along the dormant buds and left undisturbed, or the whole rhizome is put in water and divided only after the plantlets are formed. Since it usually takes some years before a fairly long rhizome is obtained and only a few young plants are developed on the rhizome, *Anubias* is very rare.

These plants rarely flower; proper identification is impossible without knowledge of the floral organs, so we are not sure that the plants cultivated in our tanks have been identified correctly.

There are many questions on the nomenclature of the genus *Anubias*, and a skillful revision is needed. Many species are undoubtedly cultivated under incorrect names. Large species reaching a height of 1 meter have usually been regarded as *A. lanceolatus* or *A. congensis*—most probably they belong to *A. heterophyllae*. Seedlings (one to three years old) are suitable for aquariums; mature plants are too large for indoor aquariums.

ANUBIAS BARTERI Engler
Syn: *Amauriella hastifolia* Hepper

A. barteri from Sierra Leone is one of the few species growing regularly submersed in nature. In contrast to other species it has arrow-shaped leaves—some authors assign it to the genus *Amauriella*. Leaves reach up to 20 to 25 cm in length. The arrow-shaped blades are triangular; at the base they are prolonged into pointed lobes.

ANUBIAS AFZELII Schott (III. 216)
This medium-size plant occurs in nature mainly submersed; thus it is suitable for aquariums. It differs from other species by its undulate margins. Growing to a height of 20 to 25 cm, *A. afzelii* is also suitable for medium ponds. The petioles are green to reddish. The blade is as long as the petiole, elliptical, and dark green with very dark nerves. It develops very well in the emersed condition but remains small under water. We prefer to cultivate *A. afzelii* in terrariums, using only well-developed plants.

ANUBIAS CONGENSIS N.E. Brown (III. 42, 217)
This species from the Congo and Guinea has leaves reaching a length of 25 to 30 cm. The blades are broad, egg-shaped, leatherlike, and blunt at the tip. The veins are usually deepened, broadest in the upper third. *A. congensis* is a very interesting species but is little known in the aquarium.

ANUBIAS LANCEOLATA Schott (III. 220)
A. lanceolata is found in Nigeria, the Cameroons, and Gabon. It is the most cultivated medium-size species. The leaves (20 to 30 cm long) have petioles usually shorter than the narrow lance-shaped blades (maximum width 50 mm, 15 to 20 cm long). They are sparkling green with dark nerves; the blade is evenly narrowed on both sides and pointed at the tip.

ANUBIAS NANA Engler (III. 221, 228)
A. nana from the Cameroons is the smallest *Anubias*, measuring only 5 to 10 cm in height. The leaf blades are narrowly ellipti-

Anubias nana.

cal to lance-shaped, 60 mm long and 20 to 30 mm wide. It is the only *Anubias* appropriate for small aquariums or for planting in the foreground of medium-size tanks.

CRYPTOCORYNE

The genus *Cryptocoryne*, with the genera *Aponogeton* and *Echinodorus*, represents the most important and most popular group of aquarium plants. All cryptocorynes come from tropical Asia.

Up to the present time about sixty species from the Indo-Malayan region have been described. They are found in the area between India, the Malayan peninsula and southwestern China; a

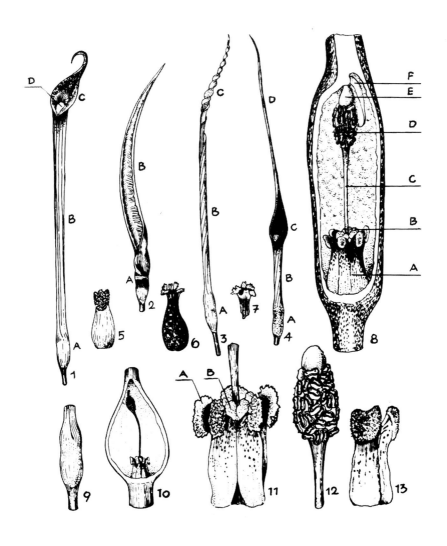

Morphological characters of the inflorescences of *Cryptocoryne:* 1. Inflorescence with a straight tube and horizontal throat (*C. cordata*). A = the kettle; B = the tube; C = limb of inflorescence; D = throat. — 2. Inflorescence without the tube (*C. spiralis*). A = kettle; B = limb. — 3. Inflorescence with twisted tube and limb (*C. retrospiralis*). A = kettle; B = tube; C = limb. — 4. Inflorescence with long caudicle (*C. johorensis*). A = kettle; B = tube; C = limb; D = caudicle. — 5. Pistil of *C. evae* with twice incised and trilobate stigma. — 6. Pistil of *C. gomezii* with horizontal stigma. — 7. Forkedly dentate aromatic corp of *C. crudassiana.* — 8. Kettle. A = pistils; B = aromatic corps; C = lower sterile part of spadix; D = fertile part of spadix with stamens; E = terminal sterile part of spadix; F = valve. — 9. A kettle constricted in the middle (*C. balansae*). — 10. Kettle not constricted (*C. bertelihansenii*). — 11. Female flowers—A = stigma; B = aromatic corps. — 12. Male flowers. — 13. Pistils of *C. hejnyi* with bilobate stigmas.

great number come from the Asiatic islands (Ceylon, Philippines, Indonesian Archipelago).

Cryptocorynes are aquatic or amphibious marsh-dwelling (rarely terrestrial) plants with a very small range of variability of living forms in both the submersed and terrestrial conditions. The petiole and the blade of the leaves are usually distinctly different. Blades may be cordate, elliptical, lanceolate or ribbon-shaped, membranous or leather-like, entire or finely dentate on the margins, smooth or crispate to undulate, and in some species they are alveolate to distinctly "blistered."

Species growing in fast-running torrents have leaves adapted to withstand the current, floating on the surface of the water or under it. Petioles are always sheathed at the base. The petiole and blade lengths in emersed forms remain constant, while in the submersed specimens the length of the petioles varies according to the depth of the water and to the intensity of the light.

Some species have green leaves, and others have distinctly colored leaf blades. The upper surface of the blades is brown-green or olive, sometimes with horizontal or vertical red-brown stripes. The dorsal side of the blades of specimens having green leaves is usually lighter, yellow-green. In species with variegated leaves the dorsal side is olive brown, light to dark red or deep purple. This coloration is not a constant character; it varies according to the light. The red color becomes more intense when the plants grow in deep shade, while the green color predominates in those plants developing with plenty of light.

The root is usually straight, often as long as the leaves or longer, and slightly branched. New plants arise vegetatively from dormant buds on the short upright rhizome of the main root. In some species there are rhizome runners on which new plants are formed at intervals of 1 to 10 cm. One of these methods of vegetative reproduction is typical for some species; others utilize both methods mentioned above. Depending on the prevailing circumstance numerous growths arise from a large number of individual plants, or a single mother plant spreads far and wide by runners, resulting in the establishment of a large colony of a monocultural character.

The inflorescence is very important for the determination of the species. The inflorescence is called a spathe, at the base of which an ovate pear-shaped kettle is situated. The kettle is joined to the tube, the terminal opening of which is called the throat. The upper part of the inflorescence is markedly colored and is called the limb.

Vegetative propagation predominates in plants found both in nature and under cultivation. The fruits of many species collected have not yet been ascertained, and it seems that these species propagate only vegetatively. Therefore many local forms have evolved, giving rise to the predominance of endemic species within the genus *Cryptocoryne.*

Most cryptocorynes are adapted to life in situations with insufficient light. In well lighted places they are not able to resist competition from other plants, their root absorption being inadequate. They occur only in the most deeply shaded places of the jungle in tropical Asia, at places without other low vegetation. It is rare to find two or more species of *Cryptocoryne* living together. One-plant cultures of a single species developed vegetatively, occupying shallow brooks with a stony ground covered with sand, are typical. In deeper waters they grow in the middle of streams, occurring in a submersed form passing over to a littoral amphibious form, rather rarely into a coastal type of vegetation. They are also found in narrow streams, often with very fast-running waters about 3 to 7 meters wide, completely shaded by thick tree vegetation. The genus *Barclaya* is very seldom seen in association with *Cryptocoryne* species. In fast-running streams with a stony to rocky bed often covered by sand *C. balansae* grows, also *C. tonkinensis* and *C. crispatula.* The water is soft, with the pH nearing the neutral value. One group of species contains those evidently preferring the exposure of the roots to air or oxygen (aerobiotic), whereas other species (such as *C. cordata, C. griffithii,* etc.) tolerate the non-exposure of the roots (anaerobiotic) well and occur both in running streams and in still waters of marshes with a thicker layer of mud.

The popular species of *Cryptocoryne* are cultivated at temperatures of about 68° to 77° F (20° to 25° C), which can be maintained all year long. Many fishes have the same temperature requirements, and this is another reason for the suitability of cryptocorynes for the aquarium. Marsh species (*C. becketii, C. nevillii, C. willisii*) growing in nature above water during a certain period are the most resistant to a cool environment, whereas the typically submersed species (*C. cordata, C. longicauda*) are sensitive to low tempeatures (below 64° F, 18° C).

Tanks with cryptocorynes should not be exposed to direct sunlight. When an aquarium is placed near the window, a position facing the north or the northeast will be most suitable. Cryptocorynes do well in an unchanging light. Most species flower, provided they are cultivated in the emersed state only.

Common species are propagated relatively quickly and during a single growing period can overcrowd a tank. Newly imported species are propagated slowly and often form only one single runner in the whole year. A resting period is required, so they should not be transplanted. Root runners are formed, but often not before one or two years after transplanting.

Cryptocorynes are ideal aquarium plants, being very varied as to form and color. Because cryptocorynes acidify the water, they form a favorable medium for the survival and spawning of many popular fish species. Certainly some species are propagated only with difficulty, but well-developed specimens are maintained easily. Only the more advanced aquarists succeed in cultivating cryptocorynes, because these plants can not tolerate any fluctuation in the temperature and require more care and knowledge than plants like *Vallisneria*, *Sagittaria*, and others.

Scientists have great difficulty with the genus *Cryptocoryne*. The various species can be reliably distinguished only by their inflorescences and many species flower rarely not only under artificial conditions but also in nature. The flowers of some species are not known at all. This is the primary reason for the incorrect determinations and incorrect nomenclature of many cryptocorynes in the existing literature. The genus *Cryptocoryne* has been revised recently by the senior author. As a consequence there are some new names in the following pages describing individual species. Incorrect or invalid names are mentioned following the valid ones. Only those *Cryptocoryne* species which have been imported and grown in aquariums are included. For those interested, information about other species can be found in the following technical literature:

Rataj, K. 1975. Revision of the genus *Cryptocoryne* Fischer. Academia, Praha, 174 pages.

Wit, H.C.D. 1970. A key to the species of *Cryptocoryne*. Belmontiana, p. 257-280.

Wit, H.C.D. 1971. *Cryptocoryne*. Aquariumplanzen, Stuttgart, p. 257-280.

CRYPTOCORYNE AFFINIS N.E. Brown (III. 41)
Syn: *C. haerteliniana* Jacobs

C. affinis is one of the most widely distributed aquarium species from southwestern Malay Peninsula. The petioles are approximately as long as the blades; the whole leaf is 15 to 30 cm long. The upper surface is light glossy dark green with light veins; the lower surfaces of well developed leaves are purple to violet, although sometimes the under surface is light green or yellow green with pale purple spots. The color of the lower surface is more intense in stronger light.

C. affinis is perhaps the most widespread and most popular *Cryptocoryne*. Given good conditions it grows very quickly; during a single summer it can overcrowd the whole tank. It is very sensitive to calcium and does not do well in alkaline or hard water. When exposed to direct light the leaves collapse and touch the ground and the plant dies. Temperatures below 68° F (20° C) stop the growth of this species.

It should be cultivated in moderately diffused or artificial light. Propagation is by root runners. Flowers are often produced under water; the inflorescence reaches up to 25 cm long, with the spathe (above the orifice) being elongated into a purple-red, spirally coiled blade. *C. affinis* is recommended for aquariums only, not for terrariums.

CRYPTOCORYNE ALBIDA Parker — see *C. korthausae.*

CRYPTOCORYNE APONOGETIFOLIA Merril —
see *C. usteriana.*

CRYPTOCORYNE AURICULATA Engler
This species grows in Borneo (Sarawak) and in the Philippines (islands of Palawan and Mindanao).

The leaves (10 to 15 cm long) have ovate blades that are dark brown-green and margins that are sometimes undulate and inconspicuously dentate. The base is abrupt or cordately lobed, and the lower third of the leaf is widest and from there, slowly becoming pointed to the tip. The blade is 5 to 10 cm long and usually 25 mm wide (sometimes with dark transverse stripes).

The inflorescence is about 50 to 75 mm long, on a short peduncle. The kettle (15 mm long) is colorless and translucent, with a tube that is 5 mm long. The ligulate limb is bent forward, smooth inside, red, and lighter in the throat.

C. auriculata is one of the most precious aquarium plants. It grows emersed as well as submersed slowly and is difficult to propagate. It endures hard water and can be cultivated in aquariums without fish, requiring an undisturbed tank with very clean water free of algae and an abundance of organic matter.

A similar plant that has not yet been reported is *C. pygmaea* Merril, hardly reaching half the height of *C. auriculata*; its inflorescence measures a little more than 2.5 cm.

CRYPTOCORYNE AXELRODII Rataj (III. 41)

Syn: *C. willisii* Engler ex Baum, *C. undulata* Wendt, *C. pseudo-becketii* Hort.

This plant really has had bad nomenclatural luck. It was described twice, in 1909 and 1920, but neither name in the two descriptions can be acknowledged as valid according to the international botanical laws.

C. axelrodii is confined to Ceylon. It links *C. walkeri* to *C. wendtii*. The leaves are 25 cm long and the petioles are approximately of the same length as the blade. The submersed plants are mostly shorter with green-brown to red leaves. The blades are oblong lanceolate, narrowing and nearly meeting at the base (margins are undulated), and 7.5 to 15 cm long and little more than 25 mm wide. Blades of emersed plants are green, with a reddish main nerve; in submersed plants they are mostly red-brown, with dark stripes. The lower leaf surface is lighter, brown-green or pink.

The inflorescence measures a little more than 7.5 cm long. It is twisted above the throat, greenish yellow or ochre yellow-brown, and the margins are slightly dentate. The throat is light green; the collar is brown, trimmed on the lower side by two very thin lines (the upper line whitish, the lower line dark green).

A typically amphibious plant growing better emersed than submersed, *C. axelrodii* flowers only when emersed with a rather low air humidity. It is easy to cultivate in the aquarium; unexacting, endures a great variety of temperature, and needs medium hard water. *C. axelrodii* propagates quickly by means of rootstocks and rhizomes. It belongs, with some forms of *C. wendtii*, to the commonly cultivated species and is the most beautiful cryptocoryne. Its leaves are mainly colored, often very dark, beautifully contrasting with other bright green plants.

CRYPTOCORYNE BALANSAE Gagnepain (III. 236)

Syn: *C. longispatha* Merril, *C. somphongsii* Hort.

C. balansae is distributed in Thailand, North Vietnam to Kwangsi Province in China, growing there in shady to poorly sunlit situations, usually in submersed forms, in various depths of slow- or fast-running water. In natural localities the water has 9° DH and a pH of 7, sometimes higher. The bed of the streams where *C. balansae* grows is stony (usually limestone) and the plants are tightly and deeply rooted in the fissures among large stones covered with sand. In water depths of 1 to 2 meters, the leaves are green-brown, floating, and very long (50 to 75 cm). In average cultivations if emersed *C. balansae* develops well and flowers easily. During the spring months it sometimes develops emersed, nearly upright, long elliptical blades, with hardly any noticeable "blisters"—other emersed leaves being typically bullate. The root is straight, with numerous secondary roots. The leaves (25 to 50 cm long) have petioles usually shorter than the blades. The leaf blades are long, elliptical, sometimes with parallel margins; in the middle both sides are narrowed, along the midrib strikingly bullate, on the margins almost even. Leaves of emersed plants reach a length of 5 to 10 cm; their blades not more than 10 mm wide, as with the submersed form they are green, bullose, rarely even. The smooth, entire blades develop temporarily, mainly during the change from the submersed state to the emersed state. Typical submersed plants have blades measuring 10 to 20 cm long and 10 to 35 mm wide that are olive green or olive brown, while the petioles are often reddish.

The inflorescence is 15 to 25 cm long. The kettle is widest in the lower third of the inflorescence; the upper part is constricted, deep red-brown, covered vertically with purple dots. The length of an almost upright or twisted tube changes according to the depth of the water. The limb (50 mm long) is upright, ligulate with short or long caudicle (up to 35 mm), usually entire in the lower two-thirds of the limb, or only the caudicle is twisted two to three times. The inside wall of the limb is yellow, or yellow-green trimmed with striking wine-red lines of different lengths, shortened in the throat sometimes to dots.

The plant is relatively modest in its requirements for cultivation and is not too sensitive even to direct sunlight, but it can not tolerate low temperatures. It propagates very slowly by rhizome runners, forming not more than two to three individual plants per year. Plants that are several years old can be propagated by cutting off the rhizome on which five to fifteen new ones appear.

CRYPTOCORYNE BOGNERI Rataj

C. bogneri was found in Ceylon and is an important evolutionary link, the discovery of which helps our understanding of the evolution of a species. Previously it was difficult to explain the presence of *C. thwaitesii* in Ceylon, because it completely differs from other *Cryptocoryne* species found in Ceylon. *C. bogneri* explains its presence there, as its leaves resemble the shape of those of *C. thweitesii* and its inflorescence shows a remarkable relationship to that of *C. walkeri*.

Cryptocoryne balansae.

The leaves are about 10 cm long, their petioles brownish and longer than the blades. The blades are elliptical and the base is moderately cordately lobate, while the tip is nearly blunt. They are deep green, brown-green or red-brown, occasionally alveolate, and 50 mm long and 25 to 30 mm wide. Their margins are undulate or crispate, appear dentate, and the texture is leather-like.

The inflorescence is about 75 mm long; the kettle is red-brown, and the tube is only 10 mm long. The limb is ligulate (30-35 mm long), longer than the kettle and the tube together. The outside is reddish; the inside (including the throat) is clear yellow. There is no collar, and the upper part and the margins are warty.

C. bogneri is one of the most decorative species. It grows emersed as well as submersed—there are no records yet of its cultivation in aquariums. There are only a few specimens of this plant existing in artificial cultivation at present.

CRYPTOCORYNE BECKETII Thwaites ex Trimen   (Ill. 360)

C. becketii comes from Ceylon and is related to *C. petchii*. The most resistant species among cryptocorynes, it is suitable for all aquarium conditions.

The leaves are 15 to 26 cm long; petioles are olive-brown and longer than the blades, which are oblong, abrupt or shallowly lobate at the base, rarely decurrent. They are widest at the lower third, acuminate to the tip. The upper surface of the leaf is olive brown-green with darker veins, while the lower surface is purple-brown to pink. The lower parts of the margins are usually undulate, and the blade is 75 mm long and 25 mm wide.

The inflorescence is 7.5 to 10 cm long, with a kettle that is 15 to 17 mm long. The tube is upright, pinkish like the kettle. The limb is 30 to 45 mm long; at the base of the dilated part it is usually inconspicuously dentate, brown-yellow or olive-brown. A collar separates the surface of the limb from the purple to chocolate-brown throat.

C. becketii is easy to maintain, enduring even hard water and strong light. It can be propagated rapidly from rhizome runners; after transplanting it soon takes root and grows abundantly within the same year. This is the most suitable *Cryptocoryne* for beginners.

CRYPTOCORYNE BLASSII de Wit — see *C. siamensis*

CRYPTOCORYNE BULLOSA Beccari ex Engl.   (Ill. 361, 365)

C. bullosa is better known from imported and cultivated plants than those coming directly from their natural environment.

It occurs probably only in Borneo.

The leaves are 10 to 30 cm long. The petioles are green, the upper parts are sometimes red. The petiole is sheathed almost in its full length with the exception of the upper fourth and is as long as the blades or longer. The blades are oblong-lanceolate, with the tip narrowed, and the base is decurrent, abrupt, or indistinctly lobate. The blade is 5 to 15 cm long and 15 to 30 mm wide, and the whole surface is covered by rows of blisters. The upper surface is green or brown-red, while the lower surface is whitish or pink, but always lighter.

The inflorescence is shorter than the leaves and has a length of about 50 to 75 mm. The kettle has a short peduncle. The tube is upright, not more than half as long as the kettle, colorless or pink with fine purple dots. The ligulate limb is 15 to 20 mm long, purple red, and indistinctly wrinkled. The collar is distinct and rarely indicated.

C. bullosa is a typically submersed plant belonging to the most decorative and attractive representatives of the genus. Although known for a relatively long time, it is only recently that an ample supply of plants has become available from natural sources; these plants are now imported. Propagation is very slow. Its cultivation is similar to that of *C. balansae*.

Note: *C. scurrilis* de Wit, a recently described species from Sumatra, is doubtful. Herbarium plants of this species do not bear any characters distinguishing them from *C. bullosa*. Prof. de Wit mentions that *C. scurrilis* differs in the coloring of the limb of the inflorescence, but this cannot be proved from plants deposited in the herbarium. At present it is regarded only as a variety (*C. bullosa* var. *scurrilis*).

CRYPTOCORYNE CILIATA (Roxb.) Fischer ex Wydler

C. ciliata is distributed from the eastern state of India across the coastal areas around the Bengal Gulf to Thailand and Malaysia (both Malay Peninsula and Sarawak) as far as the Indonesian Archipelago (Java, Sumatra, Celebes, Bintan, Moluccas, Siberut) and New Guinea including Papua.

This species has the widest geographical distribution among the cryptocorynes, occurring in large mangrove areas of tropical Asia, where it occupies the solid banks of larger streams on sufficiently lighted situations. A typical terrestrial species, *C. ciliata* occurs rarely in shallow inundated places. The leaves and inflorescences are always emersed. They are found mostly on loamy clay

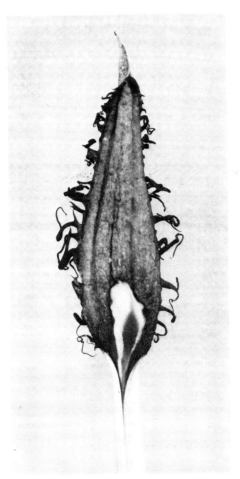

Limb of the inflorescence of *Cryptocoryne ciliata* with the excrescences distinctly visible.

soils on the coastal plains to a height of 50 meters and extend to a distance of about 50 km inland from brackish water areas into fresh water in thickly wooded areas.

There are two varieties of *C. ciliata*. The basic variety (*ciliata*) is 1.2 meters tall and propagates by long rhizome runners; the second variety (*latifolia*) is only 15 to 25 cm tall and does not propagate by rhizome runners.

CRYPTOCORYNE CILIATA var. *CILIATA* (Ill. 239, 361, 416, 417)

The leaves are 0.5 to 1 meter long, with strong green petioles; the lower third of the petiole is sheathed. Leaf blades are leather-like, fleshy and thick, dark green, and smooth; the lower surface is somewhat lighter than the upper surface. They are 20 to 35 cm long and 5 to 12.5 cm wide, long or short lanceolate; their bases are abrupt, decurrent, usually cordate. Six to fifteen thin recurved lateral ribs run out from the strong main rib.

The inflorescence is 20 to 37 cm long. The kettle (20 mm long) is constricted in the middle. The tube is straight, not twisted, white-yellow or pink, and the throat is yellow, red spotted, and smooth. The limb is purple-red (rarely pink or olive-yellow-green), vertically wrinkled or smooth, remotely veined, and about 75 mm long and 15 to 20 mm wide. There is a distinct collar at the base. Outstanding excrescences reaching to a length of 5 to 15 mm and branching at the tip or the middle adorn the margins of the limb at intervals of 5 mm. These are purple-red or brown.

This variety propagates vegetatively by rhizome runners, 30 to 40 cm long, on which new rooting plants develop in intervals of 7.5 to 10 cm; thus they can be found occupying several square meters of area on the banks of streams.

CRYPTOCORYNE CILIATA var. LATIFOLIA Rataj

The leaves are 12.5 to 20 cm in length, with leather-like cordate or lanceolate blades whose bases are deeply lobed and measure from 5 to 10 cm in length and 25 to 50 mm in width (twice as long as it is wide). A purple-red limb is characteristic of the inflorescence.

Long rhizome runners do not arise with vegetative propagation, but new plants develop either directly on the rhizome from dormant buds or on very short (only 10 to 20 mm long) runners. Numerous tufts of growth gradually develop from several plants.

C. ciliata var. *ciliata* is suitable only for a large paludarium or terrarium, and under favorable conditions this plant reaches a good size even in the aquarium and grows out of the water. Unlike other cryptocorynes, moreover, it requires a good light or indirect sunlight; thus in order to limit its exuberant growth it is cultivated in partial shade on a rather poor substratum. Hard water is tolerated well by it. For the aquarium, var. *latifolia* is the most suitable; it is not too large and submersed conditions are tolerated all year round.

CRYPTOCORYNE CORDATA Griffith (Ill. 416, 420)

Syn: *C. grabowski* Engler, *C. purpurea* Ridley, *C. grandis* Ridley

In comparison with other species, *C. cordata* is distributed over a large geographical area, from southeastern Malay Peninsula to Borneo and Java. It is a very variable species with regard to the size and color of the leaves and the limb of the spathe. *C. cordata* can exist in the most deeply shaded areas. In this condition, the coloring of the flowers will depend on the intensity of the light. This reality led to a lot of confusion concerning the exact characteristics of *C. cordata*.

Plants growing as emersed forms in shallow water are abundantly leafy, while those found in deep water and shady places often develop only three to four leaves per plant. The leaves are 20 to 40 cm long with green or red-brown petioles which are slight, sheathed at the base, twice as long as the leaves but seldom of the same lengths. The leaf blades are typically cordate, lobate at the base, on the average half as long as wide, rarely of the same length and breadth or more rarely lanceolate, and the base is smooth or remotely alveolate. Both cordate and lanceolate blades can occur simultaneously on a single plant. The upper surface of the blades is deep green, while the lower surface is green, red-brown to intensive red; in a well-lit situation they are greener, when in the shade redder. Blades measure from 7.5 to 12.5 cm in length and 25 to 75 mm in width.

It is typical for *C. cordata* to have inflorescences that are longer than the leaves; the inflorescence is upright and 10 to 50 cm long, usually reaching about 7 to 17.5 cm in submersed plants. Extremely long ones arise in deep water, extending the tube. The kettle is colorless or pinkish; the limb is funnel-shaped with a ligulate base. Including the caudicle (13 to 40 mm long), the limb is 50 to 75 mm long. The tube dilates into a funnel-like shape, so that the throat is wide and occupies usually a third of the surface of the limb, which is most often purple, brown to vermilion red, or dirty yellow, but can also be light yellow or colorless. Our experiments showed that flowers of plants situated in well-lit places are always purple; the same plants when situated in deep shade can have yellow flowers. However, the existence of forms or varieties always flowering yellow cannot be denied.

In nature *C. cordata* is found in places with soft, neutral or slightly acid water that is usually exceptionally clean. These places are flooded occasionally by brown, muddy, and acid water. In its natural habitat *C. cordata* occurs in such deep shade that no other plants can exist, but it has been proved that in emersed artificial cultivation *C. cordata* prefers plenty of light. In the aquarium this species is cultivated in clean washed sand without peat. The sand should be supplied sufficiently with mineralized detritus. For this reason *C. cordata* can be cultivated successfully only in mature aquariums with crystal-clear water with a perfect biological balance. It does not tolerate fresh water poor in nutrients, so it is not for beginners. *C. cordata* is currently imported but is an exacting species. This plant is very decorative (especially the violet undersides of the leaves), but diffused light is required; in the shade the leaves lose the violet color and turn green on both sides.

CRYPTOCORYNE COSTATA Gagnepain
Syn: *C. hansenii* S.Y. Hu   (III. 64)

C. costata comes from Thailand; it is a typical species of coastal vegetation rarely descending into the beds of streams. It prefers to grow on sandy ground.

The leaves are 10 to 15 cm long; the leaf blades are lanceolate, 7.5 to 10 cm long and 10 to 15 mm wide, with a large main rib. Their margins are usually entire or undulate (sometimes inconspicuously dentate at the base). Emersed plants have red-brown leaves which are trimmed with vertical red-brown lines on the petioles and blades. Submersed forms have green leaves, but the red-brown lines are present and these are typical for this species. The inflorescence is about 10 cm long. The kettle is dark purple in the upper third, white in the lower two-thirds, with indistinct red dots. The tube (usually twisted two or three times) is yellow-brown and the limb, which is three to five times wider than the tube and nearly upright, is sometimes prolonged into a short caudicle. The inner surface of the limb appears cream-white with numerous small and fine dots.

C. costata grows well in the emersed state. Under water it requires the same conditions as other species, but cannot endure great temperature changes. It is very rare and one of the more sensitive species which take root slowly. Both the shape and color of the leaves differ greatly from other *Cryptocoryne* species, so it is a very valuable addition to our hobby. This species is suitable for aquariums, paludariums, and terrariums.

CRYPTOCORYNE DIDERICII de Wit   (III. 243)
The origin is uncertain, probably Malacca in Malaysia.

The leaves are 7.5 to 15 cm long; their reddish or green petioles are as long as the leaves or slightly longer and sheathed at the base. The ovate leaf blades, 50 to 75 mm long, are deep green (lower leaf surface is green or brownish), nearly blunt at the tip, and usually lobate at the base.

The inflorescence (about 75 mm long) is shorter than the

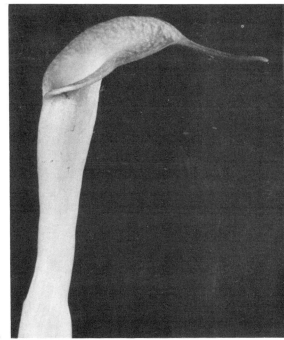

Inflorescence of
Cryptocoryne didericii
showing the warty
condition of the limb.

Cryptocoryne didericii.

leaves and the peduncle is very short. The kettle as well as the tube are white or pinkish, and the limb (2.5 mm long), which is warty or nearly smooth, has two layers of color (the lower one being yellow, the upper red), so that there are areas of intensive yellow with brown to reddish tinges on the limb. The limb is usually yellow in the middle, pinkish or brown in the lower part on the margins. The uniformly colored bright yellow throat is without a collar. The tip of the limb is elongated; the caudicle is approximately 10 mm long.

C. *didericii* is cultivated in the same way as C. *cordata*.

CRYPTOCORYNE EVAE Rataj (Ill. 417, 425, 428)

C. *evae* is one of the most decorative species of *Cryptocoryne*. Its origin is unknown, probably Thailand. Except for C. *ciliata*, it has an inflorescence with the largest limb. C. *evae* is commonly cultivated under the incorrect name of the narrow-bladed C. *blassi*.

The leaves are 40 to 60 cm long, with petioles twice as long as the blades or equally as long, which are green or red-brown. The blades are lanceolate (both sides nearly symmetrically narrowed); their upper surface dark green or olive-brown and very smooth and shiny, while the lower surface is red-brown to violet and also shiny. The blades are 15 to 22.5 cm long and 50 to 75 mm wide.

The inflorescence is 12.5 to 17.5 cm long. The kettle is slightly constricted in the middle, light yellow brown, and covered thickly and irregularly with purple dots while its lower half is purple inside. The throat is funnel-shaped, dilated, and bright yellow. The limb is cordate, 25 to 50 mm long and about 20 mm wide at the base, bright yellow, and slightly wrinkled or has small, closely grouped, merging brown-orange dots on a yellow background. In this case the limb is decidedly darker than the bright yellow throat. The stigmas are vertical, twice incised above; therefore trilobate.

C. *evae* is cultivated like C. *cordata* but it tolerates hard water well.

CRYPTOCORYNE FERRUGINEA Engler
Syn: C. *fusca* de Wit, C. *tortilis* de Wit
Incorrect name: C. *longicauda*

This species comes from Sarawak and is very rarely cultivated (usually under the incorrect name C. *longicauda*).

The leaves are 15 to 25 cm long; the petiole is usually as long as the blade or shorter. The blades are cordate, lanceolate to ovately rounded. The base is lobate or nearly abruptly lobate and the tip is usually sharp, elongated, rarely blunt. The upper surface of the blade is green while the lower surface is white-green or reddish, nearly smooth, irregularly alveolate to bullate. The blades are 10 to 15 cm long and about 50 mm wide. The reverse side is sparsely or densely haired; the prominent, reddish brown hairs are setiform and intermingled with silver-white, glossy crystals that are 2.5 to 5 mm long.

The inflorescence reaches a length of 7.5 to 12.5 cm. The kettle, symmetrically curved inside, has the lower half deep purple with light red points; the upper half is lighter, with purple spots. The tube is absent and the limb is constricted above the kettle; it opens through a lateral suture. Above (outside) it is light yellow to chocolate-brown or reddish, often vertically striped; inside the lower part (about 25 mm) is brown-red, finely spotted and the upper part is brown-red or yellow-brown, strikingly ciliated.

C. ferruginea is a rare species, only seldom imported. It grows better emersed with 100 % humidity than when submersed. In aquariums it is best cultivated in diffused light and in crystal clear, aged water.

CRYPTOCORYNE GRACILIS de Wit

C. gracilis is native to Sarawak and without any doubt closely related to *C. elliptica.*

The leaves are 50 to 75 mm long, with petioles that are as long or a little longer than the blades that are ovate to elliptical, abrupt, or lobate at the base. The upper surface of the leaf is green or bronze-brown-green; the lower surface is usually purple, remotely and slightly alveolate or smooth. The blades are 25 to 50 mm long and 15 to 30 mm wide. The color of the leaves is very variable, ranging from dark bronze-green to yellowish brown and dark purple. The leaf blades are often lattice-like, trimmed with darker stripes.

The inflorescence is 50 to 75 mm long. The kettle and the tube are nearly colorless and translucent. The limb reaches up to 40 mm long; the broad base is prolonged into a caudicle, 15 to 30 mm long. At the base of the limb there is a dark red or violet spot covering two-thirds of the broadened base. The tip and the caudicle are light purple or nearly colorless. The throat inwards is violet or spotted with purple and the collar is inconspicuous, but a dark black-violet zone is present in its place.

C. gracilis is one of the rarest species in our aquariums. Its small size makes it useful for small aquariums. The cultivation of *C. gracilis* is similar to that of *C. cordata.*

Mr. T.J. Horeman photographing a collection of *Cryptocoryne evae* at a typical site in Thailand where cryptocorynes are found.

CRYPTOCORYNE GRIFFITHII Schott (III. 433)

The habitat of this species is the Malay Peninsula and it differs from *C. cordata* by its shorter growth and inflorescence. Without the flower plants can hardly be distinguished. In contrast to *C. cordata*, the inflorescence (7.5 to 12.5 cm long) of *C. griffithii* is usually shorter than the leaves. The peduncle, often reaching a length of 75 mm, is variable. The colorless or pink kettle appears sometimes very thin, otherwise swollen, and the upright tube is either only as long as the kettle or much longer. The ligulate triangular limb has a dilated base; it is almost without a caudicle, purple, very warty and rough, and 20 to 30 mm long. A distinct collar is present in the red throat.

The name *C. griffithii* is frequently cited in aquarist literature, but it seems that this species has not yet been imported into Europe.

CRYPTOCORYNE HEJNYI Rataj

Incorrect name: *C. purpurea* Ridley (III. 432)

With its dark-striped leaf blades and bright limb of the spathe this species, belonging to the most beautiful representatives of *Cryptocoryne*, is commonly cultivated in aquariums and probably comes from Malaya. It is distinguishable from *C. cordata* by a vermilion red limb and a throat that is not funnel-shaped, and from *C. griffithii* by the absence of a collar.

The leaves are 10 to 15 cm long, with petioles varying in length. The elliptical or cordate blades (base is abrupt or indistinctly lobate) are usually twice as long as they are wide and with transverse purple, pink or red-brown stripes. They are often 67 mm long and 25 mm wide.

The inflorescence (10 to 20 cm long) has a white or pink kettle. The throat is not dilated (not funnel-shaped); it is smooth, yellow or light orange and much lighter than the limb. The limb is usually 40 cm long, bright vermilion red, finely veined, without a collar, and with a caudicle up to 20 mm long.

Cultivation is similar to that of *C. cordata*.

CRYPTOCORYNE JOHORENSIS Engler (III. 437)

C. johorensis is native to the Malay Peninsula (Johore), but according to the information of professional collectors *C. johorensis* is also to be found in Sarawak (Tekalong-Dor) and perhaps also in Sumatra (Djambi, Palembang). However, this information has not been verified.

From an oblique rhizome up to four to seven leaves (10 to 20 cm long) develop. The leaf blades are green (lighter on the reverse side) and cordate; the base is lobed, elongated and pointed on the tip. Their margins are finely dentate and the surface of the blade is smooth or slightly bullate, usually 75 mm long and 50 mm wide. Emersed plants found in sunny situations have red-brown areas among the secondary nerves.

The inflorescence is longer than the leaves, reaching 17.5 to 25 cm; the length of the caudicle is usually 60% of the whole length. The limb is dish-shaped in the basal part, 15 mm wide and 30 mm long, wine-red and slightly wrinkled at the inside. A collar separates the limb from a colorless throat.

This species requires diffused light and a planting medium that is poor in nutrients. It is not exacting in its requirements but propagation is slow. This is why we rely mainly on imported specimens.

CRYPTOCORYNE KORTHAUSAE Rataj
Incorrect name: *C. albida* Parker (III. 246, 437)

The leaves are 10 to 15 cm long, with elliptical narrow leaf blades that are up to 10 cm long and 10 to 15 cm wide; the margins are usually undulate. In both emersed and submersed plants the leaves are always green without red lines.

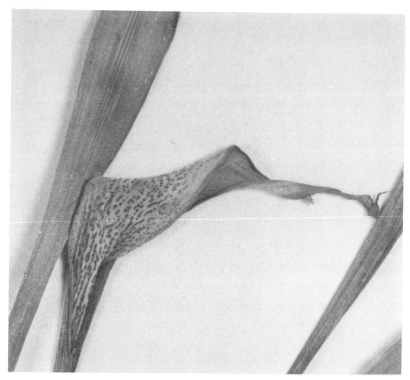

Beautifully patterned and twisted limb of the inflorescence of *Cryptocoryne korthausae.*

The inflorescence is usually 10 cm long. The kettle is one third from the top of the inflorescence and turns inward and is very constricted; it is purple along the whole length on the inside, deeper purple in the upper part. The tube is twisted once to three times or nearly upright. The limb (25 to 40 mm long) is cream-white with pink or red dots, elongated at the tip and is usually horizontally twisted backwards into a spiral.

C. korthausae has been mistaken for *C. albida* and was cultivated under that name. Its origin is not known. *C. korthausae* prefers the emersed to the submersed conditions. It differs from *C. costata* by having: (1) the inner part of the kettle red, (2) a limb that is elongated and twisted horizontally backwards, and (3) green leaves that are without red lines.

CRYPTOCORYNE LEGROI — see *C. walkeri*

CRYPTOCORYNE LINGUA Beccari ex Engler
Syn: *C. spathulata* Beccari ex Engler (III. 436, 440, 441)

This species is a native of Borneo. It closely resembles *C. versteegii*, but differs from the latter mainly in its smaller size.

The leaves (usually 12.5 cm long) are arranged in a rosette; the petioles are broad, a little longer than the blades. These flat, fleshy, thick blades are spoon-shaped or spathulate and about 50 mm long and 25 mm wide. The base of the blade is decurrent, rarely lobate, pointed at the tip with hardly visible nerves.

The inflorescence is 50 to 75 mm long. The limb, widely open at the basal part, is light yellow in the throat with deep purple spots. The rest of the limb is extended into a long, upright dark purple caudicle. These two colored areas of the limb are not separated by a collar.

C. lingua requires higher temperatures (68° to 77° F or 20° to 25° C), acid water, and a fair amount of light. Like all bright green species it can withstand sunlight. It is propagated best in the emersed condition in paludariums and terrariums; propagation under water is very slow.

CRYPTOCORYNE LONGICAUDA — see *C. ferruginea*

CRYPTOCORYNE LUCENS de Wit (III. 441)

This cryptocoryne probably originates from Ceylon and was described from plants cultivated in artificial conditions.

The leaves, 15 to 30 cm long, have petioles that are red at the base and usually one and a half times longer than the blades. The exceptionally long blades are oblong, lanceolate (both sides decurrent), and are usually widest at the middle part, where the margins are nearly parallel. The blades are usually 75 mm long and 15 mm wide, bright green (lower leaf surface is lighter than the upper). The main rib is elevated and the tip of the blade does not bend downwards.

The inflorescence is about 75 mm long and often has a very long peduncle. The limb (13 mm long) is twice as long as it is wide. It is triangular, without a caudicle, sometimes twisted, reddish brown, dull and warty. The limb is separated by a collar from the throat which is of the same color as the limb or bright red.

C. lucens is cultivated like *C. nevillii*.

CRYPTOCORYNE LUTEA — see *C. walkeri*

CRYPTOCORYNE MINIMA Ridley (III. 444)

C. minima comes from the Malay Peninsula.

The leaves (5 to 10 cm long) have petioles that are as long as the blades or a little longer. The long, ovate blades have decurrent bases, are usually widest in the lower third, and have undulate margins. The blade is 25 to 37 mm long and about 25 mm wide; the upper leaf surface is green, while the lower surface is purple-red and occasionally alveolate (only in the submersed form).

The inflorescence is 50 mm long, but considering that the limb is bent downwards it is in fact only 25 mm tall. The terminal part of the tube is constricted. The limb is as long as the kettle and the tube taken together. The tip of the limb touches the ground. The warty and dull yellow limb is spotted brown and separated by a distinct collar from the glossy, brownish black throat.

The cultivation of *C. minima* is similar to that of *C. cordata*.

CRYPTOCORYNE NEVILLII Trimen (III. 445)

This plant is known only from Ceylon.

The leaves (5 to 10 cm long) have narrowly elliptical to lanceolate blades that are 37 to 75 mm long and 10 to 15 mm wide. The blade is narrow or abrupt at the base and the widest part is directly above the base and from there to the tip it is acuminate and sometimes recurved. The green lower leaf surface is somewhat lighter than the upper, with hardly visible nerves. There are stabilized forms with elliptical blades (about 10 mm wide, decurrent at the base) and forms with lanceolate blades (15 mm wide, cordate at the base).

The inflorescence is 50 to 75 mm long and the bright, warty, rough limb is about 20 mm long (3 to 3.5 times longer than the width). It has a short caudicle and a base with a distinct collar which separates the purple surface of the limb from the yellow throat of the tube.

C. nevillii can be easily cultivated in the aquarium and paludarium; it is not exacting with regard to the environment. Because the leaves are stiff, they are not susceptible to injury. It can withstand a bright light and is not affected by low temperatures. *C. nevillii* is especially suitable for foreground planting in the aquarium; propagation is by means of the long rhizomes.

CRYPTOCORYNE NURI Furtado (III. 444)

C. nuri originates from the Malayan Peninsula. The plants with dentate leaves offered in the trade under this name usually belong to *C. siamensis* var. *ewansii*. Both species are distinguishable only when in flower.

The leaves (10 to 15 cm long) have petioles that are as long as the blades or slightly longer. The blades are usually elliptical, widest in the middle (both sides nearly symmetrically narrowed). The lower third to half of the blade (90 mm long and 25 mm wide) is distinctly dentate and the upper surface is glossy green (sometimes with transverse stripes) while the lower surface is rarely green, usually dark red-brown.

The inflorescence is 7.5 to 15 cm long and is shorter than the leaves or of the same length. The white kettle is slightly constricted at the center. The tube is white or pink. The ligulate limb (38 to 50 mm long) is sometimes extended into a caudicle. The base of the limb is distinctly dilated up to 25 mm, dark red or purple, warty and rough. The collar is distinct and the throat is light red.

This species is one of the most decorative plants, but its propagation is difficult and slow. Aquarium shops are entirely dependent on the imports from natural sources. *C. nuri* is cultivated like *C. cordata*.

CRYPTOCORYNE PARVA de Wit (III. 113)

A species (probably from Ceylon) that was described from plants commonly imported into Europe for aquariums. It is one of the most easily cultivated plants both in emersed and submersed forms. It easily propagates vegetatively and as new plants arise on a strong rhizome (often longer than the leaves), they grow in abundant groups with numerous plants.

The leaves are 50 to 55 mm long; the petioles are usually twice as long as the blades. These blades are narrowly elliptical (both sides nearly symmetrically narrowed), widest at the lower third or in the center and the tip is usually bent downwards. The grass green blade with hardly visible nerves is 25 mm long and 5 to 7.5 mm wide.

The inflorescence (25 mm long) has a white kettle and a white or pink tube narrowed a little at the throat. The triangular, ligulate limb is about 10 mm long, without a caudicle, twice as long as wide, warty and rough, and bright purple red; this coloring is separated from the whitish throat by a nearly black collar.

CRYPTOCORYNE PETCHII Alston (III. 56, 61)

Another plant from Ceylon and without doubt related to *C. becketii*. It differs from *C. becketii* by its smaller growth and by having an inflorescence with a distinctly darker green limb and a red throat in the tube. The limb is wartily dentate on the margins on the whole length (only in the base with *C. becketii*). *C. petchii* has forty-two chromosomes while *C. becketii* has only twenty-eight. Sterile and submersed forms are scarcely distinguishable.

Emersed leaves (10 to 20 cm long) have petioles that are reddish brown and one and one-half to two times as long as the blades. The lanceolate blades are cordate at the base, or elliptical and narrowed at the base, rarely shallowly lobate, and widest in the center or in the lower third. The upper surface of the blade is olive-brown or brownish red, the lower surface red or pink. The blade is usually 75 mm long and 20 mm wide. Submersed blades are narrower with undulate margins.

The inflorescence is 7.5 to 10 cm long; the kettle as well as the tube is pink or light brown. The limb is ligulate, upright (37 mm long), olive-green, dull, silky smooth and finely wrinkled. The margins are warty and dentate along the whole length. The very dark purple-brown or chocolate-brown throat has a distinct dark brown collar.

This amphibious plant tolerates hard water and low temperatures and is also not affected adversely by either bright light or rather shady conditions. Propagation is like that of the preceding species.

CRYPTOCORYNE PONTEDERIIFOLIA Schott subspecies SARAWACENSIS Rataj (III. 56, 61)

C. pontederiifolia comes from Sumatra and is not cultivated. In recent years there are plants imported to Europe from Borneo described as C. pontederiifolia subsp. sarawacensis in 1975.

The leaves (10 to 15 cm long) have petioles that are as long as the blades. The blades are cordate and elliptical, sometimes indistinctly undulate (the base with dentate margins), membranous and both sides of the blade are green.

The light purple inflorescence is 7.5 to 10 cm long. The kettle is dilated upwards; in the lower half in the inside, finely wrinkled vertically; in the center constricted, and from there upwards, deep violet or spotted wine-red. The tube is as short as the kettle. The basal part of the limb is wine-red inside; without a collar, transversally wrinkled and warty; the throat is oblique so that the caudicle part of the limb is at the side of the extended axis of the tube.

C. pontederiifolia subsp. sarawacensis grows well both emersed and submersed. Emersed plants are more decorative and variegated, and also flower easily. It is one of the most hardy cryptocorynes, requiring little attention. It propagates easily from root runners, will stand diffused as well as direct light, and will be popular among aquarists.

CRYPTOCORYNE PURPUREA Ridley — see *C. hejnyi*.

CRYPTOCORYNE RETROSPIRALIS (Roxb.) Fischer

C. *retrospiralis* ranges from India to Thailand and Laos. The green leaves are 10 to 30 cm long, linearly narrow (2.5 to 10 mm wide). *C. retrospiralis* does not do well underwater; it thrives practically only in the emersed state and is therefore wrongly included in aquarium literature. Plants offered under this name in aquarium shops are usually *C. tonkinensis*.

CRYPTOCORYNE SCHULZEI de Wit   (III. 260)

Only very few plants of *C. schulzei* have been cultivated in indoor aquariums. It is one of the new varieties and it originates from Malaysia (Johore).

The usually horizontal, rarely upright leaves (10 to 15 cm long) have green or brown-red petioles that are as long as the blades or up to one-third to a half longer. The elliptical blades are one and a half to twice as long as wide (either side almost equally narrowed). The base of the blade is slightly lobulate. The upper leaf surface is green or brownish red with irregular stripes while the lower leaf surface is red-brown to bright purple. The blade measures 50 to 75 mm in length, about 25 mm in width.

The inflorescence is shorter than the leaves, usually 75 mm long. The tube and the kettle are colorless, in the upper third olive-pink. The limb is 25 mm long (including a 10 to 15 mm caudicle); the throat is brown-purple, the collar and the limb are yellow, warty and rough.

C. *schulzei* is cultivated like *C. cordata*.

CRYPTOCORYNE SIAMENSIS Gagnepain

Thailand is the home country of this species. Three varieties, each differing in the shape of the blade, are known: var. *siamensis* has elliptical blades, var. *kerri* has cordate blades, and var. *ewansii* has blades that are distinctly dentate in the lower third (similar to *C. nuri*).

CRYPTOCORYNE SIAMENSIS Gagnepain var. *SIAMENSIS*

The leaves are 15 to 20 cm long; their petioles are longer than the blades or nearly as long both in the emersed and submersed forms. The elliptical blades are widest in the lower third, 7.5 to 10 cm long and 37 to 50 mm wide.   (III. 257)

CRYPTOCORYNE SIAMENSIS var. *KERRI* (Gagnepain) Rataj
Syn: *C. kerri* Gagn., *C. blassii* de Wit   (III. 40)

The leaves (10 to 25 cm long) have petioles that are two to

three times longer than the blades (in submersed plants), or as long as the blades (in emersed plants). The blades are cordate and measure 37 to 75 mm long and 25 to 50 mm wide.

CRYPTOCORYNE SIAMENSIS var. EWANSII Rataj (III. 57)

The leaves of this variety are 15 to 25 cm long and the petioles (in both emersed and submersed plants) are very variable in length measuring 7.5 to 10 cm in the emersed plants and up to 25 cm in the submersed ones. The limb (25 to 45 mm long and 10 mm wide). has a short or long caudicle; it is uniformly colored bright yellow inside; the funnel-shaped throat is light yellow or whitish.

C. siamensis is cultivated like *C. cordata* but it comes from Thailand and is usually found growing on limestone. It is easily cultivated and tolerates hard water very well.

CRYPTOCORYNE SPIRALIS (Retz.) Fischer (III. 272)
Syn: *C. unilocularis* (Retz.) Roxb., *C. huegellii* Schott, *C. tortuosa* Blatter ex McCann

C. spiralis inhabits India, Bangladesh, and probably Ceylon.

The leaves (10 to 20 to 75 cm long) have ribbon-like or oblong blades that are lanceolate and green. The inflorescence is 10 to 25 cm long and without a tube. The limb is usually 75 mm long, spirally twisted and longitudinally ligulate. It is purple-red, obliquely wrinkled and warty inside.

C. spiralis is mainly an emersed species and not a true aquarium plant.

CRYPTOCORYNE THWEITESII Schott (III. 257, 273)

Cultivated plants of *C. thweitesii* from Ceylon grow very well both in submersed and emersed forms. They are cultivated emersed on a neutral peat substratum; plants propagate quickly and the typical bronze colored leaves develop if regularly exposed to sunlight. The plants flower easily and often.

The leaves (10 to 15 cm long) are spread out almost horizontally and the petioles are shorter or as long as the blades which are entire; the margins (at least the lower third) are distinctly dentate. The blade is widely elliptical; the base is slightly decurrent or shallowly cordate and the tip is blunt. The main rib is much more prominent than the secondary nerves. Blades in the emersed form are bronze, brownish red and dull. They are finely granulated on the upper side and 50 to 75 mm long and 15 to 37 mm wide.

The inflorescence measures 7.5 to 10 cm in length. The kettle is colorless; the tube is only 15 mm long, in the lower part colorless, toward the top pink. The limb (25 to 75 mm long) is inside of the widened basal part cream white to yellow, dark purple, densely spotted. It is elongated into an upright caudicle which is somewhat longer than other parts of the inflorescence.

Like *C. cordata*, this species is cultivated under water.

CRYPTOCORYNE TONKINENSIS Gagnepain   (III. 256)

This plant from Vietnam is wrongly offered as *C. retrospiralis*.

The roots are banded, with numerous sprouting leaves (20 to 40 cm long); the blades are linear to strap-like with parallel margins. In emersed plants they are olive-green, 15 to 20 cm long and about 5 mm wide; in submersed plants they are reddish brown, 20 to 40 cm long and 5 to 15 mm wide. Their margins are always alveolate so that the margins appear distinctly and thickly undulate. The inflorescence of emersed plants is 10 to 15 cm long while in the submersed plants it is 20 to 25 cm long. The kettle is constricted in the upper third; the top is reddish, the base lighter. The brown-green tube is spirally twisted. The twisted limb is not dilated at the base; inside it is light olive-green or red.

These plants are adapted to the submersed way of life. In the emersed form they can only be cultivated as dwarf forms in 100 % humidity. *C. tonkinensis* differs from *C. retrospiralis* by having bullate and undulate leaf blades both in submersed and emersed forms and by having a uniformly colored limb in the inflorescence. Growing in nature on limestone, *C. tonkinensis* tolerates hard water. It is cultivated like *C. balansae* and grows well in artificial light.

CRYPTOCORYNE USTERIANA Engler
Syn: *C. aponogetifolia* Merril

C. usteriana is endemic to the Philippines.

The leaves are 20 to 70 cm long and the length of the petioles is very variable. The leaf blades in emersed plants are oblong-lanceolate with abrupt, cordate or decurrent bases 15 to 25 cm long and 25 to 50 mm wide, and bullate (embossed). In emersed plants the leaf blade is 20 to 40 cm long and usually 37 mm wide, ribbon-like, green-brown, trimmed on both sides with two to three rows of prominent and deep blisters.

The inflorescence reaches a length of only 50 to 75 mm in emersed plants but in submersed plants the length of the tube is adapted to the height of the water and the complete inflorescence reaches up to 25 cm. The upright, ligulate limb is usually 37 mm long and uniformly colored dirty flesh-red.

Cryptocoryne tonkinensis.

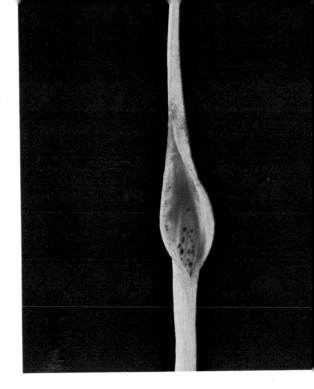

Opened inflorescence of
Cryptocoryne thweitesii
showing the purple
spots inside the limb.

Cryptocoryne siamensis var. *siamensis*.

C. usteriana is cultivated in moderately acid water in artificial as well as natural light; the amount of light is not critical. It does not withstand being transplanted and needs a long time before it can resume its growth. Propagation by rhizome runners is slow. On account of its robust growth, it serves as a contrast to shorter *Cryptocoryne* species with colored leaves. *C. usteriana* is rare but it grows well in submersed conditions.

CRYPTOCORYNE VERSTEEGII Engler in Lorentz   (III. 259)

This cryptocoryne is found only in New Guinea. The leaves (10 to 15 cm long) have thick, green petioles that are as long as the blades or twice as long. The blades are fleshy thick, green, cordate or nearly spathulate-triangular and with abrupt or cordately lobate bases. The lower third of the blade is widest and from there narrows into a rather blunt tip. They are usually 50 mm long and 25 to 37 mm wide.

The inflorescence is 5 to 10 cm long. At the basal opened part of the limb the throat is uniformly colored yellow and the remainder of the limb is extended to a very short, purple-red caudicle.

In nature it generally grows in emersed condition and is therefore suitable for terrariums; if cultivated under water it needs more light than other species. Even under favorable conditions the growth is slow and propagation is difficult; not more than one or two runners a year are formed. *C. versteegii* closely resembles *C. lingua.*

CRYPTOCORYNE WALKERI Schott   (III. 260-1, 264, 269, 276)

This *Cryptocoryne* species is confined to Ceylon. Three varieties of *C. walkeri* are known. Emersed and submersed forms of var. *walkeri* and var. *lutea* have green leaves, while the emersed plants of var. *legroi* have red-brown leaf blades. The blades of var. *lutea* are shorter and narrower than those of var. *walkeri.* The submersed forms of all three varieties are hardly distinguishable from each other.

The leaves are 10 to 15 to 25 cm long. The petioles in emersed plants are two to three times longer while in submersed plants they are one and one-half to twice as long as the blade. The oblong, lanceolate, green or red-brown blades are three to four and one-half times longer than the width, usually 5 to 10 cm long and 12.5 to 37 mm wide.

The inflorescence (7.5 to 12.5 cm long) is upright or loosely twisted, with a light pink tube. The tip of the ligulate limb is sometimes arched downwards. Initially the limb is yellow, after two to

Cryptocoryne versteegii.

three days it becomes darker yellow-green; the throat is light, often with pink points. The collar is sometimes hardly visible, but at least indicated. *C. walkeri* can be grown in both submersed and emersed conditions and it is one of the more resistant *Cryptocoryne* species. Cultivation is similar to that used for *C. becketii*; propagation is by way of rhizome runners.

CRYPTOCORYNE WENDTII de Wit   (Ill. 74)

C. *wendtii* comes from Ceylon and having five varieties it is the most variable species among the cryptocorynes.

The leaves are described in the discussion of the individual varieties.

The inflorescence (25 to 75 mm long) has a limb that is twisted directly above the throat, so that the throat sometimes has a narrow fissure (hardly visible); otherwise the throat is partly opened but it is always oblique. The limb is purple-brown, finely wrinkled, and the margins are dentate. The collar is distinct, dark purple to black and the throat is dark violet with fine white points.

Cryptocoryne schulzei with inflorescence. Photo by T.J. Horeman.

Cryptocoryne walkeri var. *lutea.*

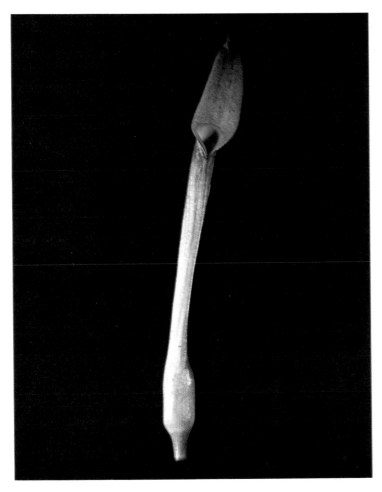

Inflorescence of *Cryptocoryne walkeri* var. *lutea*.

CRYPTOCORYNE WENDTII var. WENDTII (III. 265)

The leaves are 15 to 20 cm long; the petioles are green or reddish, approximately as long as the blades. The elliptical blades are 7.5 to 10 cm long and 25 to 37 mm wide, with truncate or cordate bases. The upper surface in emersed forms is distinctly bullose, green while the lower surface is lighter. In submersed forms the "blisters" are sometimes visible and the blades are green or olive-green with transverse stripes.

The inflorescence is usually 50 mm long.

CRYPTOCORYNE WENDTII var. JAHNELII Rataj
Incorrect name: *C. wendtii rubra* (III. 265)

The leaves of var. *jahnelii* are 15 to 20 cm long and the brownish red petioles are as long as the blades. The elliptical blades are 5 to 10 cm long and 25 mm wide, red-brown, and irregularly bullose (blistered). The "blisters" in submersed plants are not always indicated. The margins are always distinctly undulate.

The inflorescence is 50 to 75 mm long, usually darker as in *C. wendtii* var. *wendtii.*

CRYPTOCORYNE WENDTII var. KRAUTERI Rataj (III. 263)

The leaves are 15 to 20 cm long. The elliptical blades (7.5 to 12.5 cm long and 25 to 37 mm wide) are widest at the center, smooth, and with slightly undulate margins. The lower third of the blade is distinctly dentate. The upper surface is bronze-green or bronze-brown, dull and granulate, while the lower leaf surface is lighter green or pink.

The inflorescence is 7.5 to 10 cm long.

CRYPTOCORYNE WENDTII var. NANA Rataj

The leaves of var. *nana* are 7.5 to 12.5 cm long and the blades are 25 to 50 mm long and 15 to 17 mm wide. The shape of the blade is variable, from lanceolate to elliptical. The upper surface is green while the lower leaf surface is olive-green to olive-brown.

Its inflorescence is only 50 mm long.

CRYPTOCORYNE WENDTII var. RUBELLA Rataj

The leaves are 10 to 15 cm long with brown petioles. The blades in the submersed form are 75 mm long and 10 mm wide, green-brown or red-brown with undulate margins, usually with transverse dark stripes.

The inflorescence is 50 mm long.

All of the varieties of *C. wendtii* are easily cultivated. They reproduce as quickly as *C. becketii* and being more decorative than other species cultivated up to now they should be regarded as popular cryptocorynes for aquariums and terrariums. These varieties can withstand subdued as well as direct light. They tolerate temperatures down to 59° F (15° C) but grow best at temperatures between 68° to 77° F (20° to 25° C).

CRYPTOCORYNE WILLISII — see *C. axelrodii*

CRYPTOCORYNE ZEWALDAE de Wit

This plant is probably from Malaya and whether this species has ever been cultivated is not certain.

The leaves are 15 to 25 cm long. The cordate blades have undulate margins and are slightly alveolate. The blades measure 50 to 75 mm long and 37 to 45 mm wide. The upper surface is green or olive-brown while the lower surface is purple-red and glossy.

Cryptocoryne wendtii var. *krauteri*, emersed form.

Inflorescence of
Cryptocoryne walkeri
var. *legroi.*

Cryptocoryne walkeri
var. *legroi.*

Cryptocoryne wendtii var. *wendtii*.

Cryptocoryne wendtii var. *jahnelii*.

The inflorescence is 75 mm long but its limb being bent downward, it reaches to only about 35 mm high; the tip of the limb touches the ground. The limb is glossy, dark purple, distinctly warty, and dilated at the base.

CRYPTOCORYNE ZONATA de Wit

C. zonata is found only in Borneo (Sarawak, Brunei).

The leaves (10 to 20 cm long) have cordate blades that are distinctly bullose or irregularly alveolate over the surface. The upper surface is deep green while the lower surface is purple. The leaf blade is 50 to 75 mm long and 25 to 50 mm wide. They are sometimes cordate, membranous, and quite smooth in submersed plants.

The inflorescence is 10 to 15 cm long. The kettle is red at the base and at the tip, much lighter at the center. The limb (25 to 37 mm long) is widely opened; in the throat it is light bright yellow, on the surface deep bright yellow, and on the margins often darker (orange). The upper two-thirds of the limb and the caudicle are slightly warty (yellow red-bordered warts). The caudicle is sometimes darker, orange to red.

Cultivation is like that of *C. cordata*.

CRYPTOCORYNE ZUKALII Rataj   (III. 267, 268)

C. zukalii is a species probably originating from Malaya.

The leaves (15 to 30 cm long) have blades that are cordate to round, slightly dentate, slightly bullose, and with short acuminate or blunt tips. The upper surface is dark green while the lower surface is usually red-violet. The blade measures 7 to 10 cm in length and 50 mm in width.

The inflorescence is 10 to 15 cm long. The upright tube is colorless and has thick purple dots and stripes. The throat is as narrow as the tube and not funnel-shaped. The ligulate limb is 35 to 50 mm long including a 10 to 20 mm long caudicle. The whole limb is uniformly colored brown-orange, smooth, and without a collar. The throat is of the same color as the limb except a little brighter.

C. zukalii is cultivated like *C. cordata*.

Cryptocoryne zukalii,
cultivated emersed.

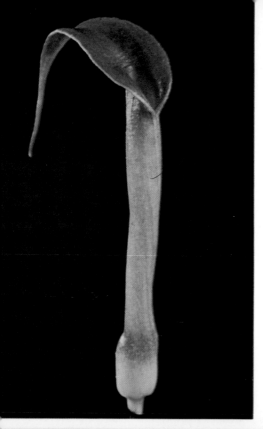

Inflorescence of *Cryptocoryne zukalii.*

Cryptocoryne zukalii, cultivated submersed.

Opened kettle of *Cryptocoryne walkeri* showing the female flowers at the base and the male flowers at the top. Photo by T.J. Horeman.

KEY TO THE IDENTIFICATION OF THE SPECIES OF THE GENUS CRYPTOCORYNE

Not enough distinctive characters are present in the leaves of *Cryptocoryne* species to enable us to identify safely all the cultivated species. Both leaves and inflorescences are absolutely necessary for their determination. The following key is arranged according to these structures. The numbers enclosed in parentheses refer to the alternate choice or the second half of the couplet.

Key to Cryptocoryne Species

1 (4) Tube absent, inflorescence opening through a vertical suture 2

2 (3) Leaf blades oblong, lanceolate or ribbon-like . . *C. spiralis*

3   Leaf blades cordate or ovate . . . . *C. ferruginea*

4   Tube present, opening through a horizontal throat. . . .5

5 (6) Limb of inflorescence on the margins fringed . . . *C. ciliata*

6   Limb not fringed 7

7 (20) Leaf blades oblong, lanceolate, 8 to 20 times or even more times longer than wide 8

8 (17) Limb in the basal part at most half as wide as the tube 9

9 (12) Leaf blades entire or undulate only on the margins; if bullose, then always narrower than 1 cm 10

10 (11) Limb trimmed with red dots and lines . . . . *C. retrospiralis*

11   Limb uniformly colored red or yellow-green . . . . *C. tonkinensis*

12   Leaf blades bullose 13

13 (16) On the blade only, one row of blisters on both sides 14

14 (15) Blades ribbon-like, margins alveolate and densely undulate . . . . *C. tonkinensis*

15   Blades oblong, lanceolate, in the center alveolate, margins nearly entire . . . . *C. balansae*

16   On the leaf blade both sides 2 to 3 rows of blisters . . . . *C. usteriana*

17   Limb distinctly dilated, 3 times wider than the tube . . . 18

18 (19) Emersed leaves red, limb with distinct caudicle . . . . *C. costata*

19   Emersed leaves green, limb without caudicle, horizontally twisted . . . . *C. korthausae*

Inflorescence of *Cryptocoryne spiralis* with the characteristic spirally twisted limb.

Cryptocoryne thweitesii, emersed plant.

73	Limb and throat not bright yellow, usually purple, rarely dull brown-yellow . . . . *C. cordata*
74	Throat not funnel-shaped 75
75 (76)	Blades smooth, limb vermilion red . . . . *C. hejnyi*
76	Blades blistered, limb orange-brown . . . . *C. zukalii*

JASARUM STEYERMARKII Bunting

This plant is undoubtedly the newest import at present. It was found and described a few years ago in Venezuela. The elliptical leaf blades of *J. steyermarkii* are bullose (embossed); the petioles are rather short. Living plants were imported for the first time to Europe by Mr. J. Bogner from Munich. Without doubt this import represents a unique material cultivated under artificial conditions.

LAGENANDRA

Plants of this genus are found in Ceylon (four species) and in the southern part of India (three species). They are perennial plants with a robust rhizome. In the emersed form a firm, woody stalk is developed. The leaves with long petioles have ovate or lanceolate blades. The flowers are similar to those of the cryptocorynes but the pistils are arranged in spirals (not in a circle). *Lagenandra toxicaria* is one of the most poisonous plants known.

LAGENANDRA DALZELLII (Schott) Rataj
Syn: *L. meeboldii* (Engler) Fischer

L. dalzellii originates from India and Ceylon and it resembles some of the cryptocorynes. The plant is only 5 to 10 cm tall. The leaves with typically heart-shaped blades are green or bronze reddish brown as in *Cryptocoryne thweitesii*. *L. dalzellii* was first imported in 1974. It seems to require the same conditions of cultivation as *Lagenandra thwaitesii*.

LAGENANDRA KOENIGII (Schott) Thwaites (III. 277)

L. koenigii is from the same area as the preceding species. The leaves are 10 to 15 cm long. The deep green blades (10 to 20 mm long) are usually longer than the petioles and narrowly lanceolate. Unlike *L. thwaitesii* their leaf margins are not silvery. This species is among the newly imported novelties. It is suitable for smaller and medium size tanks.

LAGENANDRA LANCIFOLIA (Schott) Thwaites (III. 277)

This plant grows in Ceylon in periodically flooded marshes within the jungle and on the shady banks of moving as well as still waters. It will tolerate permanent cultivation under water. *L. lan-*

Cryptocoryne walkeri from Ceylon (Sri Lanka) with inflorescence.
Photo by T.J. Horeman.

Lagenandra koenigii.

Lagenandra lancifolia.

cifolia is substantially smaller than *L. ovata* and it reaches a height of 25 to 30 cm.

The petiolate leaves have blades that are as long or shorter than the petiole, oblong-lanceolate, generally 75 mm long and 30 mm wide. The upper leaf surface is glossy grass-green; the lower surface is light green with white spots, especially along the center, about the midrib.

L. lancifolia is cultivated under conditions similar to those of *Cryptocoryne* spp., i.e., in moderately acid water with a richer planting medium. It requires plenty of diffused light and temperatures above 72° F (22° C). At lower temperatures the plant develops very sluggishly and eventually stops growing. Reproduction is slow; rhizome runners usually develop only after two to three years. Plants are most easily propagated from rhizomes cut off from the parent plant and cultivated in emersed conditions.

LAGENANDRA OVATA (L.) Thwaites (III. 279)

This inhabits the same place as the preceding species but allegedly it is also found in India. *L. ovata* is less suitable for aquariums because the leaves reach a length of up to 90 cm and under good conditions these can easily grow out of the water. The rhizome is robust, reaching up to 50 mm in diameter. The petiolate leaves are oblong-oval, acuminate. The blades in the submersed state are usually 20 cm long and about 75 mm wide, in the emersed form growing to 40 cm long and 12 cm wide. The upper leaf surface is glossy green while the lower surface is lighter in color.

L. ovata is cultivated like *Cryptocoryne ciliata*, i.e., in a poor medium and a moderately bright situation to prevent the leaves from growing out of the water. Propagation is more or less the same as the preceding species.

LAGENANDRA THWAITESII Engler

L. thwaitesii is native to Ceylon and is the most beautiful and at the same time the smallest member of this genus. In the wild it may reach a height of 25 cm but in the aquarium and the greenhouse emersed cultivated specimens do not grow more than 15 to 18 cm. The petiolate leaves are grass-green or grayish green. The whole blade is covered with silver-gray flecks. It is elongated lanceolate and about 10 cm long and 30 mm wide.

The plants are best cultivated in a temperature of about 72° F (22° C), in soft and moderately acid water, and a medium rich substrate. This species can stand more light than *L. ovata*. It is suitable for terrariums as well as aquariums.

Lagenandra ovata
growing emersed.

ORONTIUM AQUATICUM L.

O. aquaticum occurs in shallow water in eastern North America and is frequently cultivated as a decorative plant in garden ponds. The often floating leaves are 15 cm long, with oblong blades. It is not suited for indoor tanks.

PELTRANDRA

There are three species of *Peltrandra* from eastern North America. They are found in shallow water and swamps. *Peltrandra virginica* is cultivated in garden ponds. Petioled leaves, up to 40 cm high, have sagittate blades that are 25 cm long. This plant is not suitable for aquariums.

Schismatoglottis.

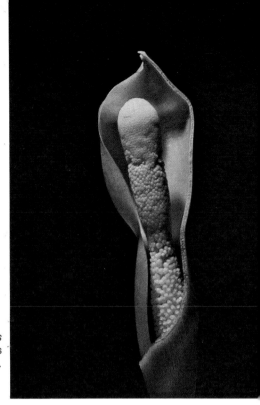

Inflorescence of *Schismatoglottis* with the male and female structures exposed.

Pistia stratiotes together with *Salvinia* (smaller floating plants). Photo by Dr. Herbert R. Axelrod.

PISTIA STRATIOTES L. (III. 281)

This plant, often called water lettuce, is distributed throughout the tropical regions and occasionally penetrating into the subtropical zones. The main area of distribution extends from Paraguay and Argentina across Central America and the West Indian archipelago to the southern part of the U.S.A. (Texas and Florida). In Africa it is found throughout the whole equatorial region, including Madagascar. In Asia this plant is found everywhere between eastern India and the Philippines. It has become a serious pest in many regions.

The leaves, on a shortened axis, form a rosette and are of most varied shapes—round, or cuneate, lingulate, reversely cordate, etc. The rosette is 10 to 20 cm in diameter. The upper leaf surface is light green, sparsely haired; the lower surface is greenish. Flowers in short, laterally vented spathes develop from the axil of the leaf.

Having a dense root mass, up to 20 cm long, this plant is very useful as a spawning medium for various species of fish. Unfortunately it grows only on a very well lighted surface where it produces tender root runners at the ends of which the young plants develop. For cultivating this plant, temperatures around 64° to 72° F (18° to 22° C) are required, and it can be cultivated successfully even in garden ponds during the summer. However during the autumn it is very sensitive to the shortening of the daylight hours; it can hibernate in aquariums, but only if given plenty of additional artificial light. The plant should have light for approximately twelve hours each day.

Water lettuce can be kept only with difficulty if additional light is not provided; if this is not possible, the plants should be transferred to small, flat dishes filled with sand and covered by about 25 mm of water. This is done as early as September. As soon as they have taken root the water can be left to evaporate and the plants are watered only moderately afterwards. They can then lie dormant safely.

Since *Pistia* produces seeds easily, it can be sown in dishes of water every spring. As soon as the seedlings are about 10 mm long they are transferred to the water surface in the aquarium where they propagate vegetatively very fast.

SCHISMATOGLOTTIS (III. 280, 281)

Plants representing the genus *Schismatoglottis* have been imported from the Malay Peninsula but the species is not yet determined. The leaves are 30 to 60 cm long (in the aquarium only 20 to 25 cm long). The blades are elongately cordate, acuminate at the tip, green, and trimmed with a broad, irregular silver stripe along the middle rib. Emersed plants flower easily. The spathe is green and the flowers on the spadix are divided into the lower female and upper male parts.

Cultivation is similar to that of *Aglaonema.*

SPATHIPHYLLUM Schott   (III, 421, 429)

Spathiphyllum is found mainly in South and Central America, and less frequently in Southeast Asia. The genus is represented by thirty-six species. Many are popular as ornamental indoor or greenhouse plants. Although a number of them grow in moist places, only one species has been tested successfully for permanently submersed growth.

SPATHIPHYLLUM WALLISI Regel   (III. 284)

This *Spathiphyllum* from Colombia is a perennial marsh plant. It is 50 cm tall but when cultivated under water it grows generally only to a height of 30 cm. The rhizome, from which petiolate leaves with a long lanceolate blade arise, measures up to 40 mm thick. The petiole is usually longer than the blade. The bright green blade is 30 to 60 mm wide and has margins that are moderately undulate. The blade is ornamented by fairly well elevated veins.

The cultivation of S. *wallisi* is similar to that of *Cryptocoryne* species, but unlike them it is not sensitive to excess light and it tolerates lower temperatures. In the water it remains in good condition all the summer but grows extremely slowly and often forms but a single leaf during the whole year. There are no known cases in which the plant developed runners under water; only emersed cultivated plants are propagated. They do well in flowerpots, provided they are treated in the same way as other plants commonly cultivated in greenhouses. Ten to fifteen young plants can be obtained by cuttings from the rhizome.

SYNGONIUM ALBOLINEATUM   (III. 285)

This liana resembles the growth of plants belonging to the genus *Philodendron*. It is commonly cultivated as an indoor plant reaching a height of several feet. Petiolate leaves grow on its climbing stem at intervals of 5 to 15 cm. Their sagittate blades are about 7.5 to 10 cm long, green and trimmed with a silvery white or yellow line along the main nerves. If we wish to use this species for our tanks, we should cut the stem into pieces with a single leaf on

Spatiphyllum wallisii.

Opposite: *Syngonium albolineatum.*

each of them. These cuttings are then planted in fertilized peat and watered well. They will take root within a short time and form rosettes of five to ten leaves, 10 to 15 cm long. They are then transplanted in this form into the aquarium. Their multi-colored and interesting leaves are very beautiful. They prefer diffused light, crystal clear acid water and are not sensitive to temperature changes.

TYPHONIUM FLEGELLIFORME (Lodd.) Blume (III. 288, 424)

T. flegelliforme is now imported regularly from Malaya. The leaves (up to 20 to 25 cm long) develop from little round tubers. The petioles are longer than the sagittate blades, which are deep green, 5 to 10 cm long, and have pointed lobules at the base.

Typhonium grows well emersed as well as submersed. In emersed cultures it propagates very quickly by producing new little tubers and flowers easily. The shape of the inflorescence is most attractive. An extended whip-shaped sterile part of the spadix grows from the kettle.

Very little is known about the cultivation of these plants in aquariums except that they propagate in an emersed form. They are planted under water with as few as four well developed leaves. Plants do not tolerate new water and they should be transplanted into mature, biologically balanced tanks with clean sand enriched with detritus and in places with indirect illumination.

ASTERACEAE (COMPOSITAE)

This very large family (900 genera) includes many well known decorative plants, such as the daisy, chrysanthemum, sunflower, etc. Many species grow in marshes but only ten genera include submersed plants. Most of them have not been imported yet and tested for aquatic purposes.

GYMNOCORONIS SPILANTHOIDES DC

G. spilanthoides is from tropical South America, where it occurs mainly in still or flowing waters and in marshes. The stems (about 10 to 15 mm thick) are erect at first, later becoming prostrate, rooting richly in many places. The elliptical to lanceolate leaves (5 to 12.5 cm long and 15 to 20 mm wide) are deep green and have inconspicuous undulated margins. The inflorescence is white (15 to 20 mm); the flowers are arranged on heads.

This plant can be propagated from any part of the stem having a pair of leaves. Emersed plants transplanted under water grow quickly and extend above the water surface. They do best when planted in tanks with a shaded surface illuminated only from the sides. Plants acclimatized to submersed life can be used in any aquarium. They are extremely hardy and do well in clean neutral water. The plants are 30 to 40 cm long and in order to get widely branching bushes they are pinched at the tips.

BRASSICACEAE Burnett (Cress Family)

This family (formerly Cruciferae), with 375 genera and 3200 species, is very abundant and is widely distributed all over the world. A great number of representatives grow amphibiously. However only a few species can be used in the aquarium. *Cardamine lyrata* and the beautiful *Rorippa aquatica*, rarely *Subularia*, are cultivated.

CARDAMINE LYRATA Bunge (BITTER CRESS)   (III. 424)

C. *lyrata* is distributed in East Asia and Japan. In the land form the plant has a prostrate or twisting stem but under water the feeble stems float vertically, up towards the water surface. The leaves are alternate, lyre-shaped, pinnate, round with short petioles, light green. The whole plant is very fragile. The inflorescence is a cluster; flowers are white, 5 to 10 mm in diameter.

It is best cultivated in shallow water, in well lighted conditions. This species can stand medium temperatures (about 68° F, 20° C) and tolerates a fall in temperature to 59° F (15° C) better than it does an increase. Propagation is by the division of stems, with roots forming below the petiole of each leaf. During winter it should be given additional artificial light or it can hibernate in shallow dishes. Water snails often damage this plant.

There are about 160 species in the genus *Cardamine*. Most of the species are marsh or bog plants. C. *lyrata* Bunge, C. *prosperens* Fischer, and C. *variabilis* Philippi are found growing submersed. *Cardamine rotundifolia* Michx., from North America, is now cultivated in aquariums by the same methods used for C. *lyrata*.

RORIPPA AQUATICA (Eaton) Palmer   (III. 289, 369)
Syn: *Neobeckia aquatica* Greene, *Armoracea aquatica* (Eaton) Wiegland

The genus *Rorippa* includes 70 species, but according to some authors it is divided into several other genera (*Nasturtium, Neobeckia, Armoracea*). About four species of *Rorippa* are aquatic, but they are usually emersed and not suitable for aquariums.

R. *aquatica*, from the U.S.A., is the species most often cultivated and is undoubtedly the most beautiful aquarium plant of the family Brassicaceae.

Typhonium flegelliforme.

Minute flowers of *Rorippa aquatica*.

Rorippa aquatica, cultivated emersed.

Living plants are extremely variable. The land form is 7.5 to 12.5 cm and has strikingly odd-pinnate and very deeply incised leaves arranged in a rosette. A stem develops at the time of flowering. Its leaves are alternate; the lower ones are deeply incised, the upper ones entire, with the edges more or less dentate. The flowers are white. *R. aquatica* develops submersed leaves that are quite different from the emersed ones. They are divided into fine narrow thread-like cuttings 25 to 75 mm long, bright green in color. *R. aquatica* can be cultivated in old clean water with a poor planting medium. Its greatest advantage is that it grows exceptionally well in a submersed form in winter, even in tanks with inadequate light. The beauty of its fine leaves equals that of the most beautiful tropical plants, and it belongs without any doubt to the most interesting novelties for aquariums. It does not tolerate overly acid conditions and when grown in shallow aquariums will produce emersed leaves in summer.

SUBULARIA

These plants are annual, tufted, glabrous herbs. The stems are reduced to corm-like structures. The leaves (25 to 75 mm long) are numerous, arranged in a rosette, subulate or linear. Only two species are known growing submersed in pools and lakes. *S. aquatica*, with subulate leaves, is found in North America, northern Europe, and central Asia and can be used for the aquarium only in summer. It is difficult to hibernate. The second species, *S. monticola* A. Br. ex Schweinfl., with linear leaves, comes from the mountains of Uganda, Congo, Kenya, and Tanganyika.

CABOMBACEAE (Fanwort Family)

The family Cabombaceae includes perennial aquatic herbs having floating or submersed leaves. White, yellow, or purple flowers are developed above the water. Only two genera, *Brasenia* and *Cabomba*, are known.

BRASENIA SCHREBERI Gmel. (WATER SHIELD)

Water shield grows in the Americas, from the southern states of the U.S.A. to the tropical area of South America; it occurs also in West Africa, tropical Asia, and in Australia.

From a stiff rhizome, long petioles extend upward, leading into the center of shield-shaped leaves of round or moderately oval form. The blade is 25 to 75 mm long, submersed or floating on the surface; the upper blade is dark brownish green, the lower surface red-brown. Flowers (which rarely appear in aquaria) are purplish red.

B. schreberi requires a fairly fertile substratum, very soft water of moderately acid reaction and sufficient light. It does poorly in deep water. It is cultivated most easily in the shallows, with adequate light from above.

The plant is interesting on account of its unusual leaves, but as a rule it does not live long and thus it does not belong in aquariums.

CABOMBA (FANWORT)

These are exclusively submersed plants which, when natural waters dry out, may form only two to three emersed leaves. In the emersed stage fanwort can exist only for a limited time.

The stem branches strongly under water and may reach a length of 2 to 3 meters or even more. Submersed leaves are filiform and divided into fine segments of varying size (25 to 50 mm long). During the flowering stage some species develop floating leaves which are oval or linear and about 30 to 40 mm long. The flowers (on the surface) are yellowish, white, or purple-red.

Cabomba is native to the American continents, ranging from the southern U.S.A. to tropical South America. About seven species are known. These species are all very decorative, but are delicate. *Cabomba* does well in old water in a reasonably well lighted aquarium without snails and with few fish, because the stems as well as the leaves are fragile, tender, and damage easily. It requires ordinary aquarium temperatures, about 68° F (20° C), but does not grow at lower temperatures, although it survives them well. The existing literature mentions the most frequently cultivated *Cabomba*, *C. caroliniana*, as having floating sagittate leaves and white flowers that are clear yellow at the center. *C. aquatica* comes from the tropical area of the Amazon River and evidently has not yet been imported to Europe, its name appearing in the literature by mistake. Authors are wrong in assuming that it is possible to determine individual species according to the width of the leaf segments. The reliable determination of cultivated species depend entirely on the flower structure. It appears that only the three following species are cultivated in aquariums.

CABOMBA CAROLINIANA A. Gray (III. 292, 293, 296)

This species from the southern part of the United States also extends to South America. The leaves are divided into narrow segments. The floating leaves are sagittate and the flowers are white,

Cabomba caroliniana var. *multipartita*.

Cabomba caroliniana var. *paucipartita.*

Flower of
Cabomba caroliniana.

293

yellow in the center. Leaf blades are 30 to 40 mm long and up to 60 mm wide. The flower is star-shaped; petals (crown leaflets) are narrow, not covering each other.

C. caroliniana is not a typically tropical species. It endures a relatively shorter day in winter and is able to winter even with a small amount of light. It is not difficult to cultivate and therefore is used frequently by aquarists.

This plant exists in several natural and horticultural forms, the best known of which is C. caroliniana var. multipartita Hort. It is a horticultural form, obtained by selection, which has abundant leaves (75 mm wide) with a greater number of segments.

C. caroliniana var. paucipartita Van. Ramsh. et Florsch. is, on the other hand, very delicate in appearance. The leaves have only a few thin segments. It is of little value for aquariums.

C. caroliniana var. pulcherrima Harper differs from the preceding species in having a more abundant foliage and purple-red stem and leaves (a most beautiful plant). It is rarely found in European tanks, though quite capable of tolerating a rather shady environment.

CABOMBA AUSTRALIS Speg. (III.   , 337)

C. australis is found in southern Brazil, Uruguay, Paraguay, and Argentina. It occurs between the southern subtropical and the temperate zones. It needs the same attention as C. caroliniana and is probably unrecognized in the aquarium of aquarists until the time of flowering. The leaves are rather small, up to 20 to 30 mm wide and 50 mm long; the leaf segments are medium in size, about 0.5 mm wide. The flowers are clear yellow with a striking orange spot at the base. It differs from other species in the shape of the flowers, the crown leaflets being egg-shaped and so broad that they overlap each other; the flowers are not star-shaped, but are round and slightly campanulate.

CABOMBA PIAUHYENSIS Gardner (III. 296, 325)

This species is distributed over a large area extending from Central America to South America, reaching to the area of the Amazon River. This is a typical tropical species that grows slowly and is fragile and also sensitive to algae. It can only be cultivated in clean water without snails, which often damage it. C. piauhyensis is sensitive to a short winter day and requires extra light hours, otherwise it will die. It roots poorly and slowly. Newly imported plants coming from natural environments have bright red to purple-violet stems and leaves. In aquariums this wonderful coloring usually disappears after a while. The plants will keep the red-brown color only in very well illuminated places. The flowers, situated on 2.5 cm pedicels, are star-shaped, purple-red to violet, with a yellow spot in the center.

CERATOPHYLLACEAE (Hornwort Family)

The family Ceratophyllaceae is composed exclusively of perennial plants and includes only the genus *Ceratophyllum* (foxtail) with two species. Some authors list up to 30 species, which are probably mostly local varieties. These are submersed plants with only their tips reaching the surface. The leaves, arranged in whorls, are forked. True roots are absent and are replaced by short "rhizoids."

CERATOPHYLLUM DEMERSUM L. (III. 297)

C. demersum is distributed all over the world. The leaves have two-forked divisions. This species is commonly found in backwaters and pools of both lowland and hill countries and prefers swampy soils. Propagation is mainly by stem breakage.

CERATOPHYLLUM SUBMERSUM L.

This plant is found throughout the world. However, in the temperate zone it is found only in the lowlands of the warmer regions, being absent over wide areas. It is found more frequently in slightly brackish waters, where *C. demersum* is not present. It differs from *C. demersum* in having three-pronged leaves.

Plants of both species originating from the temperate zone are not suitable for aquariums. They become spindly and the distance between the whorls of the leaves increases as much as five times while the leaves become thin and short, so the plants lose their natural decorative character. The plant usually dies in the summer. In recent years a species of *Ceratophyllum* has reached the European market from Cuba. Its whorls are very abundant and dense, even when maintained in a warm aquarium. It is a very decorative plant.

CLUSIACEAE (Guttiferae)

This family, with about 40 genera and about 100 species, contains only one unique water plant.

HYPERICUM ELODES L.

This plant can be found growing in bogs and marshes of western Europe and is rarely cultivated in aquariums. The leaves are opposite, rounded, sessile, and partly surround the prostrate stem.

Cabomba piauhyensis.

Flowers of *Cabomba caroliniana* var. *pulcherrima*. Photo by T.J. Horeman.

Ceratophyllum demersum.

It propagates easily by rooting part of the stems with leaves. For its cultivation, old neutral water that can be medium hard is used. *H. elodes* must receive the maximum amount of illumination in winter, otherwise it will die.

COMMELINACEAE

Many representatives of the family Commelinaceae are commonly cultivated as indoor plants—*Tradescantia, Commelina, Cyanotis*, etc. They are known to be extremely hardy and simple, rooting easily in tanks with tap water. Many experiments undertaken to acclimate these plants under water have so far produced negative results. There is a species found in nature, *Murdannia blumei* (Hassk.) Brenan, which is a weed in the ricefields of Asia. Plants of an undetermined species of the genus *Floscopa* are also currently being imported.

FLOSCOPA   (III. 301)

Emersed stems of *Floscopa* plants are prostrate, rooting in many places. The alternate leaves are sessile with inconspicuous fine hairs, lanceolate, and about 50 to 75 mm long. Vegetative tips (10 to 15 cm long) with five to six leaves can be transplanted under water. They root quickly; the fine hairs disappear, blades turn light green and conspicuously extend up to a length of 10 to 15 cm. Being most decorative, *Floscopa* is among the very attractive novelties of recent time.

CRASSULACEAE (Orpine or Crassula Family)

This family consists mostly of drought-loving herbs, undershrubs and bushes. Only a very small percentage of about 1500 species live in a moist medium and are able to grow amphibiously.

CRASSULA (TILLAEA)   (III. 300)

The genus *Crassula*, with about 300 species, comprises mainly succulent herbs. Only a few species, with creeping floating stems, are found in wet places and may tolerate long periods of submergence. *Crassula aquatica* (L.) Schonl. from Europe and *C. vaillantii* (Willd.) from the Mediterranean area and the United States are annual plants. They are not suitable for the aquarium. *C. helmsii* Kirk from New Zealand and *C. bonariensis* (DC.) Camb. from South America are commonly cultivated in indoor tanks. These are always perennial and fit for aquariums, although they are not very popular.

Species of this genus reach a height of 40 cm. The leaves are about 15 mm long and 1 mm wide, needle-shaped, opposite and arranged cross-wise. The land form has distinctly shorter leaves. Minute reddish or white flowers develop at the axil of the leaves.

Crassula plants are best cultivated in well illuminated situations. In other respects (composition of water, temperature) they are not particular. They do not flower when submersed and propagate by stem division. These plants are not too decorative.

CYPERACEAE (Sedge Family)

This family contains perennial, or more rarely annual, plants. Compound inflorescences of the most varied types are present. The family Cyperaceae contains 60 genera with 3,700 species distributed all over the globe from the tropics to the Arctic regions, including high mountain habitats. Various species are confined to special locations (sand, rocks, steppes, woods, meadows); many grow in marshy to bankside conditions but are adapted solely to an amphibious life and can live under water only temporarily.

CYPERUS (CYPRESS GRASS)

This genus is distributed mainly in the tropical and subtropical zones of the world. Some more resistant species grow even in the temperate zones. They are absent only from high ground. These are low, medium, and tall plants, usually with a leaved culm. Altogether more than 900 species are known; some of them are commonly cultivated in greenhouses and as indoor plants. The best known species is *C. alternifolius* L. from Madagascar, known by the incorrect name *"papyrus."* The real *C. papyrus* L. inhabits the Mediterranean area (principally Egypt) and reaches a height of 1.2 to 3.0 meters; in ancient times a paper was made from it.

Almost all the perennial species can be used in terrariums and paludariums. Since the majority of *Cyperus* species grow in moist, periodically flooded places, some of them can be cultivated as aquatic plants at least temporarily.

CYPERUS ERAGROSTIS L.   (Ill. 302)

Of more than 100 species tested by the senior author for underwater cultivation, this species has been found to be the best. It forms a white rhizome (up to 7 mm thick), from the lower part of which a sparsely leaved culm develops with a typical fan of linear leaves at the upper end. In the emersed state in terrariums it flowers readily and produces a great number of fertile seeds. Under water this species reaches a height of 20 to 30 cm and is propagated by buds on the rhizome, which produces a group of very decorative plants of unequal sizes.

Crassula aquatica.

Phyllanthus fluitans.

Floscopa species.

Bird's eye view of the terminal rosette of leaves and flowers of *Cyperus eragrostis*.

It requires a sandy substrate, generous daylight, and a temperature of about 68° F (20° C); it can stand lower temperatures (down to 50° F or 10° C) for a short while.

ELEOCHARIS (SPIKE RUSH)

These plants (minute to medium height) are found in marshes, on the banks of rivers, and on the bottom of stagnant or slow moving waters. The genus consists of more than 200 species growing all over the world, from the tropics to the Arctic. Many of them can withstand great fluctuations in temperature and are suitable for both coldwater and tropical tanks. In appearance they differ greatly from the majority of aquarium plants, so they form an appropriate complement to the specimens usually maintained.

They are content with a very poor planting medium but require a fair amount of light, especially if they are to be kept in good condition through the winter months.

Many native and foreign species, such as *E. palustris* (L.) R. et S., *E. obtusa* (Willd.) Schult., etc., can be cultivated in aquariums. They are more robust and often form tufts, but drop their leaves for the winter period. The following two species are the most suitable for aquariums.

ELEOCHARIS ACICULARIS (L.) R. et Sch.

Hair grass grows in the temperate, subtropical, and tropical zones of the world, excluding Africa. It is found on the sandy banks of rivers and lakes and is as a rule amphibious. The rhizome is thread-like, creeping, with long rooting runners forming minute tufts of delicate, slender, light green stems. The submersed stems are from 40 to 60 cm tall; the culms produced by land forms are shorter and the dense rootstock creates a conspicuous carpet. The emersed form will flower if kept in containers with a thin layer (25 mm) of earth.

In the aquarium the plant should be cultivated in a poor sandy medium under fairly good illumination; if the tank is given additional artificial light in winter, the plant grows all through the year. It is not particular with regard to temperature (50° to 77° F, 10° to 25° C). Propagation is by root runners and nutlets; in deeper waters it rarely forms rooting bud-plants that are arranged in tiers, one series above the other. This plant is easily obtained from our waters and marshes.

ELEOCHARIS VIVIPARA Link (= *E. prolifera*)

E. vivipara comes from the warm southern parts of the United States, growing in situations similar to those where *E. acicularis* is

Eleocharis minima, submersed plant.

Flowering *Eleocharis minima.*

found, but in comparison to the latter it is better adapted to submersed growth. Under water it forms long and slender stems with groups of fine linear leaves that are arranged in linear whorls, one above the other (rather like upturned umbrellas). On each stem there are ten to fifteen whorls, each with roots at the base; by dividing the stem into individual whorls the plant is readily propagated.

Its cultivation requires the same conditions as those of the preceding species: a sandy soil and plenty of light. Temperature requirements are not too critical. If kept in tanks without additional warmth it often dies in winter.

A similar plant cultivated in aquariums is *Eleocharis minima* from South America. Both species are hardly distinguishable when cultivated submersed in the aquarium.   **(III. 304-305)**

ISOLEPIS

Of about 60 species of *Isolepis* growing in shallow water, only *I. setacea* is commonly cultivated in aquariums. Under water it resembles *Eleocharis acicularis*. Emersed, flowering plants are distinguished according to the position of the inflorescence. In *I. setacea* it is located a short distance before the tip of the stem, while in *E. acicularis* it is exactly at the tip of the stem. Cultivation of both plants in aquariums is the same.

DROSERACEAE (Sundew Family)

This family is represented mostly by perennial herbs, of which only the genus *Aldrovanda* is bound with an aquatic medium. The genera *Drosera* and *Dionaea* grow on peat soils, *Drosophyllum* on dry soil. It is a family of typically carnivorous plants. The aquatic genus *Aldrovanda* contains a single species, *A. vesiculosa.*

ALDROVANDA VESICULOSA L.

This European perennial plant grows on the surface layer of water. It has no roots, only a thin stem which is 25 to 100 mm long. Leaves are arranged in whorls, and their round blades are equipped with large bristles. On the upper surface of the blade there are numerous digestive glands which absorb the captured minute animal organisms. Flowers are greenish white. The fruit is a pod with ten black seeds.

A.vesiculosa is rarely seen, is not a popular plant, and is difficult to cultivate in aquariums, where it grows very slowly and soon dies. The carnivorous embossments are sufficiently large to endanger both the fish fry and their living crustacean food. Medium to low temperatures and acid water are required. The plant is propagated by stem division and winter buds.

ELATINACEAE (Waterwort Family)

The family Elatinaceae has two genera, *Bergia* with about twenty species and *Elatine* with about twelve species; both genera contain amphibious plants. Some species are able to survive under water for a long time and are useful in aquariums; others flower readily and form seeds capable of germinating.

ELATINE (WATERWORT)

Elatine is suitable only for aquariums. In terrariums and paludariums the plants are basically annuals; even with sufficient moisture they flower and then die. *Elatine* has been cultivated recently, but only very rarely. Often mistakenly offered in the shops under the name "Elatine" is *Lilaeopsis lacustris* or *Lilaeopsis novae-zealandiae* (see the family Apiaceae).

ELATINE HYDROPIPER L.

In the aquarium it does not thrive as successfully as the next species. Although it is an annual, in submersed conditions it lasts longer.

E. hydropiper should be cultivated under conditions similar to those used with *E. macropoda*, shallow water with plenty of light; it is not quite so particular with respect to the type of soil. As a rule it hibernates well. Because of the very feeble root system, the plants are often pulled loose, especially in tanks with fish foraging close to the bottom.

Other species are less suitable for aquariums and hibernate badly. Examples are *E. hexandra* (Lap. Dc.) with six stamens and *E. triandra* Schkuhr. with three stamens. Both species are rare in nature and are mostly annual.

ELATINE MACROPODA Guss.

This plant is distributed through southern France, Sicily, Malta, Spain, Algeria, and Morocco. In nature it is an annual, 25 to 50 mm tall with a creeping, well branched stem.

Submersed forms are perennial in aquariums, take root abundantly, and form characteristic tufts of prostrate stems with spatulate leaves 10 to 18 cm long and 10 to 30 mm wide; the leaves are light green in color.

E. macropoda grows faster than all other species of *Elatine* and forms rich carpets close to the bottom of the tank. The plant requires temperatures from 55° to 77° F (13° to 25° C). It is not particular in other respects, but it does not stand lime salts and does well only in shallow water. It hibernates readily and its root

Myriophyllum aquaticum, submersed form.

Myriophyllum aquaticum, emersed form.

system is sufficiently robust to prevent the plant from being pulled out easily. In paludariums it usually dies at the approach of winter.

BERGIA

This genus has about twenty species distributed throughout the warmer regions of the world. About ten species are aquatic or semi-aquatic. *B. capensis* L. and other species are known as weeds in rice fields and have not been imported as yet.

ERIOCAULONACEAE

Many typical aquatic plants are contained in this very interesting family. It is strange that none of them have been imported. Some species closely resemble such classical aquarium groups as *Myriophyllum* or *Mayaca*.

Worthwhile mentioning are *Eriocaulon melanocephalum* Kunt from South America, *E. setaceum* L. from Southeast Asia, and *E. bifistolosum* v. Heurck. et Mueller from Africa. *Leiothrix fluitans* (Mart.) Ruhl. from Brazil occurs submersed in streams. *Mesanthemum reductum* Hess from Angola, *Syngonanthus hydrotrichus* Ruhl. from Brazil, and *Tonina fluviatilis* Aubl. from tropical America grow permanently under water.

EUPHORBIACEAE

The family Euphorbiaceae contains 6,000 species growing in most varied conditions. It is interesting that along with the gigantic plants of the genus *Euphorbia* growing in deserts and resembling enormous cacti are plants floating in the water but belonging to the same family.

PHYLLANTHUS FLUITANS Mull   (III. 300, 421)

This species from Brazil, Ecuador, and Paraguay is a free-floating plant, annual or perennial, green when young and becoming red at maturity. The stems are floating, up to 75 mm long, and sparsely branched. Floating leaves (about 15 mm diameter) are rounded, sessile, overlapping, and alternate in two rows.

These floating plants resemble *Salvinia*, which is very often found with it in nature. *P. fluitans* will grow on the surface in well illuminated tanks. In the summer it grows very well and quickly in water of any quality, but it hibernates poorly.

An extremely interesting plant, although it needs attention in winter, *P. fluitans* is hibernated in shallow dishes with about 10 mm of peat. In spring it can be cultivated again on the surface of the water.

HALORHAGACEAE (Water Milfoil or Marestail Family)

The family contains herbs, undershrubs, or bushes with leaves that are opposite or arranged in whorls. Only two genera are represented by aquatic plants: *Myriophyllum* (water milfoil) and *Proserpinaca* (mermaid weed).

MYRIOPHYLLUM (WATER MILFOIL)

The forty species of this genus, all of them perennial plants, are distributed from the tropics to the temperate zone. Australian species are largely amphibious, while American species are usually aquatic (although some are amphibious). For aquariums the aquatic species are the most suitable, and to these belong the majority of species from the temperate zone including some from the tropical zone.

The leaves of aquatic species are mostly arranged in whorls, rarely opposite. They are divided into numerous segments. The flowers are arranged in a spicate inflorescence that emerges above the surface of the water. The shape of the flower, especially of the calyx, is an important character for identification of individual species.

Members of this genus are popular aquarium plants for the back, sides, and corners of tanks; they are not exacting as far as the composition of the bottom and water is concerned, and they grow in practically all common aquarium conditions. The plants require good light and can withstand great fluctuations in temperature. They do best in deeper tanks (30 to 60 cm), where the stems branch out abundantly.

Old stems often lose the leaves on the lower parts, so they should be pinched out. This way they are stimulated to form leaf whorls only a few inches above the bottom, thereby increasing their decorative character.

Some species from the temperate zone that are often cited in aquarium literature are not suitable for aquariums because they require cooler water (*M. alterniflorum* DC., *M. verticillatum* L.).

MYRIOPHYLLUM AQUATICUM (Velloso) Verde.
Syn: *M. brasiliense* Cambess (III. 308-309)

This species from the southern parts of the United States and Central and South America has become naturalized in many countries. The submersed leaves are in whorls of four to six and a light to grass-green color; those on the emersed parts of the stem are shorter, stiff, and have a velvety sheen. Upper parts of stems protrude above the water and tend to hang over the edge of the tank.

Myriophyllum spicatum.

Myriophyllum hippuroides;
emersed form.

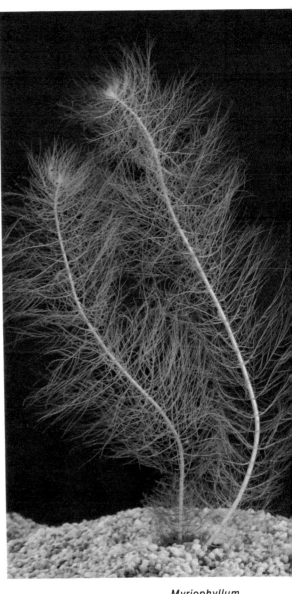

*Myriophyllum
hippuroides;* submersed
form.

Myriophyllum spicatum (left) and its inflorescence (right).

Plants require lighted conditions and neutral to slightly alkaline water. Temperatures between 77° to 86° F (25° to 30° C) in the summer and in winter 59° to 68° F (15° to 20° C) will do. They are also good plants for paludariums and terrariums.

MYRIOPHYLLUM HIPPUROIDES Nutt. (III. 313)

North America and Mexico are the native habitats of *M. hippuroides*. This aquatic to amphibious plant develops creeping rhizomes and stout, thickened stems up to a meter long. Leaves are in whorls of four to six (often pseudowhorls). Submersed leaves (50 mm long) are pinnate, with shorter filiform segments at the tip; aerial leaves are linear to lanceolate, serrate or smooth-edged, and 25 mm long by 2.5 mm wide.

MYRIOPHYLLUM SCABRATUM Michx.
(= *M. pinnatum*/Walt./Britt.) (III. 316)

This species, distributed in the southern parts of the United States and Cuba, includes aquatic to amphibious plants. The stem is profusely branched; thin green leaves are arranged in pseudowhorls of three to five parts. *M. scabratum* stands cooler as well as warm waters (above 68° F, 20° C) which are slightly alkaline to neutral.

MYRIOPHYLLUM SPICATUM L. (III. 312, 314, 317)

M. spicatum is found in Europe, North America, and North Africa, but it is absent from South America and Australia. The conspicuous reddish stems in the adult stage are up to 2.1 meters long. The leaves are in whorls of four or five and are 25 mm long. It is not too exacting with respect to the substrate and is less particular than the preceding species to the light requirements. It tolerates both cool and warm water also. The plant is very decorative because of its red coloration, but in winter it adopts a dwarf form and often loses most of the leaves.

MYRIOPHYLLUM USSURIENSE (Regal) Maxim
(= *M. japonicum*)

This is one of the most popular representatives of the genus and it is distributed in eastern Asia, Manchuria, and Japan. The delicate leaves are arranged in whorls of three or four, with eight to twenty-six segments 10 to 50 mm long. It practically never flowers in the aquarium; aerial leaves are very rare.

In recent years several new species of *Myriophyllum* have been imported to Europe. The most interesting is the red-leaved water milfoil from South America (probably *M. matogrossense*).

PROSERPINACA

The genus *Proserpinaca* comprises aquatic plants with prostrate stems. The leaves are alternate and pinnately divided or the upper leaves are occasionally entire. They are very seldom cultivated. *Proserpinaca palustris* is the most common species.

Myriophyllum scabratum

Ottelia species growing in a fast flowing stream in Curitiba, Brazil. Photo by T.J. Horeman.

Inflorescence of *Myriophyllum spicatum*.

HYDROCHARITACEAE Jass (Frogbit Family)

This family contains both floating and submersed plants; leaves develop above the water only in certain species. The external appearance of the stems and leaves is varied to such an extent that the plants of individual genera do not resemble each other at all. The flowers are either small and inconspicuous or large and very attractive. Some species are dioecious, some are hermaphroditic. They are pollinated under water (in marine species) or on the surface. Female flowers usually grow on the surface while male flowers, as in the genus *Vallisneria*, are virtually sessile and before maturing become detached, rise to the surface and only then open; pollen is dispersed by water. Pollination in most other species of this family is based upon a similar principle; only a few groups of the Hydrocharitaceae are insect pollinated (*Stratiotes*, the water soldier, and some species of *Ottelia*).

The family consists of marine and freshwater plants distributed over all continents in the tropical and temperate zones. In the northern temperate zones the genera *Stratiotes*, *Limnobium*, and *Hydrocharis* are found. In the tropical and subtropical zones there are three marine genera and the freshwater genera *Lagarosiphon* (only in Africa), *Vallisneria*, *Blyxa*, *Ottelia*, *Hydromistra*, *Egeria*, *Hydrilla*, etc. Some of these genera reach to the temperate zone.

Most widely distributed is *Vallisneria spiralis* L., which is the only representative of the frogbit family found in both the eastern and western hemispheres. *Elodea canadensis* (Casp.) from North America has spread from there to central and northern Europe. *Hydrilla verticillata* Casp. also has a wide distribution; it is found from Pomerania and Lithuania to Japan and Australia, and even in Africa.

Many representatives of this family can be considered to be the most popular and readily cultivated among aquarium plants. With a few exceptions—plants coming from tropical Asia (*Blyxa*, *Ottelia*)—they tolerate very hard water, drawing from it the limy salts and thus making the water soft. *Vallisneria*, *Elodea*, *Lagarosiphon*, and *Hydrilla* are practically the only ones able to tolerate all kinds of aquarium water.

European plants of the family, such as *Stratiotes aloides* L. and *Hydrocharis morsus-ranae* L., are unfit for aquariums but can be used as a temporary decoration in paludariums.

Belonging to this family are very interesting, but not yet imported, plants probably most suitable for aquariums; these are

Maidenia rubra Rendle from Australia and *Nechamandra alterni-folia* (Roxb.) from Southeast Asia.

BLYXA

Representatives of this genus are found in the tropical areas of Asia and Africa. The leaves are narrow, sessile, pointed at the apex, and alleged to be able to grow up to 50 cm long (in tanks they do not grow longer than 20 cm). They are practically never cultivated in aquariums and require extraordinary care to ensure hibernation. About ten species are known.

BLYXA AUBERTII Rich.
Syn: *B. oryzetorum* Hook. F.

This plant comes from Madagascar, tropical Asia, and Australia. It has twenty to fifty leaves (in a rosette) that are green or yellow-green, sometimes brownish, band-shaped, and indistinctly denticulate on the margins. In the aquarium they are 20 to 40 cm long; in nature, up to 1.5 meters. This species flowers regularly in aquariums; it is self-fertile and mature seeds can be obtained.

B. aubertii is the most often cultivated species of the genus. It is very hardy, found in nature on mountains, and tolerates low temperatures.

BLYXA ECHINOSPERMA (Clarke) Hook f.

B. echinosperma comes from an extensive area, from Ceylon and eastern India, Malaya and Australia to North China and Japan, growing under conditions similar to those of the genus *Cryptocoryne*. In nature an annual, it can hibernate in the aquarium, but it flowers so extremely rarely that propagation from seeds cannot be considered.

A leaf rosette is planted in the tank; as soon as it has developed, a stem arises (2.5 to 10 cm long) between the root collar and the leaf fan. This stem is irregularly leaved and has roots at the axil of each leaf. The plant can be divided further, if required, into two or four parts. Plants systematically rejuvenated in this way can be hibernated during the resting seasons.

B. echinosperma should be cultivated in soft, moderately acid water. It is very exacting with respect to external conditions and is easily damaged by snails. The plant is most readily maintained if given illumination from above and kept in shallow water (about 15 to 20 cm deep). It definitely requires additional light in winter.

This is one of the rarest and most decorative aquarium plants, but due to the difficulties associated with its cultivation it is not too certain to be accepted for popular use in aquariums.

Egeria densa.

Male flower of
Egeria densa.

Elodea nutalli.

BLYXA JAPONICA (Miq.) Maxim.

This species inhabits more or less the same areas as *B. echinosperma*, but it is more restricted to eastern Asia (China, Korea, Japan, Thailand, Vietnam, Malaya, Borneo). It resembles the preceding species in structure, although its leaves may not be only grass-green but also olive to golden in color. *B. japonica* can be propagated faster and maintained more easily than *B. echinosperma*.

EGERIA (III. 320)

Egeria is similar to *Elodea*. There are only two species in the genus. *Egeria najas* Planch has not yet been imported.

Egeria densa Planch is originally from the warmer parts of the temperate zone of South America, but has been introduced into North America, Africa, Europe, and Japan. It is a fairly long plant (stem reaching 3 meters), but sparsely branched; at the points of branching adventitious roots develop. Leaves are arranged for the most part in whorls of five and are light to bright green and narrowly lanceolate, about 20 to 30 mm long and 2.5 to 5 mm wide. The margins are finely serrated. Male flowers are white (about 10 mm in diameter); female flowers have not yet been recorded in aquariums.

As stated in the introductory paragraphs to these genera, this plant consumes a large amount of limy salts and softens water. Although coming from the tropical and subtropical areas, it is not a forest plant and is found in the waters of open areas with plenty of light and with great fluctuations in temperature. Thus it requires a generous light but is not too exacting with respect to temperature, growing well in both tropical and coldwater tanks.

E. densa is quite modest in its requirements as to the composition of the substrate, because it usually anchors itself by means of its roots while receiving nutrients through the surface of the leaf; it can be cultivated even when floating freely.

ELODEA Michx. (= *Anacharis* Rich.) (WATERWEED)

Elodea is distributed mainly over the American continent, but such species as *E. canadensis* and *E. nutalli* have been taken to Europe.

Plants of this genus have a long, branching stem. The leaves are in whorls of various densities and are narrowly lanceolate to linear with the margins finely serrated. The plants are dioecious; on one plant there are only male, on another only female flowers. In aquariums they flower very rarely and are propagated by planting detached fragments of the stem.

These plants grow in any kind of water. In neutral to alkaline water, especially if subjected to good illumination, the whorls of leaves are dense and profuse. In a more acid and darker environment they develop thin stems with somewhat distant whorls of shorter and more delicate leaves. Elodeas stand even hard water very well, drawing limy salts from it and making it soft; in this way they provide good conditions for species that do not tolerate hard water. Consequently, they should be present in any aquarium that contains hard water; quantities of this plant will permit the growth of species that are less tolerant of such conditions.

E. canadensis Michx. is unsuitable for tanks because it cannot withstand high temperatures and lack of light. *E. callitrichoides*, often cited in the literature, is not cultivated in aquariums; plants offered under this name are all *E. nutalli* Planch.

Of seventeen known species only *E. nutalli* is cultivated. What has been stated about this genus is applicable for *Egeria*, *Hydrilla*, and *Lagarosiphon* as well.

ELODEA NUTALLI Planch. (III. 321)

E. nutalli originates from North America and has become naturalized in recent years in Germany and the Netherlands. Being a plant of the temperate and subtropical zones, it is found, unlike *E. canadensis*, in areas situated more toward the south. It adapts to external conditions very well and does not react unfavorably in warm water or diffused light; consequently it is suited, just like the preceding species, for tropical and coldwater aquariums.

This is one of the smallest species of the group. The stem (3 to 12 cm long) is much branched and bears whorls of minute leaves (each about 5 to 10 mm long) that are sometimes moderately curved, with minutely serrated margins. There are male as well as female plants in our aquariums, but they flower very rarely.

E. nutalli is cultivated under conditions similar to those of *E. densa*. It is a good plant for use as a spawning medium.

HYDRILLA VERTICILLATA (L.f.) Royle

H. verticillata, the only species of the genus *Hydrilla*, is distributed over an extensive area, from northeastern Europe (Pomerania, Lithuania) across southern Asia and Indonesia to China and Japan, as well as in Australia, West Africa, Mauritius, and Madagascar. It grows therefore in the temperate, subtropical, and tropical zones and is very accommodating in its requirements.

The stem (up to several meters long) is profusely branching, with three to nine whorls, much thinner than those of *Elodea*.

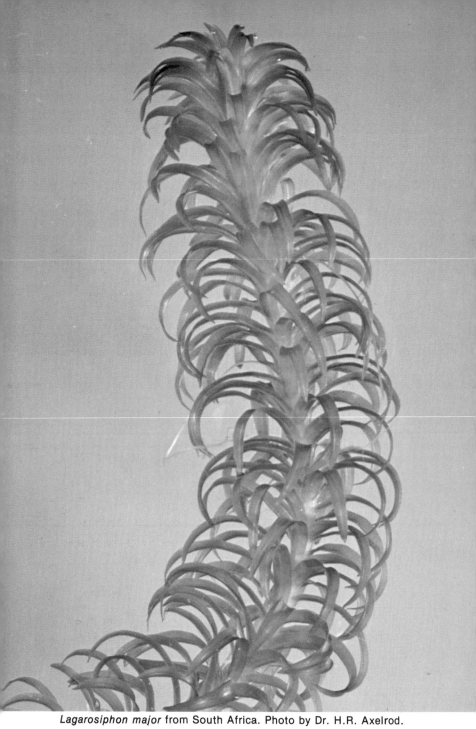

Lagarosiphon major from South Africa. Photo by Dr. H.R. Axelrod.

Flowers of *Cabomba piauhyensis* (top) and *Cabomba australis* (bottom).

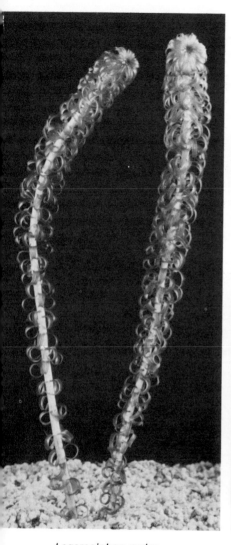

Lagarosiphon major.

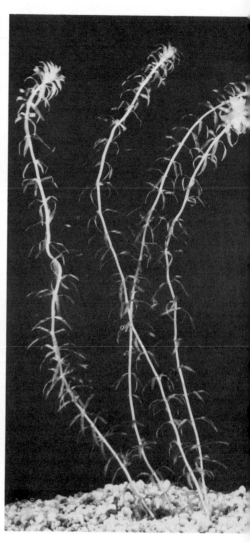

Lagarosiphon muscoides.

326

Leaves are narrowly lanceolate, 15 to 25 mm long and 1 to 2 mm wide; their margins are unmistakably dentate, not like the leaf margins of *Elodea* which are only finely serrated and seem to be entire unless examined closely. Methods of cultivation and propagation agree largely with those of preceding species of the frogbit family, but *Hydrilla* is even more modest with respect to temperature. It grows in heated aquariums all the year round; in cold tanks it stops growing in winter at 41° to 45° F (5° to 7° C) and survives this period in the form of winter buds.

LAGAROSIPHON

Lagarosiphon differs from *Hydrilla* and *Elodea* by having numerous flowers in the male spathe. The leaves are usually arranged in spirals. About sixteen species are known from Africa and Madagascar.

LAGAROSIPHON MADAGASCARIENSIS Casp.

This species was imported, only with the last decade, from Madagascar. It has fine stems, up to 50 cm long and about 1 mm thick, that are abundantly branched. The leaves are linear, pointed, bright green, only 10 mm long (at the most 20 mm), and rather narrow. These are arranged in irregular whorls in spirals. Imported plants cultivated in aquariums flower relatively easily.

L. madagascariensis demands very soft water and pH from 5 to 7.5. Nutrients are accepted, as with related plants, directly from the water.

LAGAROSIPHON MAJOR (Ridley) Moss
Syn: *L. muscoides* Harvery var. *major* Ridley
Incorrect name: *Elodea crispa* Hort.   (III. 324, 326)

This plant, a native of South Africa, is usually offered in the trade by the incorrect name *Elodea crispa*. It is the most beautiful representative of the whole family. It differs from *Elodea* and *Hydrilla* in that its leaves are not arranged in whorls but are sessile and in dense spirals. The leaves (medium to bright green) are about 20 mm long, recurved, and substantially stiffer than those of other species, with margins minutely serrated. *L. major* rarely flowers in the aquarium.

It is cultivated in the same manner as the preceding species, but it is somewhat more exacting in that it requires neutral to moderately alkaline water; in acid water it grows slowly. This species does best in intermediate to generous light at temperatures around 68° F (20° C), but tolerates both warmer or cooler water. Hard water is softened by it, but it stops growing when limy salts are

Inflorescence of
*Echinodorus
maior.*

Echinodorus maior.

Ottelia species found on
the borders of Bolivia
and the Mato Grosso,
Brazil. Photo by T.J.
Horeman.

Inflorescence of *Ottelia*
species. Photo by T.J.
Horeman.

329

absent; some aquarists add chalk (calcium carbonate) to the water. In this manner, however, the hardness of the water is substantially increased, which prevents other plant species from growing and makes the conditions bad for most fish. If tap water is used in the tanks, it is not necessary to add limy salts.

During the winter months the plant stops growing and requires additional light. If it does not have a sufficiently long period of adequate light it does not die, but the young stems (about 10 mm long) cease further development until the beginning of spring and start growing when the days get longer.

LAGAROSIPHON MUSCOIDES Harvey (III. 326)

This species, also from Africa, appeared in our tanks only in the last few years. Its leaves are not curved as much as those of *L. major*. As to the height, *L. muscoides* stands between the two earlier mentioned species. On the average leaves are 12 to 15 mm long. It tolerates acid water, but the plant becomes less attractive.

LIMNOBIUM (FROGBIT)

Floating or rooting in shallow water, these plants have petiolate leaves with blades that are floating or emersed, elliptical, ovate, or orbicular; the tip is rounded or obtuse, the base usually cordate. The reverse side of the leaves is often covered by a thick aerenchymatous cushion. All three known species come from the warmer parts of America. Only two species are cultivated.

LIMNOBIUM STOLONIFERUM (G.F.W.) Gris (FROGBIT)
Syn: *Hydromistra stolonifera* Meyer (III. 331)

The American *L. stoloniferum* can be found from Mexico to Paraguay, the whole tropical and subtropical area. A floating plant, the leaves grow in a rosette. They have short petioles, are round, cordate at the base, 25 to 50 mm in diameter, pulpy, 5 mm thick, and formed largely of spongy tissue which enables them to float on the surface. The plant is dioecious and readily flowers in the greenhouse. In aquariums only female plants occur; the flower is conspicuous, with a three-parted stigma that is 10 mm long.

As with all floating plants, it is exacting with regard to light and humidity above the water surface; consequently it does well in the greenhouse or in well lit tanks covered with a piece of glass. It also thrives in terrariums. It requires temperatures above 68° F (20° C). With favorable conditions the plant develops very quickly and soon covers the whole surface of an aquarium. It can be cultivated even in moist sand, where it tolerates lower temperatures and hibernates readily.

This fully floating plant forms a tangle of delicate roots on the surface layer of the water. It is very suitable for aquariums.

OTTELIA (III. 316, 329)

Ottelias are among the most beautiful aquatic plants but are unfortunately of an annual character. Hibernation in the tank is possible, but difficult to ensure. *Ottelia* species bloom readily, however, and each flower produces seeds; the flowers are hermaphroditic and self-fertile.

Limnobium stoloniferum.

Unlike other members of the Hydrocharitaceae, these plants grow in moderately shaded environments and in water with slightly acid reaction; they are plants of the forests and jungles. Leaves are either with long petioles and broad blades or without petioles and broadly strap-shaped; they are often somewhat spirally coiled.

After maturing the seeds can be dried and preserved for a maximum of one year; after this time they lose their capacity to germinate. When sown in medium fine sand at temperatures above 77° F (25° C) they germinate very readily. The seedlings should be developed in diffused but adequate light; upon reaching a height of 5 to 10 cm they are transplanted into the aquarium. They can easily be damaged by snails.

Vallisneria portugalensis.

Vallisneria tortissima.

The forty species of this genus are distributed throughout the tropics. In recent years some Australian and American species have been imported to Europe, notably *Ottelia brasiliensis* (Planch.) Walp., that has leaves which are dark green with red-brown stripes, strap-like, and 20 cm by 50 mm wide.

Only the species *O. alismoides* has been cultivated in aquariums, and it is the least demanding.

OTTELIA ALISMOIDES (L.) Pers.

O. alismoides is found over an extensive area from northern Africa (Egypt) across tropical southern Asia and the Philippine Islands to Australia and Japan. It is an annual plant that rarely hibernates. The leaves of seedlings are strap-shaped and almost sessile. Adult plants have leaf blades that are 5 to 10 cm long and 25 to 75 mm wide, on petioles with a length of 10 to 15 cm. The leaves are light green, elliptical, cordate at the base, and moderately undulate or spoon-shaped. The flowers open at the surface and consist of an ovate green calyx with three white petals.

This *Ottelia* species is cultivated in a diffused but adequate illumination, at temperatures from 72° to 83° F (22° to 28° C). It does not stand cold water and is very sensitive to lime. It can not be propagated vegetatively, and over winter can be maintained only in a well lit heated tank with additional artificial light; snails should not be present, nor too many fish kept in the tank.

VALLISNERIA (WILD CELERY, EEL GRASS) (Ill. 24, 98)

Vallisneria is the genus most commonly seen in aquariums and which has become a symbol of the hobby. These plants grow in any type of water, even a very hard medium, and are unexacting with respect to both the nature of the substrate and the pH of the water. They require a generous light, but if the aquarist is content with slow growth he can cultivate them in the subdued light of an indoor aquarium without artificial illumination.

Vallisneria species are dioecious and both male and female plants are found in our aquariums. The female flowers grow on long, thin, spirally coiled scapes; they are inconspicuous, greenish, and float on the surface. The male flowers develop at the base of the plants, become detached, and then rise to the surface, where they open and the pollen is carried by the water to the female flowers. In spite of flowering abundantly in tanks, seeds are not produced even if both male and female plants are present.

Vallisneria species are ideal for background planting in the aquarium. Their leaves are as a rule very long and coil close to the surface so they form dense tangles suitable for breeding purposes of a great number of fishes. The tallest species of *Vallisneria* produce firm ribbon-shaped leaves 30 mm wide which are useful for spawning the bigger fishes of the family Cichlidae. All species of *Vallisneria* propagate readily.

Through selective cultivation a great number of forms have been obtained differing from each other in size, structure, and color of the leaves. Various apparently distinct kinds of *Vallisneria* have recently come onto the market, but it is not clear which of these have come into existence artificially and which may be new varieties or forms developed in nature.

The genus is distributed all over the tropical and subtropical regions, in some places penetrating into the temperate zone. About seven species are known, four of which are cultivated in aquariums.

VALLISNERIA AMERICANA Michx.
Syn: *V. spiralis* f. *tortifolia* Wendt; *V. torta* Hort. (III. 336, 339)

This *Vallisneria* species is found in the southern part of the United States. Its leaves are substantially shorter (30 to 40 cm long) than other species and closely coiled.

V. americana is exacting with respect to the composition of the water but less particular as to illumination. It grows badly in hard water, where coarse crystals of limy salts are secreted on its leaves. It requires higher temperatures than *V. spiralis*. *V. americana* is commonly known among aquarists by the incorrect name *V. spiralis* forma *tortifolia* Wendt., abbreviated to *V. torta*.

VALLISNERIA ASIATICA Miki (III. 339)

This species from eastern Asia and Japan resembles *V. spiralis* except that its leaves are grass-green and in well developed specimens they are stiff. The leaf margins are finely serrulate.

It is cultivated in the same way as the other species, but it reproduces more slowly; it is not common. *V. asiatica* is more suitable for ordinary aquariums than the better known *V. spiralis* because its leaves do not form tangles below the surface and consequently do not shade the bottom; neither do their tips tend to rot and disintegrate.

VALLISNERIA GIGANTEA Graebner (GIANT VAL) (III. 67, 336)
The giant val is found in the Philippine Islands and in New Guinea. It has a bulbiform rhizome with a tangle of not very long roots. From the rhizome ten to fifteen ribbon-like leaves arise that are about 20 to 35 mm wide and 0.9 to 2 meters long; they are bright green, usually with fifteen longitudinal obliquely connected

Vallisneria gigantea. Photo by T.J. Horeman.

Vallisneria americana. Photo by T.J. Horeman.

Bright yellow inflorescence of
an unidentified *Cabomba*.

Cabomba australis.

337

veins. The plant is dioecious; female plants are the ones most generally present in aquariums.

This tall plant requires a large (deep) aquarium where it can develop properly. It is not exacting with respect to the composition of the substrate and water, but needs a higher temperature than the other common species of *Vallisneria* (above 68° F, 20° C). Plants blossom throughout the summer but do not produce seeds and are propagated vegetatively by separating young plants from the rhizome runners. Propagation is much slower than that of smaller species of *Vallisneria*. If the aquarist wants to obtain a greater number of individuals, he has to replant them repeatedly from March to August. Two to three weeks after being established, one parent plant produces two to three root runners on which three to seven new plants arise; after this, usually no further runners appear. As soon as the runners have grown sufficiently strong they are uprooted, together with the parent plant, and planted again. Propagation then continues.

VALLISNERIA GIGANTEA var. RUBRA Hort.

Var. *rubra* has been imported only lately. It resembles the preceding green form, but its leaves are red-brown with distinct dark veins. It is not known whether it is an undescribed natural variety, a new species, or a horticultural form obtained by selection. As alleged by importers it occurs in nature in association with the initial species, *V. gigantea*.

VALLISNERIA PORTUGALENSIS Hort.   (III. 332)

The origin of this plant is unknown; it is probably some variety of *V. denseserrulata*. In the aquarium the leaves are 30 to 40 cm long (longer than those of *V. americana*), up to 10 to 15 mm wide, and coiled five to six times; margins are lighter and undulate or curled. It tolerates slightly acid water and half shade and can be cultivated with *Cryptocoryne* species.

VALLISNERIA SPIRALIS L.

V. spiralis has been recorded throughout the tropical zones, but it occurs mainly in the subtropical areas of the world; it also appears in the temperate zone of Europe (Italy and France). The character of the plant is the same as that of *V. gigantea*. Leaves are bright green, ribbon-shaped, 120 cm long or even longer, and 5 to 12 mm wide, usually with five longitudinal veins. The leaves are straight only in young plants; upon reaching a length of 10 to 15 cm they are generally moderately coiled once or thrice along their length.

Vallisneria asiatica.   *Vallisneria americana.*

Lobelia splendens.

Not all species of *Lemna* found in many ponds are suited for the aquarium.
Photo by C.O. Masters.

Mayaca growing emersed on swampy ground in Brazil. Photo by T.J. Horeman.

This species grows in any normal aquarium conditions and is the most common plant in aquariums in Europe. It is not exacting as to the composition of the planting medium or water. If given a generous light it propagates quickly and soon fills up the whole aquarium with a dense growth.

VALLISNERIA TORTISSIMA Hort.   (III. 333)

The origin of this most decorative *Vallisneria* is unknown. The leaves with a length of 40 to 50 cm are usually only 5 mm wide and are coiled fifteen to twenty-five times. This plant is very resistant and grows in the same conditions as the common *V. spiralis*.

LEMNACEAE (Duckweed Family)

The family Lemnaceae is represented for the most part by species that float on the surface of the water. They represent the smallest of the monocotyledonous plants. The body of the plant is formed by a single flat internode with a rootlet.

Minute flowers are produced very rarely (even in nature) so that the plants are virtually never propagated from seeds. Vegetative propagation is the most common method of reproduction and in good conditions a new plant may arise every thirty to forty hours; thus it is clearly capable of speedy reproduction.

The family is distributed from the tropics to the temperate zones and contains the genera *Lemna* (duckweed), *Spirodela* (great duckweed,) *Wolffia* (watermeal), and *Wolfiella*; altogether there are about thirty species.

Since they reproduce very quickly they are not suitable for aquariums, covering the surface with a closely intermeshed growth so that the space below is deeply shaded. If the surface needs to be shaded there are other, taller plants at hand whose growth can be regulated. An aquarium infested by duckweed can not be cleaned properly because the individual plantlets sink and get caught in the tangle of other plants at the bottom, where they escape our notice. Later they rise again and create new colonies. For this reason they are regarded as a weed in the aquarium and they should be destroyed as soon as possible if they happen to be brought in accidentally along with fish food or other plants. Only one species, *Lemna trisulca*, is of any use in the aquarium, while the other species can be used for covering water areas in terrariums and paludariums.

LEMNA (DUCKWEED)   (III. 25, 341)

The genus *Lemna* includes nine species which have flat, exceptionally swollen internodes with a single root. They are known to reproduce vegetatively very fast.

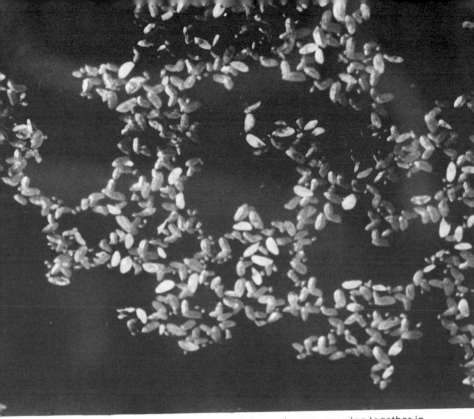

Very tiny *Wolffia* scattered among much larger *Lemna,* growing together in a pond. Photo by Dr. D. Sculthorpe.

LEMNA TRISULCA L. (CHAIN OF STARS or IVY-LEAVED DUCKWEED)

This species is found all over the·world. The translucent internodes are ovately lanceolate to lanceolate. Four to fifteen plants are connected to each other by narrow stalks so that they form pronged, branching, grass-green colonies. In nature they live on the surface of the water or in a submersed form attached to other plants. It is the only species of Lemnaceae suitable for use in the aquarium. With regard to external conditions it is not very exacting; plants hibernate readily at temperatures around 68° F (20° C).

WOLFFIA (WATERMEAL) (III. 343)

The smallest flowering plant in the world is found in the genus *Wolffia.* The body is only 1 mm long, floating on the surface of the water, without roots. The individual plantlets are hardly visible, but they can form a solid cover on the surface of the water.

A male *Colisa lalia* guarding the bubblenest situated in a clump of bladder-wort (*Utricularia*). Photo by H.J. Richter.

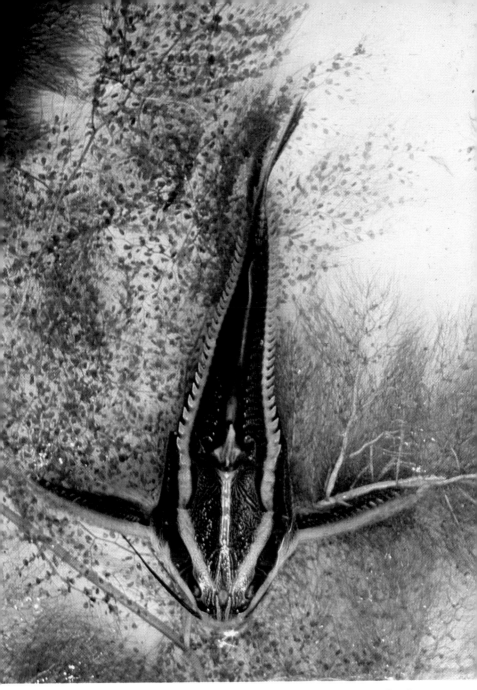

An armored catfish (*Acanthodoras spinosissimus*) resting on top of a cluster of *Utricularia*. Note the conspicuous bladders on many of the branches. Photo by Dr. Herbert R. Axelrod.

LENTIBULARIACEAE (Bladderwort Family)

Water, marsh, and land species whose leaves are adapted for catching minute animals represent this family. There are four genera altogether, and not all the species grow submersed.

UTRICULARIA (BLADDERWORT) (III. 11, 70, 344, 345, 348)

Some species of bladderwort are tropical and subtropical plants which grow as epiphytes entwined on trees and bushes and as land forms. Altogether about 260 species are known which are distributed mainly in the tropics. The aquatic *Utricularia* species of the temperate zone are mostly annual, but those from the tropics are annual and perennial as well. The leaves are filiform to hair-like segments with minute snapping bladders, some of the leaves projecting above the surface. In nature the plants flower irregularly, while in aquariums they flower very rarely and consequently are identified only with difficulty. Only the tropical species are fit for the aquarium.

UTRICULARIA EXOLETA R. Brown

In Europe this species is found only in Portugal, but otherwise it occurs in North Africa, Ethiopia, tropical Africa, tropical Asia, and in Australia. Small leaves with very minute bladders are characteristic for this species. The floral stalk is 2.5 to 10 cm long and the flowers are white or yellow, but it does not flower in the aquarium.

U. exoleta is very resistant and can withstand bright light as well as shaded conditions. It is not particular with regard to the type of water, but does best in a soft, moderately acid medium. A great range of temperatures is tolerated; it grows well at 68° to 86° F, 18° to 30° C. Bladders are developed in water containing minute animals, but the bladders are too small to capture fish fry. Dense tangles of delicate stems which grow very fast are formed. By dividing the always rootless stems, the plant is propagated.

In recent years some bigger, undetermined species have been imported. These are cultivated in the same way as *U. exoleta*.

LILIACEAE

Many of the well known garden plants, such as the tulip, snowdrop, lily, and others are included in this family. Although many representatives occur in rather moist places, these plants have not until now been cultivated in aquariums. It is only recently that the two following genera have been imported from tropical Asia to Europe.

CHLOROPHYTUM BICHETII Backer (III. 400)

This plant (native to Malaya) has twenty to thirty leaves originating from a rhizome which has whitish underground bulblets that are pointed or elliptical at the tips and 10 to 15 mm long. The leaves are strap-like, narrowed at both ends, and green with parallel nerves that are very distinct. Leaf margins are trimmed with golden yellow. Flowers are white, about 10 mm long, and resemble tiny lilies.

Chlorophytum propagates by producing tufts that can be easily separated from each other. Propagation is effective only in emersed cultivation. Plants which are transplanted under water acclimatize quickly and without difficulty. They are not sensitive to changes in the pH, but do not tolerate new water. Growth under water is rather slow. This plant is a promising aquarium novelty.

OPHIOPOGON (III. 350)

Leaves of *Ophiopogon* grow arranged in a row from the roots, not in rosettes. They are stiff, leathery, strap-like, bending in an arch on both sides, and green with distinctly protruding dark and parallel nerves.

Recently imported is *O. japonicus* Ker-Gawler, which reaches the height of 7.5 to 10 cm, and another most beautiful but still undetermined species which grows to a height of 25 to 35 cm.

Both species propagate emersed from long root runners or from short rhizome runners and can be transplanted under water easily. These species will certainly become a popular addition to the list of hardy aquarium plants.

LIMNOCHARATICEAE

This relatively small family contains just four genera. The genus *Limnocharis* (with two species) is not used in aquatics, the plants being unable to grow permanently under water. The same is valid for the genus *Tenagocharis*. Only *Hydrocleis* can be cultivated in indoor aquariums. This genus with nine species is very decorative and widely cultivated. The plants are usually partly floating and partly rooted.

HYDROCLEIS NYMPHOIDES (Humb. et Bonpl.) Buch.

H. nymphoides is found all over tropical South America and is often cultivated as a decorative aquatic greenhouse plant. It is often confused with similar species of the genus *Nymphoides* of the family Menyanthaceae.

Flower of *Utricularia* species from Guyana, South America. Photo by T.J. Horeman.

Utricularia species with beautiful purple flowers from Guyana, South America. Photo by T.J. Horeman.

Two species of *Nymphoides: N. peltata* (the single yellow flower on the left) and *N. indica* (white flowers). Photo by C.O. Masters.

Flower and bud of
Barclaya longifolia.
Photo by T.J.
Horeman.

Ophiopogon japonicus.

Hydrocleis possesses floating leaves and is seldom used in aquariums. It blossoms very readily, however, and the very beautiful flowers, up to 50 mm in diameter, campanulate, and bright yellow in color, are good for decorating aquariums.

The fast growing rhizome has creeping shoots that root in the substrate and develop long, tubular petioles (up to 7.5 mm thick), bearing at first submersed, later floating, blades about 7.5 to 10 cm long and 50 to 75 mm wide. These blades are ovate, cordate at the base, and leather-like; the upper surface is glossy grass-green, the lower surface light green. The flowers develop at the nodes of the floral stalk at the same time as the new leaves that root. In favorable conditions it flowers from spring until the end of summer.

H. nymphoides is cultivated in a rich soil in a well lit aquarium with soft water. The surface of the water should be generously supplied with light. *Hydrocleis* is content with indoor temperatures.

LOBELIACEAE (Lobelia Family)

This family contains about thirty genera including ten genera that are aquatic. Only *Lobelia* is cultivated in aquariums. There are about 365 species in this genus; many of the species are found in wet or occasionally flooded regions.

L. dortmanna, a typical submersed species, occurs in the acid lakes of North America and sub-Arctic Europe. It has a rosette of submersed leaves and an emersed inflorescence. This plant is often cited in aquatic literature, but it is not cultivated and not suitable for aquariums. Other species, such as *L. paludosa* Nutt. from North America, *L. aquatica* Cham. from South America, and *L. asiatica* Lam. from Southeast Asia, are also not suitable for indoor tanks.

Commonly cultivated in aquariums are two red flowering, paludal species (other *Lobelia* species have blue or white flowers).

LOBELIA CARDINALIS L.   (III. 352, 353)

L. cardinalis is native to the United States, where it grows from the temperate zone to the warm areas of Florida. In emersed form it develops erect stems with alternate, lanceolate leaves. The flowers are very decorative, bright red. For this reason it is often cultivated in gardens. Emersed plants are propagated; the vegetative tips (10 to 15 cm long) are transplanted under water. Plants from gardens or natural environments are not suitable for this purpose. Only plants that are grown in high humidity (such as a greenhouse) can be transplanted under water. Submersed plants are usually sold under the incorrect name of "*Cryptofolia.*" Under water they grow rather slowly; but with aged water, good lighting, and a neutral pH, they usually grow better. *L. cardinalis* is planted into groups with three to five stems. Under water the stems are white-green and the leaves are bright green, longer and wider than in the emersed forms, usually 5 to 10 cm long. The margins are dentate.

LOBELIA SPLENDENS Willd.   (III. 340)

This species from Mexico differs from *L. cardinalis* in being more robust and reaching up to a meter in height. The stems of *L. cardinalis* have underwater leaves that are always arranged alternately, while *L. splendens* in submersed conditions forms rosettes of leaves that are bright green or red and up to 10 cm in length.

L. splendens is cultivated in the same way as *L. cardinalis*. It tolerates being in half-shade and adapts well to the warm water of a tropical aquarium.

Lòbelia cardinalis.

Flower of *Lobelia cardinalis*.

Ammania senegalensis

LYTHRACEAE (Loosestrife Family)

The Lythraceae comprises herbs, bushes, or trees with opposite leaves (rarely whorled). About 500 species in 25 genera are known, the majority of which are found in the tropics (especially in America), with a few in the temperate zone. Only three marsh genera (*Ammania, Rotala,* and *Lythrum*) are distributed in both hemispheres. Seven genera of this family contain aquatic plants. Only *Ammania, Didiplis,* and *Rotala* are cultivated.

AMMANIA

Thirty *Ammania* species are known coming from the swampy areas of America, Africa, Asia, Australia, and Europe. They usually have an erect stem, leaves that are smooth-edged, grass-green, and oppositely arranged. Inconspicuous flowers are formed at the axil of the leaves. Of several plants tested, *A. senegalensis* or *A. latifolia* were found to be the best.

354

AMMANIA SENEGALENSIS Lam. (III. 354, 356)

This species is distributed in the northern parts of Africa and is also found as a weed in rice fields. The creeping stem (usually reddish) is 2.5 to 5 mm thick. There are three varieties known: one with green leaves, another with narrow leaves, and a third one with wide red leaves. Those plants with green leaves are not suitable for aquariums because they do not grow permanently under water. The leaves of the red varieties are ovate, 25 mm long and 10 to 12 mm wide, and their margins are undulate (the broad-leaved variety). The leaves of the narrow-leaved variety are about 50 mm long and 7.5 to 10 mm wide, with nearly curled margins. The flowers are pink or reddish and 5 to 7.5 mm wide.

An *Ammania* plant is cultivated in a poor substrate in soft or medium hard water with a good light. In winter it must be provided additional artificial light, otherwise the lower leaves drop so that at the beginning of spring the existing tips have to be cut off and replanted. If it grows well under water in summer, the tips can be pruned and the main stem will then branch out; in this way bright green, very ornamental bushes can be obtained.

DIDIPLIS DIANDRIA (Nutt. ex DC.)
Syn: *Peplis diandria* Nutt. ex DC.

This is the only species of *Didiplis* found in America; it occurs in the United States, from states in the temperate zone to Texas and Florida and in Mexico. *D. diandria* is an aquatic or a marsh plant. The stem is densely leaved, prostrate in emersed plants, and floats in water; the leaves (15 to 25 mm long) are linear, green, opposite, arranged cross-wise, and so dense that the stem resembles a spruce branch. Sessile reddish flowers are formed regularly under water. This is one of the most beautiful plants in our aquariums.

The plant is cultivated in soft to medium hard water in a reasonable light, but artificial light will also do. It requires temperatures about 68° F (20° C), but withstands colder as well as very warm water without being damaged. This species grows relatively slowly. The plant is propagated by planting broken fragments of the stem.

ROTALA
Rotala is widely distributed all over the world and contains fifty species. All the species are aquatic or amphibious. Many of them are found as weeds in rice fields and irrigation channels.

Ammania senegalensis, submersed plant.

Inflorescence of
Rotala macrantha.

Rotala macrantha. Photo by Rodney Jonklaas.

ROTALA ROTUNDIFOLIA (Roxb.) Koehne
Incorrect name: R. *indica* Koehne (III. 359)

R. *rotundifolia* comes from India and is found mainly in rice fields. Along with the cultivation of rice it has been dispersed over a wide area, reaching as far as the Caspian Sea.

Emersed stems are creeping, up to one meter long, and take root easily. Leaves are about 15 mm long and 12 mm wide, opposite, round, and without petioles; the lower surface reddish with very distinct veins.

After transplanting to an underwater environment, dissimilar leaves are formed on the stems; the leaves are narrowly lanceolate, opposite, and arranged cross-wise. The upper surface is olive-green, while the lower surface is red-brown. Submersed plants develop very well and branch abundantly, especially if their growing tips are cut off.

R. *rotundifolia* and D. *diandria* are cultivated under the same conditions, but R. *rotundifolia* does well in any kind of water and is less particular as to light.

ROTALA MACRANTHA Koehne (III. 357)
This plant is similar to the preceding species, but the leaves are larger (up to 10 to 25 mm long), wide, rounded not only in emersed but also in submersed cultures, and red-brown to light red. Growth is not fast, It is cultivated in half-shade with cryptocorynes.

ROTALA WALLICHII (Hook. f.) Koehne
Incorrect name: *Mayaca* sp. from India

In recent years this plant has been imported from India and is usually offered under the incorrect name *Mayaca*. Submersed R. *wallichii* resembles *Mayaca* greatly. Leaves in whorls are 10 to 12 mm long and only 1.25 mm wide, green or brown-green, and the tips are often reddish or yellow-gold. The inflorescence above the surface is similar to other species of *Rotala*. The flowers in whorls are light lilac.

Cultivation is similar to that of R. *rotundifolia*.

MAYACACEAE (III. 341)

This family comprises of the unique genus *Mayaca* with about ten species. They are found in America, from the southeastern United States to Paraguay, and in Angola (Africa). The stems are submersed, floating, or creeping; leaves are linear, very narrow, and arranged spirally. Flowers are white, pink, or violet and 10 to 15 mm wide.

Rotala rotundifolia.

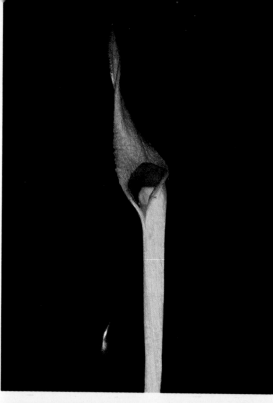

Inflorescence of
Cryptocoryne beckettii.

Cryptocoryne beckettii.

Cryptocoryne bullosa var. *bullosa*. Photo by T.J. Horeman.

Flowering plants of *Cryptocoryne ciliata* photographed in Thailand. Photo by T.J. Horeman.

Mayaca plants are occasionally imported, but being very fine and fragile they usually arrive damaged. We do not have enough experience with the cultivation of this genus. The best known species is *Mayaca sellowiana* Kunth.

MENYANTHACEAE (Buckbean Family)

Species floating on the water or growing amphibiously on the banks represent the family Menyanthaceae. There are about forty species and five genera. The genera *Nephrophyllidium*, *Menyanthes*, and *Liparophyllum* have one species each, *Villarsia* has sixteen species, and *Nymphoides* about twenty species. These are distributed mainly in the tropics and subtropics, but they also reach the temperate zone.

Most species of the genus *Villarsia* come from Australia. They are thermophilic marsh plants with beautiful yellow flowers suited for indoor cultivation under marsh conditions. Submersed they stay healthy only if given good daylight conditions.

The genus *Nymphoides* (= *Limnanthemum*, floating heart) is the only typical aquatic member of the whole family.

NYMPHOIDES (FLOATING HEART)

Plants of the genus *Nymphoides* are perennial aquatic plants developing long, thin petioles from a stiff rhizome. The leaf blades are submersed (though usually floating on the surface) and round or oval with the base sometimes cordately incised. Leaves are 5 to 10 cm long according to the species. Their flowers are campanulate, up to 50 mm long and bright yellow or white with fringed petals.

They are cultivated in deep, well illuminated aquariums; in shallow water they form floating leaves that are not too suitable for aquariums. Altogether about twenty species are known. In the temperate zone only a single species, *N. peltata* (Gmel.) O. Kuntze, is found, but it is not fit for the aquarium. *N. indica* (L.) O. Kuntze and *N. cristata* (Roxb.) O. Kuntze are common weeds in rice fields. (III. 349)

NYMPHOIDES AQUATICA (Walt.) O. Kuntze
(UNDERWATER BANANA PLANT) (III. 12)

N. aquatica comes from the United States, where it grows in shallow waters up to a depth of 60 cm. The rhizome is formed by elongated tubers (banana-shaped and in bunches) from 2 to 4 cm long. In winter the plant forms wide blades that are submersed and 5 to 10 cm long. These are green, cordate, and rounded with a lobate base and undulate margins. In summer the blades are floating and 10 to 15 cm long. The upper surface is bright green while the lower surface is purplish red and covered with spongy tissue.

The flowers grow 20 to 40 mm below the leaf blade (on the petiole) and are campanulate, white, fringed on the margins, and 15 to 20 mm in diameter. In this position the roots and leaves grow; young plants arise by this method.

N. aquatica can be cultivated permanently submersed in very poor sand and in very dark situations. If too much light is received, it forms floating leaves that shade the whole aquarium.

NYMPHOIDES HUMBOLDTIANA (Kunth) O.K.

Submersed leaves are formed by this plant only for a short period, therefore it is cultivated in greenhouse pools for its numerous beautiful lace-like white flowers with very long fringes on the margins.

NAJADACEAE (Pondweed Family)

This family (with only a single genus) consists of submersed annuals usually rooted in the ground; the tropical species do well in the aquarium. The plant is profusely branched, with simple leaves that are either opposite or in whorls. Simple, minute flowers (monoecious or dioecious) arise at the axil of the leaves.

NAJAS

About fifty species of najas are known from the tropics, subtropics, and temperate zone. The leaves are linear, with dentate and serrate margins. Najas can be found in freshwater lakes and ponds as well as in brackish waters of rivers. They are not exacting plants; some species grow very fast, very soon overcrowding an aquarium and therefore are used only as spawning plants for fish. Others grow more slowly and are successful aquarium plants. Propagation is by stem division.

They require generous lighting. Some species have no special requirements as to temperature (from 59° to 77° F, 15° to 25° C), while others grow best at temperatures above 77° F (25° C). They will also grow floating freely.

Various species, such as *Najas falciculata* Del from East India, *N. horrida* A. Br. (= *N. pectinata* Magnus) from tropical Africa, *N. guadalupensis* (Spreng.) Magnus from America, *N. interrupta* K. Schum. from Africa, and *N. madagascariensis* Rendle from Madagascar, are not suitable aquarium plants; development is very fast and in favorable conditions the plants soon overgrow the whole tank. The fragile and breakable stems give rise to new plants by stem division. The most suitable species for indoor aquariums is *N. indica; N. graminea* is very good as a spawning medium.

Aglaonema species with inflorescence collected in Brunei, Borneo and photographed by T.J. Horeman.

Collecting cryptocorynes in a river in Malaya. Some plants are seen partially emersed on a sand bank. Photo by T.J. Horeman.

Inflorescence of *Cryptocoryne bullosa*. Photo by T.J. Horeman.

Najas graminea.

NAJAS GRAMINEA Del. (III. 366)

N. graminea grows in the Mediterranean area, in subtropical
and tropical Africa, in Asia, and in Australia. In nature the stems
reach a length of 70 cm and are profusely branching from the very
bottom and densely leaved. The leaves are narrowly linear (15 to
25 mm long) with strongly undulate margins having thirty to fifty
very fine denticles. The species can be identified very easily by this
characteristic.

In the aquarium the stems of N. graminea are very fragile and
their fragments (10 to 15 cm long) form dense, light green, usually

Najas indica.

unrooted tufts. The plant requires soft water, tolerates bright as well as fairly shady conditions, and grows well even in winter.

NAJAS INDICA (Willd.) Cham.

Syn: *Najas kingii* Rendle

(III. 367)

This plant from tropical eastern Asia has underwater stems that are almost unbranched, but above the surface they are very profusely branched. Leaves are narrowly linear, up to 35 mm long, falcate, and bright green; the leaf margins have sixteen to nineteen teeth that are never longer than half the width of the blade.

Flowering *Limosella subulata.*

Rorippa aquatica, cultivated submersed.

N. indica is the most beautiful representative of the family. It requires soft or medium hard water and either a fairly good light or at least not too much shade. Decorative tufts are formed, while the stiff stems are relatively firm (not fragile). Even if fully floating it grows well and is propagated by means of fragments detached from the stems.

NYMPHAEACEAE (Water-lily Family)

The family Nymphaeaceae is represented by typical aquatic plants which are distributed everywhere in the tropical, subtropical, and temperate zones. The greatest number of these plants are found in the tropics. External organs of this family are most varied. Some plants are entirely submersed, such as the beautiful *Barclaya*. Altogether six genera with 65 species are known.

The major part of the water-lily family develops submersed leaves only for a temporary period (in the beginning of spring before the stage of sexual maturity). The typical leaves float on the surface of the water, as in the genera *Nymphaea, Nuphar, Victoria, Brasenia*, and others. Only the genus *Nelumbo* (lotus) forms emersed leaves growing out of the water on long petioles. The land forms of *Nuphar* are dwarf plants and clearly do not thrive well.

Most of the species in this family belong to the genus *Nymphaea* (water-lily) with 40 species. They are well known beautiful flowering plants with floating leaves. Some of them flower in the daytime, others at night. All of them require a resting period either at low temperatures or away from the water in dry or moderately moist sand. They are therefore of no use in the aquarium. In addition they are large plants; a single plant normally requires 10 to 30 square feet of surface area. An exception is the dwarf water-lily, *Nymphaea baumii* Rehn. et Henkel., whose floating leaves are only 20 to 30 mm long. There is another somewhat bigger horticultural hybrid, *Nymphaea daubenyana*, with leaves that are about 10 cm long. *N. daubenyana* forms only floating leaves, but the delicate blue flowers are very decorative and aromatic as well. Propagation is simple; new plants arise on the base of floating leaves. *N. lotus* is a unique species of water-lily that is commonly cultivated in aquariums.

BARCLAYA LONGIFOLIA Well. (III. 349, 373)

The most beautiful of the Nymphaeaceae in our aquariums originally came from Thailand and Burma. It is, however, a very exacting plant. Rhizomes are formed from which a rosette of leaves develops; these leaves are lanceolate, 30 cm long and 25 to 40 mm wide, cordate at the base, and gradually taper toward the apex. The upper surface of the leaf is glossy green or brown-green, while the lower surface is deep red-purple. They are very thin, nearly pellicular, and with moderately undulate margins.

A solitary flower, which opens on the surface of the water, is formed on the scape. The upper surface of the petal is purple-red, the lower surface greenish. Flowers are self-fertile and are pollinated even if the flower never reaches the surface or fails to open (this is the general rule in aquariums). Seeds are softly prickly and germinate well.

Barclaya requires a fairly rich soil without too much lime, soft water, and sufficient light. It thrives best in aquariums with illumination coming from above. The fine leaves are easily damaged by snails and fish and the plant is consequently not suitable for aquariums that are well stocked with fish.

It is exacting with respect to the temperature, which is the greatest drawback, requiring 77° to 86° F (25° to 30° C) to flower and produce seeds. For growth *Barclaya* needs a minimum of 68° F (20° C); the plant does not thrive at lower temperatures and generally dies at 59° F (15° C).

Three other species of *Barclaya* come from Southeast Asia, but only *B. mottleyi* is imported to Europe. We have not been successful in the cultivation of this species.

NUPHAR
(YELLOW POND-LILY, SPATTERDOCK)

Nuphar is distributed mostly over maritime areas of the temperate zone, although some species extend considerably toward the north. They grow in still or slowly moving waters, usually of a rather deep nature. Whereas the genus *Nymphaea* develops floating leaves soon after germinating, *Nuphar* generally grows for two to three years as a submersed plant and only then develops floating leaves and flowers. The submersed leaves are quite different from those formed on the surface. Being light green, pellicular, and fragile, they appear quite decorative alongside the grass-green leaves of other plants.

Specimens obtained from seeds can be kept submersed in the aquarium for several years. In nature floating leaves appear only on plants growing in still waters, while in sufficiently fast running waters old plants (2 meters tall) can be found flowering abundantly and possessing only submersed leaves. These robust plants are not suitable for transplanting into an aquarium.

Flowers of *Nuphar luteum.*

Nuphar luteum.

Barclaya longifolia.

The yellow water-lily is propagated from seeds. By dividing the rhizome one can cultivate tall, well developed plants that, however, do not take root but die after consuming all the food reserves.

Seeds collected from nature or the aquarium are hibernated in water at a temperature around 41° F (5° C). In early spring they are sown on the surface of a bed of fine sand at a temperature of 64° to 68° F (18° to 20° C). Germination is quick and the seedlings take root; upon reaching a height of about 50 mm they are transplanted into water 10 to 20 cm deep and later, when they are about 10 cm tall, finally placed in the aquarium.

Nuphar species are cultivated in a fairly rich medium in a well lighted situation; they are not particular with regard to temperature. In nature they have a period of rest in winter; since they are not from the tropics, they often die because of high temperatures and a short day which do not suit them. On account of the latter point they should be given additional artificial light in winter.

About twenty species, all capable of cultivation in aquariums, are known. In Europe there are strictly speaking two native species, of which *N. luteum* is the most common species. The yellow water-lilies do not flower in aquariums and are identified only with difficulty.

NUPHAR LUTEUM (L.) Smith (III. 372)

N. luteum grows in Europe, North Africa, and northern Asia. Plants living in nature reach a height of about 2 meters. Submersed leaves are round, with the leaf base cordately or sharply incised; in the aquarium they are generally 10 to 15 cm in diameter, light green, moderately undulate, and with petioles twice as long as the blade. It is cultivated in a tolerably rich medium with adequate illumination. This plant can stand lower temperatures (about 53° to 59° F, 12° to 15° C) but does best at 68° to 77° F (20° to 25° C). In dark aquariums it often dies in winter, especially young seedlings with insufficiently developed rhizomes.

NUPHAR PUMILUM (Timm.) D.C.

This species is found in central and northern Europe and in Siberia. The flowers are conspicuously smaller than *N. luteum,* but otherwise resemble it very strongly. In the aquarium the two species are not distinguishable. *N. pumilum* is not suitable for indoor aquariums. In nature it grows in cool places, so the plant can not endure warm water (above 68° F, 20° C); it can be induced to hibernate only with difficulty.

NUPHAR SAGITTIFOLIUM Pursh.

N. sagittifolium is native to South Carolina in the United States and belongs to the subtropical group of aquarium plants. The most beautiful *Nuphar*, it is very rarely seen in European aquariums. The leaves are long, arrow-shaped, much longer than the petiole (up to 50 cm long), which varies according to the depth of the water. The leaf blade is 20 to 40 cm long, its base 7 to 10 cm wide. The whole leaf surface is strongly undulate, with the margins curved upward. Leaves are light green and pellucid. This species does not produce floating leaves and is fully adapted to submersed existence, thus it is of greater value to aquarists.

It withstands high temperatures (to 82° F, 28° C) very well and hibernates very well, too. A most beautiful and rewarding aquarium plant which however does not usually flower in the aquarium and is propagated only with great difficulty. The plant requires soft, moderately acid or moderately alkaline water and generous light; mature plants are not sensitive to the composition of the substrate.

NYMPHAEA LOTUS var. JAPONICUS Hort. (III. 376, 377)

As far as it is known this is a unique species of *Nymphaea* fit for aquariums. We are not sure if it is really the species *N. lotus*. If the plant receives enough light; it forms floating leaves and consequently is not fit for aquariums. If it is cultivated only in the shade to half shade (lit from the side, not from above), only submersed decorative leaves are formed. The leaves are 20 to 30 cm long; their petioles are about twice as long as the blades, which are membranous, transparent, round, with pointed lobes at the base, at the most 10 cm long and about the same width, with distinct nerves. There are several very colorful varieties. The basic forms have green blades, but some varieties have red-brown blades or green blades with brown spots.

In containers well illuminated from above, floating leaves develop instead of submersed ones and possibly flowers. The flowers are 75 mm in diameter, snow-white, and open at night. They only open in the morning for a short period, then close. The flowers are self-fertile, so it is possible to collect from each bloom several hundred seeds that are easily germinated. However it takes a long time to cultivate seedlings, so the generative mode of propagation is seldom used. *N. lotus* is propagated by very long root-runners, at the tips of which new plants arise vegetatively. The leaves, being membranous, fragile, and soft, are very often damaged by water snails.

A horticultural variety of *Nymphaea lotus* var. *japonica*.

A horticultural variety of *Nymphaea* species called pink pearl. Photo by C.O. Masters.

NOTE: The large tropical members of Nymphaeaceae, such as *Victoria* and *Euryale*, are only suitable for large tropical ponds. The smallest species of *Nymphaea*, *N. micrantha* Guill. and Perr. (only 50 mm tall), has not yet been imported to Europe. Another very interesting plant is *Ondinea purpurea* Hartog from northwestern Australia. It is similar to *Barclaya longifolia* and occurs in small streams, up to 60 cm depth, that dry out for five to seven months of the year. During the dry period it aestivates as corms. Its cultivation is still unknown. See the family Cabombaceaea for the genera *Cabomba* and *Brasenia*.

ONAGRACEAE (Oenotheraceae) (Evening Primrose Family)

This family consists of annual to perennial herbs, also (rarely) bushes and trees. The family is divided into more than twenty genera with about 650 species, the majority of which come from the temperate to the subtropical zone of the Americas (principally California, Mexico, and Brazíl); few are found in the tropics. Many of them are well-known indoor flowering.plants, such as the South American genus *Fuchsia*. Africa, Asia, and Europe are relatively poor in representatives of this family. Many of the species are cultivated in gardens and rockeries. Some species grow on river banks, but only *Ludwigia* can grow permanently under water.

LUDWIGIA (FALSE LOOSESTRIFE) (III. 71)

Ludwigia has small, inconspicuous flowers and is mainly found in North and South America. Only a few species grow in tropical Africa, Asia, and Australia, while only one species is found in Europe.

In aquariums or terrariums they should be cultivated on medium rich to poor substrates. The plants can stand hard water, but grow better in soft water, and require a generous light and temperatures from 54° to 77° F (18° to 25° C). Note that *L. palustris* growing in Europe is even fit for coldwater aquariums. Propagation is accomplished by planting the stem cuttings. When cultivated as an emersed form, they flower readily and produce seeds, but cultivation from seeds is a lengthy process. Only the following plants are of practical use for indoor aquariums.

LUDWIGIA ARCUATA Walter

L. arcuata comes from Virginia and Florida. Emersed parts of the stems are prostrate, 30 to 60 cm long, and only the tips are erect. Leaves (15 to 20 mm long and usually only 2.5 mm wide) are green, sometimes reddish. The stems float under water, are 10 to

Ludwigia brevipes.

40 cm long, and are densely branched. The leaves are longer and narrower than with emergent forms, up to 30 mm long and only 1.2 to 1.8 mm wide, nearly linear, usually arched. Flowers are deep yellow, 15 mm in diameter.

It is best to plant *L. arcuata* in the center or in the corners of the aquarium. The tips should be pinched off as soon as they reach the surface.

LUDWIGIA BREVIPES (Long.) E.H. Eames   (III. 379, 381)
This species occurs in nature in the area of Long Beach Island, Ocean County, New Jersey. It is an emersed form, mostly creeping, lower than the preceding species. Leaves are narrowly lanceolate but considerably wider than those of *L. arcuata*, and in emersed forms about 5 to 7.5 mm wide, in submersed forms 2.5 to 5 mm wide. The flowers are yellow, about 10 mm in diameter.

A cluster of flowers of *Eichhornia*, probably of the species *E. azurea.* Photo by C.O. Masters.

Flowering plants of *Ludwigia brevipes* (top) and *Ludwigia repens* (bottom).

L. brevipes was imported to Europe only in 1970. It is an ideal plant both for small and large aquariums, hibernates very well, and is able to tolerate hard water.

LUDWIGIA REPENS (III. 381)
Incorrect names: *L. natans* Elliot, *L. mullertii* Hort.

L. repens grows in marshes and shallow waters in the southern parts of North America. The leaves are opposite and broadly lanceolate to ovate; the upper surface of the leaf is dark glossy green, the lower surface brown-red or purple, about 20 to 30 cm long and 15 to 20 mm wide. Veins are hardly visible. In emersed plants minute yellow flowers arise in the axil of the leaves.

It is cultivated in a lighted situation at temperatures from 64° to 82° F (19° to 28° C). This plant can be used in coldwater as well as in tropical aquariums, equally in paludariums and terrariums.

L. mullertii, with leaves up to 40 mm long, is a horticultural form of *L. repens*. It is very decorative because the lower surface of the leaf is redder than that in the original species.

PLANTAGINACEAE (Plantain Family)
These are annual to perennial herbs distributed all over the world. The best known genus is *Plantago*. *Litorella*, with three species, is the only genus with amphibious plants.

LITORELLA (SHOREWEED)
L. uniflora (L.) Aschers. is found in central and northern Europe, *L. australis* Griseb. in South America, and *L. americana* Fernald in the northeastern parts of North America. Only *L. uniflora* is cultivated in aquariums.

LITORELLA UNIFLORA (L.) Aschers.
This plant grows on the bottoms of ponds and in places that are periodically flooded. The leaves, up to 5 cm in length, forming a ground rosette, are narrowly linear or awl-like, about 1 to 2 mm wide. The flowers of emersed cultivated plants are formed on pedicels of about 20 to 40 mm in length. *L. uniflora* is cultivated in water (about 68° F, 20° C) in a poor sand medium with a reasonable amount of light; the composition of the water is not important. It forms dense carpets of delicate linear leaves and hibernates well both in the aquarium and in the terrarium.

PODOSTEMACEAE
Podostemaceae is a very interesting family with forty-six genera and about 260 species. All the species are aquatic herbs found

growing attached to rocks, stones or wood, in or near rapids and waterfalls. Most of them grow in restricted areas (a single cataract or river) and they are in several living forms very dissimilar. Species of this family have not yet been imported to Europe and we have not cultivated any of them.

PONTEDERIACEAE (Pickerelweed Family)

Pontederiaceae includes rooted or floating water or marsh plants distributed in the warm areas of the world except Europe. Some species penetrate as far as the cold region of the temperate zone. The genera *Pontederia* (pickerelweed), *Hydrothrix*, and *Reussia* grow only in America; *Eichhornia* (water hyacinth) and *Heteranthera* (mud plantain) are found in America and Africa, *Monochoria* is known from East Asia, Australia, and Africa (in the Nile area). To aquarists the genera *Heteranthera* and *Zosterella* are of the greatest importance. The genus *Eichhornia* is exceptional for the extraordinary shape of the leaves and for the extremely beautiful flowers that resemble those of the orchids. About thirty species in nine genera are contained in the Pontederiaceae. Some interesting water plants of this family, such as *Eurystemon*, *Hydrothrix*, and *Scholleropsis*, have not yet been imported.

EICHHORNIA   (III. 27, 380, 385)

There are seven species of floating or marsh plants coming from the tropics of South America and Africa in this genus. The leaf petioles of floating species are very swollen and filled with an inflated, spongy tissue. Rooted plants grow in marshes or submersed, and their leaves and flowers sprout above the surface. They are cultivated easily and their growth is regular.

EICHHORNIA AZUREA (Swartz) Kunth.

E. *azurea* from the tropical and subtropical areas of South America, being a marsh and not an aquatic plant, can not be cultivated in the aquarium, but it is very suitable for terrariums and paludariums with marsh vegetation. A long and thick rhizome produces temporarily submersed leaves (75 mm long and 50 mm wide), but the stem quickly grows out of the water and forms petiolate rounded leaves (70 mm long and 40 to 60 mm wide) with distinct veins. This species rarely blossoms, but when it does the inflorescence is racemose. The corolla is blue, the upper petal spotted with yellow.

This plant is cultivated with greater difficulty than E. *crassipes*. It requires a nutritious soil and the water must be 5 to 10 cm deep and moderately acid. Plenty of light should be provided; it

Heteranthera reniformis.

An irrigation canal in New Hamburg, Brazil covered with *Eichhornia.* Photo by T.J. Horeman.

Eichhornia species from Brazil. Photo by T.J. Horeman.

does well if placed near the window where there is sunlight for at least several hours each day. It usually flowers in the early spring or else in September, sometimes several times a year, but rarely produces seeds. The plant is propagated by separating the rooted parts of the rhizome. This is an ideal vegetation for paludariums.

EICHHORNIA CRASSIPES (Mart.) Solms.
(WATER HYACINTH) (III. 10, 62)

This well known plant has become a troublesome weed in certain tropical and subtropical regions, where it infests irrigation and transport canals as well as some parts of rivers which consequently cease to be navigable. It has spread from Africa, its original habitat.

The petioles of this plant, which is floating or rooted in shallow water, are swollen up to 50 mm in diameter. They are filled with a soft, inflated spongy tissue which enables the plant to float on the surface of the water.

The roots are robust, forming a tangle which may be as long as 20 cm. The leaves with swollen petioles form a rosette and the broad, oval leaf blades are moderately pointed, 50 to 60 mm long and 50 to 70 mm wide. These are often wider than long and distinctly veined. In the spring or autumn months a cluster of six to nine flowers develops in the center of the leaf rosette; each flower is about 50 mm long and composed of six lilac-colored petals. The central upper petal shows an irregular yellow patch.

There is no doubt that the blossom of this plant is, besides the water-liles, the most beautiful of aquatic plant flowers and greatly resembles some orchids in appearance.

E. crassipes can be cultivated as a floating plant in large, well lit aquariums. The tangle of its roots is an excellent shelter for some kinds of fishes. It requires soft water, is not particular with regard to temperature, and grows well and multiplies even on the surface of garden ponds. It is propagated by root runners.

This species can be kept indoors in containers or decorative vases with a good soil and covered by water 10 to 20 mm deep. If rooted, the plant blooms readily and hibernates successfully in terrariums; if floating freely on the surface of the water, it usually dies during winter.

HETERANTHERA (MUD PLANTAIN) (III. 23)

The genus *Heteranthera* differs greatly from all the other members of the family. These thin- to broad-leaved non-woody plants float under the water or on the surface. They can become marsh dwellers, but there producing only dwarf forms. The genus contains ten species from America and Africa.

HETERANTHERA RENIFORMIS Ruiz et Pav. (III. 384, 388)

H. reniformis is found in the temperate zone of the United States, in Central America, and in the West Indies. As a marsh plant it grows in shallow water. Petiolate leaves with broad reniform blades (each about 50 mm long and 50 to 75 mm wide) sprout from the thick rhizome. The venation of the blade is discernible. Flowers (bluish to purple) are inconspicuous.

This species can not be cultivated in the aquarium, thriving badly under water and quickly forming floating leaves. However, it is a very decorative plant for paludariums and terrariums and hibernates readily if supplied with sufficient light. In summer it requires temperatures above 68° F (20° C) and a sunny situation.

HETERANTHERA ZOSTERIFOLIA Mart. (III. 388)

H. zosterifolia is found in Brazil, growing mainly as a submersed plant there. The stem (30 to 40 cm long) is slender and feeble, somewhat branching, and very fragile. The leaves are alternate, narrowly lanceolate, 20 to 40 mm long and 5 to 7 mm wide; the upper surface is green, the lower surface red-brown or grey-green. Floating leaves sometimes appear; they are also green, with long petioles, and oblong-elliptical in shape, more or less of the same size as the totally submersed leaves but darker in color. The flowers are blue, but are rarely seen in the aquarium.

H. zosterifolia is much more exacting in its requirements than *Zosterella*, for it must have soft water, a generous diffused light, and temperatures above 68° F (20° C). The nature of the substrate is of little importance to its development. Snails and fish can easily damage the fragile leaves and stems. In normal conditions the plant produces very few branches and grows vertically toward the surface. If shorter, profusely branching plants are needed, then frequent trimming of the tips will make the axillary buds branch out plentifully.

ZOSTERELLA DUBIA (Jacq.) Small (III. 389)
Syn: *Heteranthera dubia* (Jacq.) MacM., *H. graminea* Vahl.

Z. dubia is a typical aquatic plant native to Mexico, Cuba, and the southern part of the United States. The feeble floating stem is 1.5 meters long; the alternate, linear, grass-green leaves are 25 to 75 mm long and 2 to 5 mm wide, often undulate, and curved. The flowers which appear readily in the aquarium are

Heteranthera reniformis found in swampy ground in Brazil. Photo by T.J. Horeman.

Heteranthera zosterifolia found in Brazil growing emersed. Photo by T.J. Horeman.

Zosterella dubia.

Potamogeton gayi.

star-shaped, bright yellow, formed above the surface, and 15 mm long; seeds are not produced in aquariums. It can be cultivated in warm as well as in colder water; any kind of medium is acceptable. A fast-growing plant, the stems form a dense tangle below the surface; it is not considered a particularly decorative plant. One propagates this plant by planting fragments of the stems.

POTAMOGETONACEAE (Pondweed Family)

The family Potamogetonaceae is represented exclusively by aquatic plants that are rooted in the substrate and have submersed or floating leaves. Yet in many representatives with floating leaves, land forms arise which enable the plants to survive short dry periods. They are annual or perennial plants that hibernate either as rhizomes, as winter buds, or rarely as green plants. Propagation is vegetative or generative from the fruits. Minute flowers are arranged in spicate inflorescences, more rarely in axillary position; fruits are mostly achenes.

Distributed over the tropical to the temperate zones, the family contains two genera with about 100 species. They are all very adaptable to variations in the environment. The submersed and floating leaves differ greatly in shape.

The species of the temperate zone grow very well in the aquarium over the summer but drop the leaves in autumn, while their rhizomes survive the winter period only rarely—consequently they are not suitable for aquarium life. The tropical species have been but little studied until the present time. There is no doubt that additional representatives of this family could become popular aquarium plants in the future.

POTAMOGETON GAYI A. Bennet   (III. 390)

P. gayi from South America has branching stems, submersed leaves that are green to red-brown, linear (5 to 10 cm long and 5 to 9 mm wide), and with a pointed apex.

This species is quite unexacting, growing in a sandy as well as in a rich planting medium in lighted or slightly shaded conditions. The growth slows down only in cooler water (below 59° F, 15° C). It is propagated vegetatively from rhizome runners, often so fast that it can soon overrun the whole aquarium. The development has to be regulated by occasional thinning out. Unrooted stems are suitable as the spawning medium for fish. This plant often blooms but rarely develops fruits in the aquarium.

Saururus cernuus.

Opposite:
Samolus valerandi,
emersed, with immature
inflorescence.

POTAMOGETON MALAIANUS Miq.

P. malaianus is distributed in the tropical and subtropical waters of Central and South America and in Asia. The submersed leaves are membranous and pellucid, elliptical or linearly elliptical, 50 to 75 mm long and 20 mm wide, with short petioles. Its strong midrib tapers distinctly into a point. Young leaves have finely serrated margins.

This is the most suitable species of *Potamogeton* for a heated aquarium, but unfortunately it is not often available. It is very unexacting as far as the composition of the substrate and water are concerned and flowers readily, developing fertile seeds. New plants are produced vegetatively from rhizome runners.

PRIMULACEAE Vent. (Primrose Family)

The members of the family Primulaceae are distributed throughout the world, but most of them are found in the northern temperate zone; only *Samolus valerandi* is present everywhere. Many are well-known garden plants suitable for shady or very dry and sunny places in rock gardens, such as *Primula* (primrose), *Cyclamen* (cyclamen or gravel bind), *Soldanella, Androsace* (rock jasmine), etc. Altogether thirty genera with 800 species are known. Genera with marshy or amphibious members are best represented by *Lysimachia* (loosestrife), *Hottonia* (featherfoil), *Samolus* (water pimpernel), and *Anagallis*.

HOTTONIA (FEATHERFOIL)

Hottonia palustris L. is found in ponds and slowly moving waters of Europe and eastern Siberia. The leaves are divided into comb-like segments. It can be kept only in coldwater aquariums at temperatures up to 50° F (10° C); the plant dies in warm water. Hibernating is in the form of winter buds. The plant is not really suitable for aquariums but can be used in paludariums.

Hottonia inflata Ell. is similar to *H. palustris*, but it has smaller flowers, a very much inflated stem, and comes from North America. It can be cultivated in aquariums indoors; the quality of the water is not important, but additional light is needed in winter.

SAMOLUS VALERANDI L. (WATER PIMPERNEL) (Ill. 392, 395)

The water pimpernel is found in all the continents, but more especially in the southern hemisphere. It grows in marshes and at the mouth of rivers, either submersed or emersed, and thrives best in brackish water.

Inflorescence of *Samolus valerandi.*

Bacopa monniera with flower.

Houttuynia cordata.

Bacopa amplexicaulis with flower.

The plant is in the form of a rosette of light green, ovate leaves tapering at the base into a very small petiole. The leaves are smooth-edged with clearly discernible veins and are 5 to 10 cm long. A leaf rosette is about 12.5 cm in diameter. Plants that are cultivated above the surface of the water flower throughout the year, bearing minute white flowers that are self-fertile. A great number of seeds that germinate readily are produced.

Under water this species usually produces only a rosette of leaves, although in very favorable conditions it develops a sparsely leaved stem (up to 20 cm tall) on which rooted runners are formed.

Cultivation of *S. valerandi* requires a medium rich soil, soft water, and generous light. Daylight is better than artificial light; in winter it can be maintained only if plenty of additional light is provided. A moderate addition of salt (about two teaspoons per 100 liters of water) will greatly benefit its growth.

It is propagated vegetatively by runners developing on the underwater stem. Cuttings from land plants will produce roots if they are laid on the surface of the water. However, the leaf rosettes obtained from plants propagated vegetatively are neither as regular nor as attractive as those plants cultivated from seeds. *Samolus* seedlings should be sown in moist sand, and as soon as the plants are 10 mm long the water level is raised. However, better plants are obtained faster by not putting the seedlings in water at all; they are not planted in the aquarium until they are fully developed, and are then set out in a well-lighted spot.

This is one of the most valuable plants for paludariums and terrariums.

SAURURACEAE (Saururus Family)

These are herbs with a subterranean rhizome. The leaves are arranged spirally on the stem and the inflorescence is in the form of a spike. The family contains only five genera; *Saururus* (with two species) and *Houttuynia* are primarily aquatic plants.

SAURURUS CERNUUS L. (LIZARD'S TAIL)   (Ill. 393)

A native of North America, *S. cernuus* is found particularly in the Atlantic coast and reaches rather far to the north into Canada. It is a perennial amphibious plant with a robust rhizome.

The petioles are 5 to 12.5 cm long and bear smooth glossy blades that are distinctly cordate, incised at the base, stiff to leathery, 10 to 15 cm long, and 60 to 80 mm wide. Flowers, in a spike with a length of 15 to 20 cm long, are minute, yellow-white, and fragrant.

In aquariums it grows only in very good illumination, but it often grows out of the water. A very hardy species suitable for terrarium and paludarium conditions, it stays green all year and spreads very fast in the summer.

HOUTTUYNIA CORDATA Thunb. (III. 396)

H. cordata comes from Japan, China, Taiwan, Java, and the Himalayas, where it grows as a stiff weed in ditches beside roads in the vicinity of villages. It is a perennial plant that quickly forms root runners. The leaves resemble those of *Saururus*, but are much wider. The blade is green but often red-brown near the veins and the base of the blade is cordately incised. The spicate inflorescence is much longer than the leaf.

This plant is cultivated in the same way as *Saururus cernuus*, principally in terrariums, paludariums, and in flowerpots; it is not really fit for aquariums, even though growing well underwater, for it usually emerges above the surface and then loses the submersed leaves.

SCROPHULARIACEAE (Figwort Family)

About 3000 species are included in this family and distributed throughout the world from the Arctic to the tropical zone. There are 220 genera, seventeen of which have aquatic species. Many of them grow in cold water and are unfit for aquariums (*Veronica, Gratiola*), while others are too small (only 10 to 12.5 mm) and can hardly be cultivated (*Amphianthus, Glossostigma*) or are not very attractive (*Bythophyton, Dopatrium, Lindneria, Palidium, Mimulus*). Frequently cultivated are the genera *Bacopa, Hemianthus, Hydrotiche, Limnophila*, and occasionally *Limosella*.

BACOPA (WATER HYSSOP)

Bacopa includes marsh, water, or terrestrial plants growing in the tropical and subtropical zones, principally in America. A great number of the 100 species in the genus can be cultivated in aquariums, although only two species have been commonly used up to now. They flower above water, the flowers growing on short pedicels from the leaf axil. They produce seeds readily but, being well adapted to vegetative reproduction by planting the detached stems, it does not pay to cultivate them from seeds. Roots may develop at the base of the leaves that are always opposite.

Some species, not imported at present, are characterized by polymorphism of the leaves. Leaves are smooth-edged above

Underground bulblets of *Chlorophytum bichetii*.

Chlorophytum bichetii.

Bacopa amplexicaulis growing emersed in nature in Brazil. Photo by T.J. Horeman.

Althernanthera species growing emersed from Brazil will adapt to submersed aquarium conditions quite well. Photo by T.J. Horeman.

water, but are divided under water. For the aquarium the following species can be considered: *B. repens* (Cham. et Schlecht.) Wettst. and *B. rotundifolia* (Michx.) Wettst. coming from North America, *B. myriophylloides* (Benth.) Wettst. and *B. lanigera* (Don.) Wettst. from tropical South America, and especially *B. aquatica* Aubl., which in Brazil and Guyana is used as a medicinal plant.

BACOPA AMPLEXICAULIS (Michx.) Wettst.   (III. 397, 401, 403)

This species is found in the warm southern parts of the United States, where it grows as a marsh or amphibious plant. In the emersed form the stem is about 2.5 to 5 mm thick, sparsely pilose, up to 1 meter long, prostrate, and rooting at the nodes. Erect parts of the stem are 10 to 20 cm high. The leaves are opposite (the individual pairs arranged crosswise, their bases clasping the stem), ovate or elliptical, 20 to 30 mm long and 10 to 15 mm wide; the upper surface is glossy green, the lower surface finely pubescent. Flowers are dark blue.

Submersed plants are without hair, green with darker, clearly discernible veins on the leaves which are usually moderately undulate. It is a very decorative plant. The stem is partly prostrate even under water so that the plant under favorable conditions covers a large area of the aquarium. The plant needs water with a moderately acid reaction, but it does not tolerate direct sunlight and does best in shaded aquariums together with *Cryptocoryne* species.

BACOPA MONNIERA (L.) Wettst.   (III. 38, 396)

B. monniera bears little resemblance to *B. amplicaulis*, even though it has opposite leaves that are arranged crosswise as well. In nature it grows in all the tropical and subtropical areas of the world. In the emersed as well as the submersed form it is naked (i.e., without hairs). The stem is moderately prostrate, rooting, with erect parts 15 to 20 cm high, but unlike *B. amplexicaulis* it is strongly branching. Flowers are light purple with darker veins.

The minute leaves are 10 to 20 mm long and 5 to 8 mm wide. Both surfaces are green, without distinct veins, much thicker than in *B. amplexicaulis*, and not undulate. Under water it grows relatively slowly and is not prostrate, so it does not spread, but forms small though decorative tufts. It is advisable to propagate *B. monniera* out of the water in paludariums or terrariums and then to plant the developed, branched plants under water. Light-loving, it does not prosper in dark places as the preceding species does.

Bacopa amplexicaulis.

Hydrotriche hottoniiflora.

Flowers of
*Hydrotriche
hottoniiflora.*

Limnophila aquatica forming emersed leaves.

Inflorescence of *Limnophila aquatica.*

HEMIANTHUS

Representatives of this genus are fine herbs with minute leaves and flowers arising from the stalk. They come from tropical and subtropical America where about ten species are known. These plants grow in marshes that are subject to occasional flooding. The genus *Hemianthus* was formerly confused with *Micranthemum*.

HEMIANTHUS MICRANTHEMOIDES Nutt.
Syn: *Micranthemum micranthemoides* (Nutt.) Wettst.

This species is distributed from the West Indies and extends northward to the United States and Arctic America. It is a perennial plant growing in moist soil on the banks of rivers and ponds as well as under water. Its linear stems root easily. As land plants they are creeping and reach a height of not more than 25 mm. Submersed creeping stems form erect runners (up to 20 cm high) with a dense foliage of opposite, light green, tubulous leaves about 5 to 7.5 mm long and 2.5 to 3 mm wide.

H. micranthemoides requires a generous light, sandy substrate, and temperatures about 64° to 68° F (18° to 20° C) but it can withstand very warm water and hibernates readily even without additional artificial light. The plant is suitable for enclosed spaces between rocks which it then fills with a fresh, dense, light green growth. This plant can be propagated by separating the rooted parts of the small stems.

HYDROTRICHE HOTTONIIFLORA Zucc. (III. 404)

This plant was first imported to Europe from Madagascar in 1967. The submersed stems are creeping, rooting, and reach 1 meter in length. The erect tips are 25 to 50 cm long, depending upon the height of the water in the tank. The submersed leaves are bright green, arranged in whorls, linear, and branched. Emersed leaves very rarely occur; they are wider than the submersed ones and trilobate. The flowers are emersed, 10 to 15 mm long, and white and yellow.

Hydrotriche is a perennial plant, in nature growing in a moist medium or under water. It is cultivated in conditions similar to those of *Limnophila* and *Cryptocoryne*. Moderately soft acid water at temperatures of 68° to 77° F (20° to 25° C) is best. The plant requires generous light but does not tolerate direct sunlight and grows very fast under good conditions. The leaf whorls are 10 cm wide. *Hydrotriche* is very attractive and suitable for planting in aquariums.

LIMNOPHILA (= AMBULIA]

This genus contains about thirty-five species growing in southern Asia, East Africa, and Australia. These perennial plants grow in a moist medium or under water. They form round, creeping, and rooting stems that are up to 1 meter long. The erect tips are 20 to 50 cm long depending on the height of the water in the aquarium. Aerial leaves are generally lanceolate with finely dentate margins while submersed and emersed leaves are the same: arranged in whorls of six on the average and divided into more or less thin multi-pinnate segments. Emersed and submersed plants that grow out of the water flower readily and produce a great number of minute, readily germinated seeds.

The typically aquatic plants of this genus are: *L. indica, L. heterophylla, L. racemosa,* and *L. hottonoides.* Only the three following species, however, are cultivated with certainty. **(III. 408)**

LIMNOPHILA AQUATICA (Roxb.) Alston   **(III. 405)**

As an aquatic or swamp plant, *L. aquatica* very often grows as a weed in rice fields from western India into Bengal and Ceylon. The stem can grow up to 50 cm long, but only 30 cm long in the aquarium. The submersed leaves in whorls are divided into linear, two-pronged, green segments, 50 to 60 mm long, so the plant measures 10 to 12.5 cm in diameter. In good conditions the plant will grow out of the water. The emersed leaves are lanceolate or elliptical, nearly entire, with dentate margins. Flowers are beautiful deep violet with purple-red dots.

L. aquatica is best cultivated in water with a pH of 6 or 7. It tolerates hard water very well but is sensitive to drops in temperature. Growth is fast in temperatures of about 77° (25° C).

LIMNOPHILA AROMATICA   **(III. 409)**

This unique cultivated species without divided submersed leaves originally comes from tropical Asia. Emersed and submersed cultivated plants have the same type of blades. They are lanceolate, deep green or red, 2.5 to 5 cm long and 10 mm wide, with dentate margins. The bright lilac flowers are campanulate.

L. aromatica is cultivated in a similar medium used for cryptocorynes in moderately soft, acid water of about 68° to 77° F (20° to 25° C) temperature. It is more thermophilic than *L. sessiliflora.* The plant requires a generous light, but it does not tolerate direct sunlight. When exposed to regular sunshine for a long time the leaves lose their green pigment, turn to green-yellow to almost white, and stop growing.

Limnophila heterophylla. A whorl of leaves is also shown in detail. Photo by Dr. D. Terver, Nancy Aquarium.

Limnophila aromatica with several whorls of serrate leaves near the apical end.

Flower of *Limnophila aromatica*.

LIMNOPHILA SESSILIFLORA (Wahl.) Blume (III. 412)

Distributed over the whole tropical area of Asia, including the Indonesian area, *L. sessiliflora* is sometimes found in the subtropical zone. It can therefore withstand lower temperatures (about 68° F, 20° C) and is much more resistant than *L. aromatica*. This is the most frequently cultivated species of *Limnophila*.

The submersed leaves in whorls of six to nine are generally 20 to 30 mm long, so the diameter of the plant does not exceed 50 mm. The leaf segments are linear like those of *L. aromatica*. Emersed parts of the stem are finely pubescent with leaves in whorls of four to six and moderately incised or pinnate. Flowers are purple.

In good conditions the plant grows very fast and requires moderately acid water with a dispersed light (it becomes pale under the sun). This species grows very well along with the crypto-corynes.

LIMOSELLA (III. 368, 413)

Limosella includes eleven species of small amphibious plants occurring in shallow, still, or flowing water. Two cosmopolitan species are cultivated: *L. aquatica* L. is about 50 mm tall with ovate blades 7.5 to 10 mm long; *L. subulata* L. has linear leaves without petioles. Both species are usually annual, perennial under water. These are not too attractive for aquariums.

Glossary

These explanations and definitions are not necessarily identical with those given in more technical works but are designed to provide readers with some clarification of the unavoidable botanical and other terms used in these pages.

Words in capital letters indicate that they are defined elsewhere in the glossary.

Achene: A dry one-seeded fruit formed from a single carpel (part of a flower).

Acuminate: Of a LEAF, tapering to a point.

Alternate: Of branches and leaves, one arising from each NODE while those arising from nodes directly above and below are on opposite sides of the stem.

Annual: A plant that completes its whole life cycle within 12 months.

Apex: The free end or tip of a LEAF BLADE.

Auricles: "Little ears"; of a LEAF, the lateral LOBES at the base.

Axil: The angle between the upper side of a leaf or petiole and the stem.

Axillary bud: A bud situated in the AXIL.

Beak: The tip of a seed-pod.

Blade: LEAF blade: the thin, flattened, conspicuous part of a leaf (see PETIOLE). SPATHE blade: flattened, though may be coiled, part of the BRACT enclosing the INFLORESCENCE (SPADIX) of certain plants.

Bract: A modified LEAF, usually small and green (can take various forms).

Bulbiform: Made or shaped like a bulb.

Calyx: Outermost part of a flower, usually green and leaf-like (sepals), that protects the closed bud.

Campanulate: Shaped rather like a cup or bell.

Limnophila sessiliflora.

Limosella subulata.

Limosella aquatica.

413

Compound: Of a LEAF, formed by a combination of parts (LEAFLETS); with branched PETIOLES.

Cordate: Of a LEAF, somewhat "heart-shaped" (as in a suit of cards).

Corolla: The usually conspicuous part of a flower; a group of petals, often joined together as a tube.

Culm: A stem, especially of grasses.

Cuneate: Of a LEAF, wedge-shaped.

Dentate: Of a LEAF margin etc., toothed (denticle: a small tooth).

Dioecious: Unisexual; male and female reproductive organs borne on different individuals.

Echinate: Provided with numerous rigid hairs or prickles (like a hedgehog).

Entire: Of a LEAF, when the BLADE consists of a single piece and the margin is not conspicuously indented (see SIMPLE).

Elliptical: Of a LEAF, OBLONG and with bluntly pointed ends.

Embossed: Decorated with raised "blisters"; closely pimpled.

Falcate: Of a LEAF, hooked; bent like a sickle.

Fibrilla: A minute fiber; tiny divisions which end branching roots.

Filiform: Long, slender, of unvarying thickness; threadlike.

Follicle: Dry fruit from a single carpel which splits along a single line.

Glandulose: Characterized by the presence of small glands (glandules).

Globular: Shaped like a globe, a sphere.

Glume: A kind of BRACT, a pair of which are present at the base of a grass spikelet.

Hibernation: "Winter sleep"; dormancy.

Incised: Of a LEAF margin, cut into and forming a toothed or other edge (DENTATE).

Inflorescence: The flowering shoot; the arrangement of the flowers; the collective flower or flowers of a plant.

Internodes: The part of a plant stem lying between two NODES.

Lanceolate: of a LEAF, lance-shaped; longer than broad, widest about two-thirds of the way up the leaf from base to APEX.

Leaf: A two-part organ consisting of a BLADE (or lamina) attached to the stem by a stalk or PETIOLE, though the stalk may not be present. (See SESSILE and also PHYLLODE.)

Leaflets: "Little leaves"; the leaf-like divisions of a compound leaf, often with each having its own PETIOLE. (See PINNATE.)

Leaf segments: Small and/or thin LEAFLETS.

Ligule: Membranous outgrowth arising at the junction of the LEAF BLADE and the leaf sheath (in grasses); one of the rays of a composite plant; strap-shaped.

Linear: Of a LEAF BLADE or a PHYLLODE, long and very narrow, with parallel margins.

Lines: Twelve parts of an inch; twelfths.

Linguate: Tongue-like, tongue-shaped.

Lobe: A division of a LEAF (or other organ), larger than a tooth (see DENTATE) and without a separate stalk.

Lobate: Characterized by, or having LOBES.

Midrib: Central raised vein of a LEAF.

Monoecious: Having separate male and female flowers on the same plant.

Node: That part of the stem where one or more leaves (see LEAF) arise, usually swollen and clearly visible.

Oblong: Of a LEAF, having parallel margins, with equally blunt rounded ends.

Opposite: Of branches or leaves, placed in pairs on contrary sides of the stem.

Oval: Of a LEAF, shaped nearly to represent a closed convex curve with one axis longer than the other; more or less egg-shaped in outline.

Ovate: Of a LEAF, characterized by being more or less egg-shaped in outline; OVAL.

Paludariums: Containers, usually tanks, in which a marsh-like environment is maintained; a tank suitable for amphibious plants and animals.

Cryptocoryne ciliata growing up to four feet tall alongside jungle plants in Malaya. Photo by T.J. Horeman.

Cryptocoryne cordata growing in shady conditions in Malaya. Photo by T.J. Horeman.

Close-up of the inflorescence of *Cryptocoryne ciliata*. Photo by T.J. Horeman.

Cryptocoryne evae with inflorescence growing emersed in Thailand. Photo by T.J. Horeman.

Panicle: A loose and irregular flower cluster.

Pedicel: The stalk of an individual flower of an INFLORES-CENCE.

Pellicular: Resembling a thin skin or a membrane.

Pellucid: Translucent (not entirely clear or transparent).

Perennial: A plant that lives for more than two years.

Perianth: The outer part of a flower, the floral envelope.

Petiole: The LEAF stalk, joining the BLADE to the stem (not always present).

Phyllode: A flattened and leaf-like PETIOLE.

Pilose: When the outer skin of an organ is sparsely covered by long and simple hairs.

Pinnate: Of a LEAF, divided into LEAFLETS.

Polymorphism: Of leaves, etc., having several different forms.

Pubescent: When the outer skin of an organ is covered by short, soft hairs.

Raceme (racemose): Where flowers are borne on PEDICELS on a single, undivided axis.

Recurved: Of a LEAF, bent backwards; reflexed.

Reniform: Of a LEAF, broader than long, somewhat CORDATE at the base, with rounded AURICLES; rather "kidney-shaped".

Rhizoids: Single- or several-celled hairlike structures serving as a root.

Rhizome: The stock, or lower part of the stem, which is like a root but differs in the presence of one or more buds, leaves or scales.

Rosette: Of leaves etc., arranged concentrically around a single center.

Scape: The leafless stem of a solitary flower or of an INFLORES-CENCE.

Self-fertile: Capable of fertilization by pollen of the same flower or a flower from the same plant.

Self-sterile: Incapable of self-fertilization; incapable of forming viable offspring by self-fertilization.

Serrate: Of a LEAF, when the margin is INCISED into tooth-like indentations (DENTATE) which are regular and pointed like the teeth of a saw.

Serrulate: Of a LEAF, when the marginal indentations are SERRATE and quite small.

Sessile: Of a LEAF, etc., when it lacks a stalk; when the BLADE meets the stem directly or practically directly, without the intervention of a stalk.

Simple: Of a LEAF, when the BLADE consists of a single piece, with the margin indented nowhere (simple is the opposite of compound; ENTIRE is the opposite of DENTATE, LOBED, etc.).

Sp./spp.: Abbreviations to permit clear differentiation between *species singular* (sp.) and *species plural* (spp.).

Spadix: An INFLORESCENCE, a form of SPIKE with a thick fleshy axis.

Spathe: The BRACT or floral envelope enclosing the INFLORESCENCE (SPADIX) of some monocotyledons (see BLADE).

Spatulate (spathulate): of leaves, when flat; when the part near the APEX is broad and short while the narrower and tapering part is long and toward the base.

Spicate: Of an INFLORESCENCE, like a SPIKE or forming a SPIKE.

Spike: An INFLORESCENCE in which the flowers are SESSILE along a simple undivided axis.

Spore: A single- or several-celled reproductive body that becomes separated from the parent plant.

Sporocarp: A "fruit" containing SPORES or sporangia.

Stellate: Of leaves, etc., when spread out, radiating from the base or nearly so; like a star; star-shaped.

Substratum: The "soil" on the bottom of an aquarium; the planting medium.

Terrariums: Containers, often tanks, in which an environment is maintained that is suitable for land-dwelling plants and animals.

Thallus: A simple plant body, undifferentiated into true root, stem, or LEAF.

The open part of the inflorescence of *Cryptocoryne cordata.*

Cryptocoryne cordata.

A collection of *Nymphaea* and *Spathiphyllum* in a typical lagoon in Guyana, South America.

Phyllanthus fluitans growing as a floating plant in its natural habitat in Brazil. Photo by T.J. Horeman.

Thermophilic: "Warmth loving."

Trifoliate: A LEAF with three LEAFLETS.

Trihedral: Having three faces; of a PETIOLE, etc., having a three-sided cross-section.

Truncate: Of a LEAF, when the APEX is cut off square.

Tubercle: A small tuber (which is a short thick portion of an underground stem, set with buds).

Tubulous: Tube shaped; of a LEAF, tending to curl longitudinally.

Umbel: Of an INFLORESCENCE, when several branches (PEDICELS) appear to start from the same point and are nearly the same length: umbrella-like.

Undulate: Of a LEAF, its margin or of a PHYLLODE, when the whole or the edges are not flat but bent or curled up and down; wavy.

Whorl: Of leaves, etc., when several arise from the same NODE and are arranged regularly around the stem; platforms or tiers of leaves circumscribing the stem; "densely whorled" indicates that the whorls are set close together up the stem, the INTER-NODES are short.

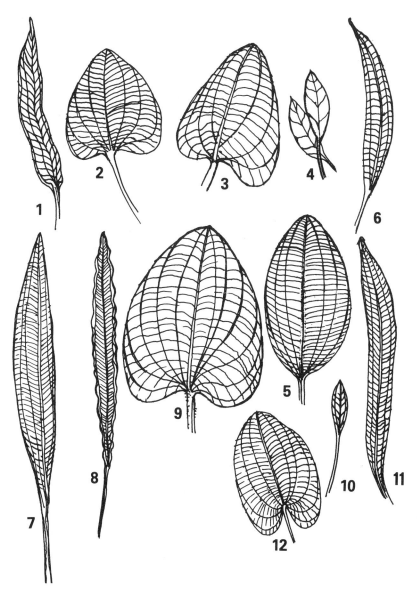

Leaf shapes in some *Echinodorus* species: 1. *E. berteroi*, submersed, 2. *E. berteroi*, emersed, 3. *E. cordifolius*, 4. *E. quadricostatus*, emersed, 5. *E. osiris*, 6. *E. amazonicus*, 7. *E. paniculatus*, 8. *E. intermedius*, 9. *E. grandiflorus*, 10. *E. tenellus*, 11. *E. nymphaeifolius*, submersed, 12. *E. nymphaeifolius*, floating or emersed.

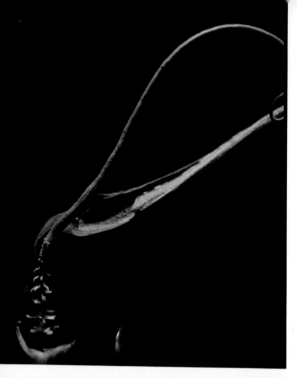

Inflorescence of *Typhonium flegelliforme*.

Cardamine lyrata.

An enlarged photograph of the male flower of *Cryptocoryne evae.* Note the presence of insects. These are believed to assist in the pollination of the cryptocorynes. Photo by T.J. Horeman.

Leaves of *Cryptocoryne evae.* The lower surface of the deep green leaf is reddish-brown in color. Photo by T.J. Horeman.

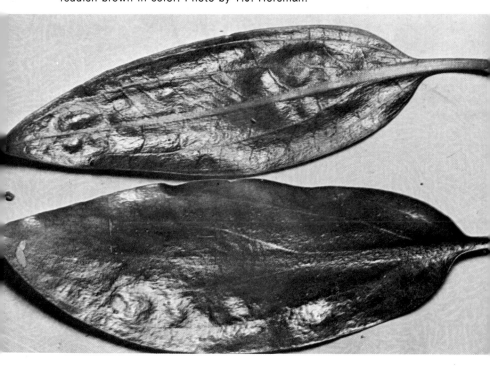

Leaf shapes in some *Cryptocoryne* species: 1. *C. siamensis* var. *kerri*, 2. *C. thweitesii*, 3. *C. versteegi*, 4. *C. ferruginea*, 5. *C. becketii*, 6. *C. johorensis*, 7. *C. cordata*, 8. *C. walkeri*, 9. *C. spiralis*, 10. *C. axelrodii*, 11. *C. retrospiralis*.

Plant Index (Scientific Names)

Page numbers printed in **bold** refer to photographs or illustrations; those in *italics* refer to the major discussion of the family, genus, or species.

Magnified view of the female flowers inside the kettle of *Cryptocoryne evae.* Photo by T.J. Horeman.

Shown are the bright yellow inflorescence and richly colored leaf surfaces of *Cryptocoryne evae* grown in the emersed condition. Photo by T.J. Horeman.

Spathiphyllum species from Guyana, South America growing amongst the trees in deep shade. Photo by T.J. Horeman.

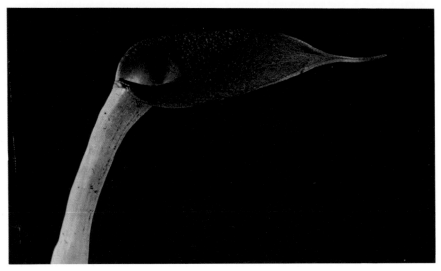

Inflorescence of *Cryptocoryne hejnyi.*

Cryptocoryne hejnyi.

Cryptocoryne griffithii with flower photographed in the greenhouse. Photo by T.J. Horeman.

Cryptocoryne lingua with inflorescence and fruit.
Photo by T.J. Horeman.

Cryptocoryne korthausae.

Cryptocoryne johorensis, emersed form.

Fruit of *Cryptocoryne lingua.* Photo by T.J. Horeman.

Cryptocoryne lingua seedling. Photo by T.J. Horeman.

Opened seed pod of *Cryptocoryne lingua* showing the ripe seeds.
Photo by T.J. Horeman.

Cryptocoryne lucens.

Plant Index (Popular Names)

Cryptocoryne minima with inflorescence photographed in its natural habitat in Malaya. Photo by T.J. Horeman.

The beautiful dark red inflorescence of *Cryptocoryne nuri* from Malaya. Photo by T.J. Horeman.

Cryptocoryne nevillii.

Inflorescence of *Cryptocoryne nevillii.*

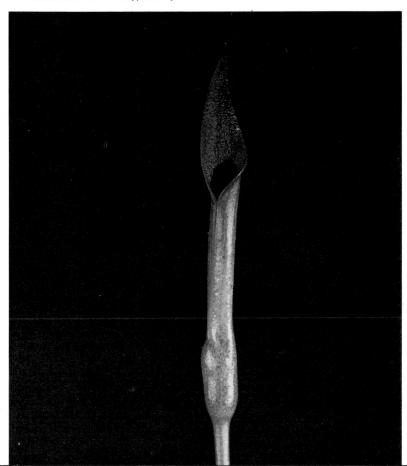

O

Orpine family, 298

P

Parsley family, 191
Pepperwort, 118
Pickerelweed, 383
Pillwort, 119
Plantain family, 382
Polypody family, 129
Pondweed family, 363, 391
Primrose family, 394

Q

Quillwort, 110

R

Rock jasmine, 394

S

Saururus family, 398
Sedge family, 299
Shoreweed, 382
Small-leaved Amazon swordplant, 144
Snowdrop, 187
Snowflake, 187
Spatterdock family, 371
Spike rush, 303
Sundew family, 306
Sweet flag, 222

T

Thallose liverworts, 102

U

Underwater banana plant, 12, 362

W

Water fern, 130
Water hyacinth, 10, 383, 386
Water hyssop, 399
Water lettuce, 282
Water lily, 370
Water milfoil, 311
Water milfoil family, 311
Water moss, 107
Water pennywort, 191
Water pimpernel, 394
Water plantain family, 139
Water shield, 290
Water sprite, 126
Water velvet, 114
Water wisteria, 135
Watermeal, 342, 343
Waterwort family, 307
Wild celery, 234

Y

Yellow pond-lily, 371

Subject Index